T0291323

PRAISE FOR *RESPONSIBLE MARKETING*

"Lola Bakare has written a ridiculously readable book about marketing that will make you laugh, cheer, and think. *Responsible Marketing* shows you how to build a better, more conscious business—starting with the topline—on the way to creating a more righteous world."
Anne Morriss, bestselling author and host of the hit podcast Fixable

"For marketing executives who want to move fast and fix things, *Responsible Marketing* is a tool you absolutely need. Equal parts passionate and pragmatic, Lola will leave you inspired with a new vision of what it looks like to drive tangible growth with a more conscious approach to free-market capitalism that is defensible for the one reason that always matters—it actually works."
Frances Frei, Professor of Technology and Operations Management, Harvard Business School

"Understanding and guiding a brand's social impact has never been more important, and never been more misunderstood. Lola Bakare breaks it all down in the most Lola way. She shows how inclusive, authentic marketing can boost not just your brand and bottom line. This isn't about being 'woke'—it's about being awoken to the real possibilities when business goals and social good align."
Greg Hann, Co-Founder, Mischief

"Consumption is undeniably a 'cultural act' in the modern era. But many brands exist outside of the culture where trust is built, where our identities are shaped. Thus, marketing is removed from high intent consumer behaviors. Lola Bakare's book offers a reminder and a refreshing take on the Marketing playbook that returns to the era when we actively looked the consumer in the eye."
Albert Thompson, Managing Director, Digital Innovation

"For everyone who believes that marketing and brand building play an essential role in shaping culture, this book is a must-read. It provides a clear roadmap for the types of stories we need to be telling in order to make positive and lasting contributions for clients, careers, consumers and the world at large. I have always believed that marketing can be a force for good; Bakare shows us how."
Emily Heyward, Co-Founder and Chief Brand Officer, Red Antler

"Lola offers a critical and transformative perspective on how brands can thrive while staying true to an ethical framework. Her insightful analysis provides practical strategies to resonate with consumers who expect their values and culture to be reflected and represented in the work. Lola's case studies and actionable insights are for anyone looking to connect integrity and positive change with authentic consumer connections and business growth. This book highlights a unique opportunity for marketers to close gaps in access and generate more equitable outcomes, paving the way for inclusive and impactful engagement, emphasizing what happens if we don't act and the opportunity if we do."
Frank Starling, Chief DEI Officer, LIONS

"At a time when marketing messages have become confused, empty and buried in greenwashing allegations, we need a new approach to communicating brand values effectively. Lola Bakare provides a constructive and practical path forward, in this smart and well-written book."
Alison Taylor, Clinical Associate Professor, Leonard N. Stern School of Business, and author of *Higher Ground*, and Executive Director, Ethical Systems

"In *Responsible Marketing*, Lola reminds us of a fundamental truth that should underpin all creative solutions: marketing is about what works, full stop. Not what works for a few individuals, but what works across a consumer landscape where change is the only constant. Rich in case studies and personal stories, it's a read that gets you thinking expansively about all the ways marketing can both delight your shareholders and drive progress through creativity."
Simon Cook, CEO, LIONS

"*Responsible Marketing* is a transformational book that guides us on how to take courageous action for change. Through her 'four keys to responsible marketing' framework, Lola Bakare masterfully leads us on the journey to

create powerful brands, stories and movements. While there's plenty of solid advice for marketing leaders, the book speaks to *all* in today's world who are operating as personal brands. Don't miss out on learning from one of the most innovative marketing experts of all time!"
Ruchika T. Malhotra, best-selling author and inclusion strategist

"*Responsible Marketing* is a light-bulb-creating marketing tome for the 21st-century marketer. Lola's model for demonstrating the relationship between social impact and commercial success is clear and brilliant and will make you critically rethink your marketing strategies. The inspiring case studies in this book are a catalyst for propelling marketers toward campaigns that are good for business, for people, and for the planet. And if we get it right, Lola may one day be able to retire the term 'responsible marketing' because it has become the inherent definition of what marketing, as a craft, is."
Onney Crawley, Chief Marketing Officer, Goodwill Industries International

"Lola has nailed it with this book. Particularly with the recognition that responsible marketing is a manifestation of the invisible hand, not a distortion of the market. It's the rational response to increased consumer demand for it in product markets, increased employee demand for it in labor markets and increased civilian demand for it in the market for public goods as well. Responsible marketing is the key to thriving in a world where constructive capitalism is taking root—and this book is the perfect tool for a marketer to ground themselves in it."
Drew Train, CEO and Co-founder, OBERLAND

"The word *responsible* is 'how we describe ourselves when we're at our best,' Lola Bakare proclaims in this book. "It's the practice of doing more than what's required, not just what we'll be accountable for." Lola reminds us that we exist to be of service, at the intersection of *all* the stakeholders we serve. She pushes us to leverage the financial pitfalls of historical exclusion thereby unlocking the upside of addressing urgent, unmet needs. Lola has served as a guiding light in our industry for the last four years and her book is a provocative and powerful summation of her framework of responsible marketing that will guide me for years to come. Keep this book close and commit to using your power for good, one 'responsible reframe' at a time."
Xanthe Wells, VP, Global Creative, Pinterest

Responsible Marketing

*How to Create an Authentic
and Inclusive Marketing Strategy*

Lola Bakare

KoganPage

Publisher's note

Every possible effort has been made to ensure that the information contained in this book is accurate at the time of going to press, and the publishers and author cannot accept responsibility for any errors or omissions, however caused. No responsibility for loss or damage occasioned to any person acting, or refraining from action, as a result of the material in this publication can be accepted by the editor, the publisher or the author.

First published in Great Britain and the United States in 2025 by Kogan Page Limited

2nd Floor, 45 Gee Street
London
EC1V 3RS
United Kingdom

8 W 38th Street, Suite 902
New York, NY 10018
USA

www.koganpage.com

Kogan Page books are printed on paper from sustainable forests.

ISBNs

Hardback   978 1 3986 1164 1
Paperback 978 1 3986 1162 7
Ebook   978 1 3986 1163 4

British Library Cataloguing-in-Publication Data

A CIP record for this book is available from the British Library.

Library of Congress Control Number

2024042685

Typeset by Integra Software Services, Pondicherry
Print production managed by Jellyfish
Printed and bound by CPI Group (UK) Ltd, Croydon CR0 4YY

To my little sister Layo and my big brother Ade.
Thank you for keeping me grounded and encouraging me to soar.
I'm so grateful to have been born in the middle
of the two most loving people I know.
Watching you move through the world with such
passion and joy enlivens my heart and frees my mind.
From the gift of your steadfast presence, I receive
the endless blessings of a sacred place of peace.
Our bond bolsters me with a true sense of belonging
that I've yet to find anywhere else in the world.
Without each of you in my corner, this book
would have been impossible to achieve.

CONTENTS

ABOUT THE AUTHOR

Lola Bakare is an Anthem Award-winning Inclusive Marketing Strategist, creator of the #responsiblemarketing movement, and founder of be/co, a boutique consultancy that empowers brands and marketing leaders with strategic guidance, coaching, training, workshops, and content creation to unleash new levels of success for clients across industries including Merck, IBM, Taylor Morrison Homes, Thought Exchange, and the Tory Burch Foundation.

With a wealth of experience on the frontlines of marketing leadership at The Daily Dot, PepsiCo, New World Pasta, Diageo, and Dell (for world-class brands including Gatorade, Ronzoni, and Smirnoff), Lola's uniquely empathetic approach comes from her deeply nuanced understanding of the distinctive challenges marketing leaders face across industries.

Lola is a LinkedIn Top Voice, a Forbes CMO Network contributor, and an Advisory Board Member at sparks & honey. Her writing and commentary can be found in major publications, including Adweek, AdAge, *Harvard Business Review*, Marketing Brew, Digiday, Campaign, SHRM, LinkedIn News, LinkedIn Collective, and Business Insider, where she is recognized as one of 13 top consultants and experts helping advertisers with diversity. She is a member of the prestigious International Academy of Digital Arts and Sciences and has served as juror for top marketing and advertising awards programs including the Anthem Awards, the Shorty Awards, and Dubai Lynx. As a keynote speaker, panelist, and moderator, she has graced the stages of global marketing and leadership conferences, including the Cannes LIONS Festival for Creativity, Sustainable Brands, Reuter's Strategic Marketing, and South by Southwest, to name a few.

Lola holds a BA in English from the University of Pennsylvania and an MBA from the Stern School of Business at NYU where, as Co-Editor-in-Chief of The Stern Opportunity along with Lisa Kravitz, she won the President's Service Award.

She lives in Philadelphia with her twin cats, aptly named Peggy and Draper (#iykyk!). Outside of work, she can usually be found voraciously consuming content from low to highbrow across media types (especially audiobooks!) or helping local non-profit Monument Lab as a Board member.

FOREWORD BY CINDY GALLOP

If there's one thing that my 39 years working in brand building, marketing, and advertising has embedded in me, it's the belief that the future of business is doing good and making money simultaneously.

So I could not have been more delighted to be invited by the amazing Lola Bakare to write the foreword to this book—because I feel confident that by the time you get to the end of this book, you'll be asking yourself, "Is there any other kind?"

There are three things I particularly loved about this book.

Firstly, *Responsible Marketing* is highly *actionable*.

Whether it's Lola's specific recommendations, her "four responsible marketing moves," the inspirational case studies she cites, or the many "Real Talk With Responsible Marketers" interviews woven into the narrative throughout, everything about this book is action-focused.

I'm a big believer in communication through demonstration: don't say it, be it and *do* it. For me, that's the true definition of authenticity—and Lola totally delivers. For any marketer, this is your indispensable day-to-day action handbook. Think of it as your personal GPS: *Responsible Marketing* helps you set your strategic direction, shows you the most efficient and effective ways to get where you want to go, and regularly updates you on how to overcome or find your way around any obstacles that appear.

Secondly, *Responsible Marketing reframes* in a way that makes you *rethink*.

Lola and I are on completely the same wavelength, but I especially appreciated the many moments within this book where Lola comes at a theme or topic from an unexpected angle, and provides the reader with a different way of looking at it—which in turn provides new ideas for how to take action, and for how to sell that action into stakeholders where necessary. *Responsible Marketing* gives you an armory of innovative thinking you can deploy both for creative strategizing and planning, but also to secure stakeholder buy-in. "I hadn't thought about it like that" is a powerful dynamic—for the reader, and for where the reader will need to take their own Responsible Marketing strategy to execution.

For example, I love Lola's injunction to "find the fun"—not something that might immediately come to mind when you hear the words "Responsible Marketing." But it should! You'll learn how to "solve real problems with a side of laughter."

Are you woke hushing and green hushing without realizing it? Do you even know what that means? I didn't! Here's where you find out, and what to do about it.

Here's where you also find out how responsible marketing can actually drive policy change; how to combat corporate fragility; dispel the myth of "cancel culture"; why there's no such thing as culture wars; and how you can get it wrong—the right way.

I especially liked Lola's advice on how to deploy FOMO—Fear Of Missing Out—to impact internal and external stakeholder behavior.

Thirdly, and importantly, *Responsible Marketing monetizes*.

As Lola says—and then proceeds to demonstrate—"Responsible marketing can actually exist in harmony with the principles of free market capitalism." Shocker! Yes, doing good and making money simultaneously is entirely possible.

In October 2023, McKinsey published a study titled, "The Power of Partnership: How the CEO-CMO Relationship Can Drive Outsize Growth." The study found that the relationship between CEOs and CMOs, especially as it related to how they jointly defined marketing's role and remit in shaping growth strategy, is highly correlated to their companies' performance. In particular, CEOs who place marketing at the core of their growth strategy are twice as likely to have greater than 5 percent annual growth compared with their peers.

Responsible Marketing *is* that growth strategy.

Nothing is as endearing to a CEO as a CMO with a Responsible Marketing strategy who's going to take responsibility for making a lot more money.

And per Lola, "What could possibly be controversial about monetizing the solutions society actually needs?"

So—are you ready to be a Responsible Marketer?

In Chapter 1 of this book, Lola says of the word "responsible," "It's how we describe ourselves when we're at our best."

I couldn't agree more. And I know that everyone who reads, absorbs and acts on this book will be operating at their very best, in the best interests of everyone.

Introduction

How It All Began

At first, I referred to it as "Maximize the Movement."

It was the spring of 2020, around that time that the reality of Covid-19's implications to life as we know it was setting in and the crisis of police brutality and racial injustice had reached a boiling point that made it impossible for us to look away. We weren't yet aware of just how much, but we knew enough to know that things would never be the same.

While the bravest of us, essential workers and on-the-ground activists, faced the daily fear of crisis on the front lines, for those lucky and privileged enough to be confined to our homes, the pregnant pause felt around the world was coupled with potent undertones of opportunity.

We began to ask ourselves heady, existential questions. If you're anything like me, your inner monologue began to sound something like this:

"What could I do with the newfound luxury of time and mental space?"

"What should I be doing to play a role in making the world a safer, fairer place?"

"Shouldn't my work be more meaningful?"

"Would I be happy with my legacy if it was all over today?"

"Is now the time to do the thing that excites and scares me most?"

Creating a content-driven "thought-leadership" brand to anchor my consulting practice and evolve to offering "one-to-many" experiences had been in the back of my mind for years, but something about the moment said now or never.

From facilitating to hosting, training, teaching, moderating, punditing, paneling, and writing, I'd always known that influencing others to "unleash their magic" was a towering professional strength and true personal joy.

I'd also always known that my passion for civic engagement and social justice was meant to somehow become a more central part of my professional life, beyond participation in employee resource groups and diversity recruiting initiatives on the side.

I began working with the inimitable Jocelyn Kelly Reid, a business coach who specializes in helping ambitious women with service-based businesses "productize" their offerings from a heart-led place. Her cohort-based coaching approach walked me through the process of tapping into a deeper level of self-awareness than I'd ever experienced. I got intimately in touch with my unique strengths, weaknesses, interests, and expertise.

From this, "Maximize the Movement" emerged as a workshop offering that teaches the practice of inclusive, social-impact-driven marketing and marketing leadership beyond the performative. As I began testing it out on live audiences, I realized that this was it. I was meaningfully filling the gap I'd spent my entire career noticing but never was quite positioned to address at scale.

#maximizethemovement became my signature social media hashtag, signature talk title, and unapologetic rallying cry for the value of a common-sense approach to embracing our "growth for good" opportunities for *all* of the reasons, not just the short-term Wall Street-driven ones.

More and more, I realized how much impact I could have by guiding those with the most decision-making power in my sphere of influence toward naturally seeking out connection points between a brand's approach to meeting the cultural moment with gusto and its potential outsized business results. I realized that my particular style of brash and sassy communication could accomplish this, even in an environment in which marketers were being systemically disincentivized to focus on the causal relationship between the two. I was able to help people see what was right in front of them clearly, and feel what was all around them tangibly—even when their insular lived experiences made this seeing and feeling much harder to do. Through teaching, I could do something to mitigate the financial and societal risks of those all-too-common, performative "Oof" moments that seemed so easily avoidable but continued to happen again and again.

As my content began to gain more traction, I was lucky enough to become a LinkedIn Top Voice in Advertising and Marketing.[1]

My luck didn't run out there.

While on a retreat for women entrepreneurs in Accra, Ghana, just after writing "Turn Maximize the Movement into a book" on my vision board, I received a LinkedIn direct message from an editor at Kogan Page who had seen me on LinkedIn's Top Voice list. As we began the process of collaborating on what would become this book, it became clear that the concept needed a less "needs to be explained to get it" title. My fantastic editor challenged me to package my points of view in a wrapper that clearly communicated their meaning and relevance at a single glance. I kept coming back to my mission of helping marketers see that the right money decision is so often the right social impact decision. Despite the growing drumbeat of cynical, shortsighted, popular belief, finding the intersection of business impact and social impact wasn't a distraction or a fad, it was simply the responsible thing to do.

From there, my use of the term "responsible marketing" was born. We'll get into a working definition in Chapter 1, but for now, sink into the spirit of it.

As the steward of a brand, isn't it on us to care for it in a way that maximizes its long-term success?

(Yep)

Knowing what we know, doesn't that *have* to involve considering its potential impact on what my friend and the CMO/CRO of Sustainable Brands Samuel Monnie refers to as the 5Ps of commerce: people, purpose, progress, planet, and prosperity?[2]

(Yep)

Could it be anything *but* irresponsible to ignore the advancement of our collective existence when making business decisions from our positions of immense privilege?

(Nope)

When we ensure our work is both inclusive and designed to make a meaningful, measurable, brand-relevant social impact that results in a positive impact on brand reputation and business results, regenerating from there, we are practicing responsible marketing that transcends the performative. We're committing to creating as much good as we can in the world, value for shareholders included.

There's a reason why every workshop I give kicks off with this classic quote from Whole Foods Founder John Mackey's most beloved book, *Conscious Capitalism: Liberating the heroic spirit of business*: "Make decisions in such a way that they have positive impacts in multiple dimensions for all stakeholders."[3]

It's just the responsible thing to do!

Why Me?

For as long as I can remember, even back to ages 3, 4, and 5, I have always been the "But what if we did it this way?" person. Recently when I asked my Mom what I was like in those days, she said a former elementary school teacher of mine once said to her, "Watch that one, she's going to be a leader someday."

Like many children of immigrants around the world, as a first-generation Nigerian American, status quo anything just was not a thing in my household growing up. In many ways, the stereotype that paints Nigerians, particularly Yoruba Nigerians, as being highly aspirational and future-focused is true for us.

As Anthony Bourdain described the place where my parents grew up, Lagos, Nigeria is "One of the most dynamic, unrestrained, and energetic expressions of free-market capitalism and do-it-yourself entrepreneurship on the planet… they long ago learned, ain't nobody going to help you in this world. Pick up a broom, a hammer. Buy a taxi, a truck. Build a bank, a billion-dollar company, and get to work."[4]

There was always a push to do better. You got four As and a B+? Well, how do we make that B+ an A? Other parents might have seen four As to celebrate, but mine only saw a B+ to fix. Our aspirational mindset doesn't extend to comfort and complacency. Why let comfort determine the way forward when there is progress to make, achievements to earn, and endless possibilities to seek?

As my mother (thankfully) never lets me forget in her guidance and the way she moves through the world from a place of service, our native culture is also rooted in collectivism.

When you have resources, you use them to take care of your own. You do this with faith in the rule of reciprocity, embracing that even if you don't have the pleasure of seeing them materialize, untold blessings to your children and generations to come is the worthiest return on your investment there is.

Then, there were the observations of how my parents charted their careers. By the time I began my own in the elite training ground of PepsiCo's marketing organization as a brand management associate on the iconic Gatorade brand, I had already observed my earliest examples of conscious capitalism from them.

One of my favorite examples of this comes from my Dad. As a successful and beloved obstetrics and gynecology (OB/GYN) doctor with his own private practice, he'd learned a lot about the unmet needs of his patients. He saw an opportunity to provide women with holistic, home-like birthing options without the risks of home birth, and he decided to pursue it by opening "The Birthing Centre" in a historic home across from the hospital where he worked in our hometown of Harrisburg, Pennsylvania. Unlike most other OB/GYNs with private practices, he also made it a point to accept Medicaid so all women could have access to the experience. It was nothing short of revolutionary and predicted trends that his industry as a whole would only catch on to decades later. It seeded my understanding of the connective tissue between service and selling in a way that has stuck with me for life.

For these and other reasons you'll hear more about throughout the book, my belief in the practice of responsible marketing and the power of a responsible marketing mindset is deeply ingrained. I believed in it even before I had a way of articulating my belief. This book is that way, and I couldn't be more honored that you believe in me enough to give it a read.

Why You?

This book is not for everyone. If you are an individual who believes that there are "good people on both sides," this book is not for you. If you buy into the narrative that there is "too much talk about race," this book is not for you. If you have ever supported, justified, or tolerated the notion of "woke talk fatigue"… this book is not for you. If, for example, you believe climate change is a hoax, I can tell you without uncertainty that this book is not for you.

But if you, like me, believe most humans have an inherent desire to connect and better each other's situation for the betterment of the collective, this book is for you. If you believe in the essence of one human family, this book is for you. If you believe that when we demand more than the status quo of ourselves as stewards of a brand, that's when we can really achieve great things, this book is for you. If you're interested in shifting from outdated, inefficient, closed-minded strategic marketing principles to a more forward-looking approach that drives new levels of growth by harnessing the power of inclusivity and social responsibility, this book is for you. If you want to better understand the relationship between social impact, reputation impact, and commercial impact to accelerate your success as a leader and create a legacy you can be proud of, this book is for you. If you're overwhelmed, scared to mess up, or lost in what feels like an endless ocean of opportunity, this book is here to help you navigate what's possible. If you see your power and influence as a privilege and not a burden, this book is for you.

What's Inside

The Framework: Reach For More

In Part One, we'll discuss how striving to achieve social impact, reputation impact, and commercial impact, enabled by inclusivity and authenticity, are the cornerstones of responsible marketing. When we embrace inclusivity, we open the door to diverse perspectives that enrich our campaigns and resonate deeply with our audiences. Authenticity ensures that our messages are not just heard but felt, fostering trust and loyalty. Social impact is our commitment to making a tangible difference in the world, demonstrating

FIGURE 0.1 The four keys to responsible marketing

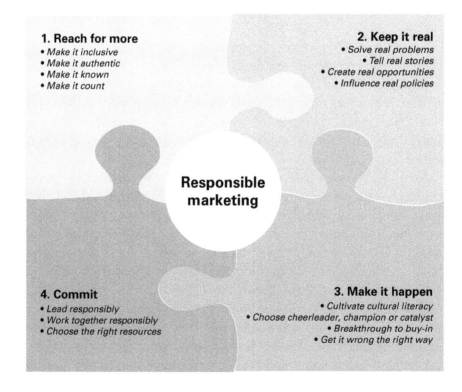

1. Reach for more
- Make it inclusive
- Make it authentic
- Make it known
- Make it count

2. Keep it real
- Solve real problems
- Tell real stories
- Create real opportunities
- Influence real policies

Responsible marketing

4. Commit
- Lead responsibly
- Work together responsibly
- Choose the right resources

3. Make it happen
- Cultivate cultural literacy
- Choose cheerleader, champion or catalyst
- Breakthrough to buy-in
- Get it wrong the right way

that we stand for more than profit. This, in turn, enhances our reputation, as consumers increasingly seek out brands that align with their values. And let's not forget commercial impact—when done right, responsible marketing drives sustainable business growth. It's a powerful reminder that doing good and doing well are not mutually exclusive but rather beautifully interconnected.

The Moves: Keep It Real

In Part Two, we'll click down on what it can and should look like within the marketing sphere of influence when we are striving for real impact and real change. This includes solving real problems, telling real stories, creating real opportunities, and influencing real policies. When we focus on solving real problems, we go beyond lip service to address the urgent needs of our communities, driving meaningful change. Telling real stories helps bring that critically important authenticity to our efforts, connecting us with our audience on a human level and making our message resonate. By creating real opportunities, we empower individuals and communities, fostering lasting growth and inclusion. And when we influence real policies, we extend our impact beyond the corporate sphere, advocating for systemic change that benefits society as a whole. Together, these elements ensure that our marketing efforts are not just effective, but profoundly impactful, reflecting our commitment to making the world a better place.

The Process: Make It Happen

In Part Three, we'll examine some of the practical tools essential to responsible marketing including cultivating cultural literacy within marketing teams and organizations, choosing exactly how involved and impactful you want to be, getting internal stakeholder buy-in, and learning how to bounce back when, despite best efforts and intent, you get it wrong. Cultural literacy allows us to navigate the diverse landscapes of our audience with respect and understanding, creating campaigns that truly resonate. Defining the responsible marketing role that makes the most sense for a particular brand in a particular moment—whether we cheer from the sidelines, champion on the field, or catalyze real change, helps us to make critical decisions about how and when to get involved. Securing internal stakeholder buy-in ensures that our responsible marketing initiatives are supported and sustained from within, aligning our entire marketing organization with our values. Finally, embracing mistakes and learning from them—getting it wrong the right way—demonstrates our commitment to growth and authenticity. Understanding these principles enables brands to drive meaningful, lasting impact through every facet of our marketing efforts.

Ready to Get Real?

I'm excited for you! Let's go over a few quick things just before you do.

Don't think of responsible marketing as an all-or-nothing proposition. There are no inherently good or bad brands or good or bad marketers; there are effective and ineffective actions and decisions, and each day is a new opportunity to make more effect and defensible ones.

Do remember that examples of what good looks like and what might be improved are learning opportunities, not endorsements of some brands as responsible and others as irresponsible.

Do keep in mind that my praise for a particular initiative doesn't mean I'm saying a company is a perfect actor. Sorry to break it to you, but there aren't any of those. In each and every case referenced, there's probably just as much going on that is worthy of critique within marketing and certainly in other parts of the organization. Two things can be true. We can want, and push for, more consistent internal alignment across functions to the campaigns and initiatives we will discuss, while recognizing the positive societal impact that responsible marketing has the power to create beyond a company's four walls, either way. When we wait for perfect conditions to do any good, we lose on two fronts instead of just one. That is bad strategy. Your responsible marketing strategy is about exploiting all opportunities to make a real social impact that drives the bottom-line—because why wouldn't you?

These pages are filled with guidance and inspiration, not hard and fast rules. It's about recreating and shaping a mindset versus following a strict playbook. I'm not suggesting we overhaul the entire marketing industry. Well... not entirely. Does the state of systemic inequity that we're in need to be overhauled? Yes. Are we doomed if we don't move the needle on climate change? Sure, yes. But is the best way to achieve progress trying to do it all in one bite? No. This book is the catalyst for taking all the bites we can and making finding those morsels an organizational habit. I'm giving a roadmap towards activation to all those who believe in the inherent importance of responsibility in the way businesses market.

Thanks for coming along for the ride.

Now without further ado—LFG!

Notes

1 LinkedIn News. LinkedIn top voices in marketing and advertising: The 15 creators to follow, LinkedIn, February 9, 2022. www.linkedin.com/pulse/ linkedin-top-voices-marketing-advertising-15-creators-follow-/ (archived at https://perma.cc/25P5-UYQB)

2 S. Monnie. Prosperity over profit with Samuel Monnie, LinkedIn, April 2024. www.linkedin.com/posts/samuelmonnie_i-can-neither-confirm-nor-deny-that-activity-7182033667714670593-Aycq/ (archived at https://perma.cc/3NYR-XV8U)

3 J. Mackey, R. Sisodia, and B. George (2013) *Conscious Capitalism: Liberating the heroic spirit of business*, Harvard Business Review Press, Cambridge, MA

4 A. Bourdain, and L. Woolever (2024) *World Travel: An irreverent guide*, Ecco, New York

PART ONE

The Framework

Reach for More

01

Make It Inclusive

How Responsible Marketing Works

I was born in 1984 and grew up in the 1990s, when catalogs were still a big thing. I'd flip through page after page of young, thin, white models in tiny clothes, imagining how perfect my life would be if I could only be one of them. While part of me found it fun and comforting to spend a few stolen moments pretending their world was my own, most of me secretly felt a deep sense of shame and sadness, knowing there was no way I'd ever belong there.

Then came Dove's iconic Campaign for Real Beauty in 2004.

It was the very first time I had ever seen bodies that looked like mine celebrated on television. Considered almost a revolutionary act at the time, the first ad became a watershed moment in the Western cultural zeitgeist, creating a ripple effect that can still be felt twenty years later. That moment was the catalyst for a major shift toward a more inclusive standard of beauty that continues today—from narrow, unobtainable, and downright danger-ous, to representative of us as we actually are, adorned with the curves, wrinkles, and so-called "imperfections" that make each of us so delightfully unique. The women in those ads posed just as confidently as the Victoria's Secret Angels who were popular at that time, but they also had real bodies that told their real stories, stories which far more of the brand's target audi-ence could delight in finally seeing themselves.

This had a profound effect on me. It changed the trajectory of my sense of self-regard and pointed it toward more self-acceptance. In changing what I believed about myself, Dove transformed my relationship with the brand into something much more visceral than it was before and, as a result, much more commercially valuable to them. Like so many others, I went from being a Dove consumer to a Dove believer, and Unilever's biggest portfolio brand got even bigger as a result. After a period of stagnant growth that was the impetus for the research behind the campaign,[1] revenues increased by 10 percent in year one.[2] As its continued success—including a recent twentieth-anniversary refresh—demonstrates, those early results were a signal of regenerative responsible marketing impact that continues to build momentum and shows no signs of slowing down.

By addressing an unmet, brand-relevant societal need (belonging and acceptance for women of all body types, ages, races, and ethnicities) in a way that grew the business, Dove's Campaign for Real Beauty lays the groundwork for understanding this book's definition of responsible marketing—the practice of ambitiously addressing brand-relevant societal needs in ways that positively impact brand reputation and deliver outsized business results.

It Cuts Through the Clutter in Name Alone

The term "responsible marketing" unlocks a level of clarity and easily shared understanding that comparable industry terms so often prevent. Purpose marketing, inclusive marketing, cause marketing, conscious marketing, multicultural marketing, social impact marketing, ethical marketing, diversity marketing, sustainable marketing, culture marketing... we've all heard and used variations of these terms and more, but we lack a shared understanding of how, why, and when to use them. By optimizing for relevance, intention, and precision, responsible marketing invites us to say "R.I.P." to unnecessary confusion that slows us down, holds us back, and leaves world-changing work vulnerable to detractors both well-meaning and otherwise.

Relevance

"Responsible" is a word that resonates with all of us. It's how we describe ourselves when we're at our best. It refers to the practice of doing more than what's required, not just what we'll be held accountable for. Being responsible involves considering the implications of our actions to all affected stakeholders, not just the ones that matter most. It drives us to be the kind of person we ideally want to be, a person who embodies an aspirational integrity. Not all professionals see themselves as purpose-driven or culturally conscious, but who doesn't see themselves as responsible, or at least as a person who is trying to be?

Intention

From an intention standpoint, I thought it was important to evolve how we talk about socially impactful marketing work to convey a sense of urgency that doesn't come through with words like "cause" or "purpose". I wanted to find a word that signaled not just what we could do, but what we *should* do. As we'll discuss more in the commercial impact chapter, my word choice of intention also served as a nod to all of the important considerations, business outcomes included. An authentic commitment to this work means recognizing that succeeding in its social mission alone does not make a marketing initiative successful. As marketers, our fiscal responsibility to the company behind our brands must always be top of mind. Does "cause" marketing evoke the importance of considering the bottom-line when we decide what approach to social impact-driven marketing to pursue? If it does at all, the word "responsible" does it better.

Precision

From a precision standpoint, the current words in our marketing lexicon are either too zoomed in or too zoomed out. Using the word multicultural to describe marketing is probably the most glaring example of being so zoomed out that all meaning is lost, like tractor trailers that look like Lego™ pieces from the vantage point of an airplane thousands of feet in the air. Multicultural compared to what? In an integrated society, isn't multicultural really the same as mainstream? More often than not, when marketers use the word multicultural, they're using it to refer to a particular racial or ethnic demographic without having to say the words. Targeting the Latine community? Call it multicultural. Targeting the Black community? Call that multicultural too! So, is multicultural marketing meant to describe marketing aimed at everyone that isn't white? Aren't white people multicultural too? Too many questions, not nearly enough precision.

Now that we've established a strong working definition of responsible marketing and the rationale for our word choice, let's dive into the handy framework I created to help you visualize exactly how it all works.

It Fuels the Marketer's Triple Top-Line Flywheel

The Framework That Explains How Responsible Marketing Works

If responsible marketing is an engine, what you feed into this foundational framework is its (100 percent sustainable!) fuel. My hope is that after reading this book, this framework becomes a lighthouse you can always trust to guide you through the process of creating authentic and inclusive responsible marketing strategies—without being so prescriptive that you don't feel free to chart your own path. I call this the marketer's Triple Top-Line Flywheel. We'll go deep on each of its three critical components in Chapters 2, 3, and 4, but here in Chapter 1 we'll begin with an overview of the framework as a whole.

As you can see in Figure 1.1, the Triple Top-Line Flywheel has three critical components, each with its own five key performance indicators (KPIs). Starting with social impact, the triple top-line depicts how—when one or more of its five conditions are met—each component unlocks the next for an ongoing cycle of regenerative impact. At its best, like Dove's Campaign for Real Beauty, we see exactly how responsible marketing leads to long-term, tangible value on all three fronts that only builds momentum as it continues to evolve.

When I spoke with veteran marketer and current Managing Director of the Forbes CMO Network Seth Matlins, I was struck by the many ways his career path itself exemplifies the very same idea. Seth's awe-inspiring journey and masterful insights are a product of his own long-term, regenerative

FIGURE 1.1 The marketer's Triple Top-Line Flywheel

Social impact
- Fosters diversity
- Enables inclusion
- Advances equity
- Cultivates belonging
- Supports sustainability

Reputation Impact
- Amplifies brand identity
- Delivers positive earned media
- Increases share of voice
- Generates word of mouth/ +NPS
- Improves brand health/sentiment scores

Responsible marketing

Commercial impact
- Drives sales
- Acquires new customers/users
- Retains customers/users
- Maximizes wallet share/frequency
- Attracts investors

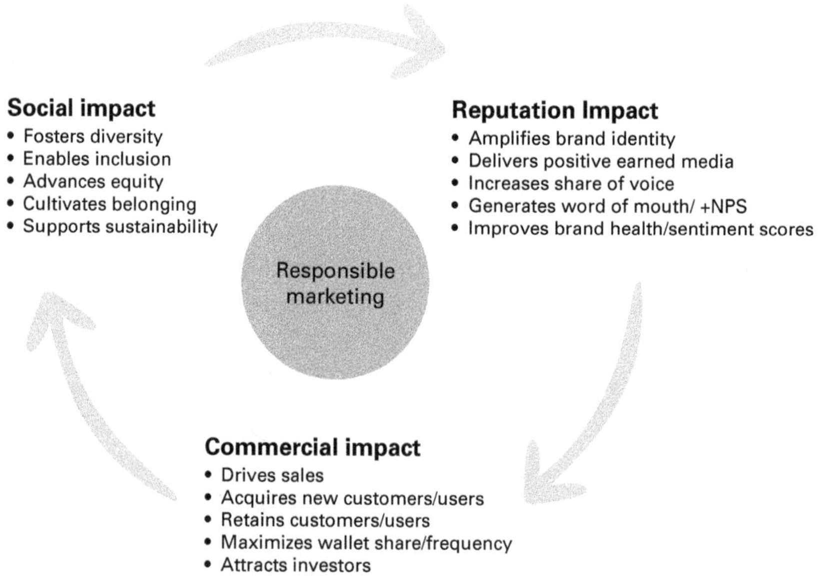

impact. His impact continues to build momentum as it evolves because it is so well grounded in what matters most to the most responsible marketers I know—ambitiously addressing societal needs in ways that lead to outsized business results. Before we move on to further unpack the triple top-line, let's get immersed in his journey for a glimpse into the real-world impact this way of thinking can help you achieve.

REAL TALK WITH RESPONSIBLE MARKETERS
Seth Matlins

Managing Director of Forbes CMO Network, Board Member at American Advertising Federation, Board Member at AdCouncil, and Advisory Board Member at Global Citizen, Seth is a versatile and universally admired operator/marketer with a career spent in and advising the C-suite of the most iconic brands globally, designing efficient, effective, and often culturally driven solutions to their most intractable problems.

Starting With a Socio-Cultural Perspective

I've always believed in the very simple premise of doing well by doing good. In 2000, I started the marketing practice at Creative Artists Agency (CAA). In our work promoting the first two Harry Potter films, we gave away tens of millions of books when we launched what I think was the largest global literacy initiative in history. We also helped Delta Airlines create the Delta Force for Social Good, through which they became the first domestic carrier to offer carbon-neutral offsets to travelers.

Advice For Marketers New to Responsible Marketing

I think the key is to understand some things fundamentally. Who they are as a brand and business. What the consequences and unintended consequences and values are of those brands and businesses. Who their audiences are, both internal and external. And what the stakeholder, if you will, cares about.

Two of my least favorite words in marketing today are *authenticity* and *purpose*. I don't even know what they mean anymore. I wrote a piece titled "The purpose of purpose is brand and business growth." That's it. That's the role. I don't believe that the greatest impact brands and businesses can have is a philanthropic impact. I believe it has to be united with marketing.

Marketing is in the practice of changing attitudes and behaviors, influencing intentions. And that's why I called the practice when I started it an "endeavor."

Branded impact. It never took, but that's the idea. Corporate social responsibility (CSR) is important, too. It's great. It's lovely, but it's table stakes. CSR is oftentimes about mitigating negatives while, in my perspective, the opportunity to create positives is equally important, if not more so.

I often refer to the old Coke campaign "Open Happiness" as a "purpose-driven" campaign because I think they were just trying to make people happier. And that's really good. Putting a smile on my face is really good. It may not solve the world's problems, but it makes my world a little bit better for even an instant. In today's world, people (I don't like the words consumer or customer very much because they relegate a human being to a functional role) want to know what you're doing to be a participant in making a world that's in crisis a better place.

To Whom Are Marketers Responsible?

I love the notion of responsible marketing because it begs the question of responsible to whom and what? The thing that keeps us from doing more good is a fundamental flaw in our thinking and framing. Making the world a better place alone cannot be the objective of a business. Growth is the objective of a business. To market responsibly, a marketer's role is to define the parameters of responsible growth. It's about identifying and activating the responsible levers of business growth.

Who is Winning at Responsible Marketing?

Obviously, you can look at some of the legacy brands—Patagonia, Ben and Jerry's, the Body Shop, and Levi's. I think those who are doing the best work are those who can measure both quantitatively and qualitatively the impact they're making on communities, brands, businesses, and arguably culture at large.

CVS is another standout. Brilliantly, their decision to remove tobacco and tobacco-related products from their stores in 2014 was a $2 billion hit to the bottom line. But they stood on principle, and it has served them well.

Walmart gets almost no credit for being, in my opinion, one of the most important players in the sustainability movement. They force manufacturers to use less plastic in their packaging and less water in their products. For example, concentrated detergent comes from Walmart. I just wish they would take the credit and find a way to let people know. Marketers that get that part right, deservedly, do really well.

It Accommodates Expansive Societal Needs

Putting the Triple Top-Line to Work

As Seth's real talk reminds us, responsible marketing combines the authentic truth of what a brand stands for with its core, fundamental purpose—driving growth. For the Triple Top-Line Flywheel to spring into action, brand-relevant social impact insights must first be identified. How work gets done is always going to vary, but no matter what exactly you're working on, chances are the process is going to involve some version of these seven steps.

1 Research/listening/analysis

2 Identifying/selecting key insight(s)

3 Creating/crafting/drafting strategy

4 Earning buy-in for strategy

5 Launching/executing strategy

6 Evaluating strategy

7 Optimizing or sunsetting strategy

Triple top-line thinking comes together because, when you solve a problem, you create brand preference and that is what makes the reputational impact turn into commercial impact. How can we be thinking about the communities, customers, and stakeholders we serve in terms of their expansive identities, and how can we use that as a way to do the thing we know marketing does well when it's done at its best, which is to make an emotional connection? It takes the push towards the diversity, equity, and inclusion movement that we've all been seeing heightened over the past few years and uses that to come up with more successful marketing strategies. And here's the true beauty of it all. It's no different than how the principles of marketing you already know work for brands. Solve problems and make emotional connections that build community.

It starts with the belief that you can have an outsized effect on something, a social impact, in a way that's relevant to the brand. That leads to a positive impact on a brand's reputation, which results in commercial impact.

It Requires Specific Business Outcomes

In a world where consumers across identities are four times more likely to trust brands that take a stand, the power of truly inclusive marketing is too often passed over. Instead, brands favor siloed multicultural marketing efforts that slice and dice the population into segments. They fail to bring us all together, or worse, attempt to check the box with surface-level visual representation.

Today's most-successful inclusive marketing moments reach for more by ambitiously addressing systemic inequities in ways that simultaneously deliver outsized business results. They show us what it looks like to embrace the reality that multiculturalism is mainstream, and a more equitable future is on all of us to create. If you're nodding your head but still not sure what to do next, just start by simply keeping it real.

Authenticity here means more than meets the eye, it also refers to being authentic to a marketer's role in the business. It all starts with choosing a social impact effort that is measurable and makes a meaningful long-term impact to the intended beneficiary. If you are doing something that actually has an impact beyond the time horizon of your marketing activity, you are on your way to the benefits of reputation impact, which leads to sales, retention, and better investor activity. It is both a framework and a flywheel that draws a clear line between what a brand does to add value to consumers, and what a brand gets in return.

We can drive the business by doing responsible marketing, and that is the link we too often ignore. As so many brands have proven, it is entirely possible to reach for more by ambitiously addressing societal needs in ways that simultaneously deliver outsized business results. Put another way, this is about finding value at the intersection of commercial goals and societal needs. With the Flywheel, marketing leaders have a tool to visualize and replicate the non-negotiable building blocks that set responsible marketing up for success. It's a tool that breaks down the causal relationship between social impact, reputation impact, and commercial impact. As I learned in an inspiring conversation with legendary marketer Derek Walker, marketing reflects the world in its most unified form. We can bring that into existence by showing people the possibilities of what that world could look like. Nobody has more power to change the way people see the world than marketers do.

REAL TALK WITH RESPONSIBLE MARKETERS
Derek Walker

Founder and Creative Director at Brown and Browner Advertising, Derek has a unique perspective shaped by a career in-house with giant brands like Pizza Hut and McDonalds, *as well as experience at TBWA\Chiat\Day. Throughout his years in advertising, Derek has been a steadfast voice on diversity and inclusion in the industry.*

His Initial Reaction to "Responsible Marketing"

I think we've made up another term and just like with any movement, they will take it and turn it into a dirty four-letter word, in the same way they did "woke" because there are individuals who just believe that organizations exist only for profit.

I have been telling brands since before the 1960s that communicating with Black and Hispanic communities can raise their profiles immensely. But something internal keeps brands from doing it, whether it be bias, prejudice, or racism. If I have a bias for Black folks, I may speak to them first. That's a bias, but I also speak to the whites and Hispanics, Asians, and all the subcultures inside of Asian and Hispanic. That's not prejudiced. That's not racism. That's bias, and bias is natural. I'm prejudiced against super thin people. Because of my culture, I think they always look like they need to eat. Therefore, I'm not going to date someone who is skinny. That's a prejudice for me. We like to say preference, but it's really prejudice. I don't think skinny people are healthy. And sooner or later, I start to think skinny people are stupid because they're not picking up weight. I'm thinking that they're lazy because they're not putting in the effort. You see how it changes and grows into something dangerous?

What happens inside a brand when that preference for that prejudice gains power? Prejudice leads to racism when it's an extreme. It creeps into something different that says this group is better than this group, which is better than this group, which is better than this group. You can change somebody who is biased or prejudiced, but once you get to the extreme racist, you can't change them.

I have sat in far too many meetings at white agencies where Black research companies have emphatically informed them that Black consumers lead their sales. Yet they completely disregard the data. How do you change that? There's something inside the decision makers that said, "We'll leave that money on the table. That money isn't good enough."

Almost two decades ago, we created a Mercedes Benz campaign that spoke about the importance of safety. We invented the airbags, but we didn't patent it so everyone else could use them. That's how important safety is to Mercedes, and isn't that responsible marketing? But we didn't call it that back then. We just called it marketing. What about the brands that divested from South Africa in response to apartheid? Wasn't that marketing? I can't delineate between the two. Yes, somebody definitely needs to come up with a definition. But they must understand that they're naming something that some brands have been doing forever.

On Companies That Have Done Well While Also Making a Measurable Social Impact

In marketing the Fusion, Ford realized that they had a couple of cars that really spoke to African Americans, and they sold a bunch of them. They put the money behind doing that. Toyota saw Ford's experience and hired a Black agency to do that with the Camry and the Corolla. The funny part is, GM was slower to do it than Ford. Subaru stumbled on the idea of speaking to the LGBTQ+ community in a couple ads and all of a sudden realized how popular their cars were in the community. They had sales in the 1990s and early 2000 that were carried by nurses and gay folks, period. They couldn't have planned that out. They could have tried but every time you try to plan something, the universe does something different. Like Dove, they had no idea. I mean, the sheer volume of positive responses to that message, nobody could have planned for that.

Most brands lack the level of patience needed to consistently work on making a social impact, but for those that want to, the first step is diversity. They have to realize they need people in the room who understand who they're talking to. So they have to change outside. Then they have to look at their partners, the agencies, and their consultants and say "You need to change too because there's a new message coming out."

On the Marketing Playbook

The playbook is simply to be human. We're trying to codify things that deal expressly with human beings. I heard this guy talking about marketing and advertising on a podcast say it's not rocket science. I'm like, you idiot. It's harder than rocket science because you deal with the heart. And the heart is not logical. The playbook should be to have a loose framework, but to understand that time is relative to humans.

Are You Solving a Real Problem For the Intended Beneficiary?

As we learned from last year's Black square-mageddon, well-meaning expressions of solidarity are no substitute for tangible solutions. In the chapters that follow, we will deep dive into some impressively impactful campaigns, such as Mastercard's True Name campaign, which masterfully showed up for the transgender community while shedding light on an over-looked indignity many face simply for being who they are.[3] When Lyft partnered with CVS to offer free rides to Covid-19 vaccine appointments for those in need, they provided a service that made a powerful emotional connection with everyone, as did Dove's championing of the CROWN Act for Black women facing race-based hair discrimination.[4]

There's no shortage of real problems for brands to solve. Addressing them in ways that also support business goals is a natural alignment with the very thing brand leaders have always been striving for: the ongoing alignment of purpose and profit.

Are You Creating a Real Opportunity?

Sephora's campaign featuring "the best of Black-owned beauty for everyone" was a powerful example of authentic allyship as an effective revenue strategy. Closing systemic opportunity gaps requires bold and corrective action, not just a simple acknowledgment. Campaigns like PepsiCo's Dig In initiative to Budweiser's Brewing Change demonstrate the unique positioning of marketers to embrace responsible marketing by using their power to address systemic inequities in ways that authentically honor a brand's purpose and create opportunities for specific communities or society as a whole. Providing help in the short term is a step forward, but creating real opportunities is the key to the type of impact with lasting societal effects.

For some brands, finding real opportunities meant facing their own histories of oppression. By committing to making banking more accessible to Black communities and acknowledging systemic injustices plaguing the financial services industry to this day, Citi's Action for Racial Equity Initiative brilliantly exemplifies what it looks like to champion inclusivity from a place of open accountability, and that's why I will refer to it often as we unpack each component of the Flywheel. The pancake and syrup brand formerly known as Aunt Jemima also faced the stereotypical tropes of its real history and rebranded as the Pearl Milling Company. This long overdue rebranding shifted outdated narratives in favor of a more inclusive reality. It shows us the extent to which cultivating a tangible sense of belonging that changes how people see and experience the world starts with facing the truth.

Reach For More—What Marketer is Satisfied With the Status Quo?

In her book *Social Impact Marketing: The essential guide for changemakers*, Maddy Kulkarni explains that social impact marketing involves the strategic use of marketing principles and techniques towards the goal of driving positive social changes.[5] She advocates moving beyond the traditional marketing strategies that focus solely on building brand equity and increasing sales, by adding an additional focus of positive impact. She says that, through the engagement of stakeholders, brands can successfully align their business goals with broader social and environmental objectives.

Overall, Kulkarni sees social impact marketing as a powerful tool for businesses to not only drive brand loyalty and competitive advantage but also contribute to the greater good by addressing pressing social and environmental challenges. It requires a holistic approach that integrates marketing principles with social responsibility, ethics, and sustainability to create meaningful and lasting impact.

When we demand more than the status quo of ourselves as stewards of a brand, that's when we can really achieve great things. That is what this book aspires to do through the lens of the most foundational level, the triple top-line framework. It is about that idea of how things can be better, and how making things better for the people that we're marketing to can actually make our marketing work better for our brand.

Using the power of social media and influences, EOS turned away from most traditional marketing methods to position themselves among young female consumers. They focused on delivering what their target market wanted, which was more about the way the product made them feel than its practicality. EOS marketed their product as one that was aesthetically pleasing and cute for the visual world of social media that matters so much to their consumers. It took less than a decade for the company to outsell the industry's most established brands, such as Chapstick and Blistex. After only six years in the marketplace, EOS accounted for 11.5 percent of all lip balm sales in the United States, second only to Burt's Bees at 12.1 percent.[6] EOS ranked fourth on Business Insider's list of the top 50 brands that young women love, ranking higher than Sephora (#7) and right under Victoria's Secret (#3).[7]

REAL TALK WITH RESPONSIBLE MARKETERS
Soyoung Kang

Soyoung Kang is Chief Marketing Officer (CMO) at EOS Products, Independent Board Member at Bob's Discount Furniture, formerly Senior Vice President of Brand Merchandising at Bath and Body Works, Adweek Brand Genius, Forbes Entrepreneurial

CMO, Campaign US CMO 50, and a Business Insider Most Innovative CMO. As a strong
proponent of diversity, equity, and inclusion, Soyoung serves on the industry DEI councils
and as co-chair of the CMO vertical for Ascend Executive Network.

Changing the Game in a Space Where the Needs of the Most Loyal Consumer Had Been Ignored

Though women purchased 80 percent of all lip care products, there was nothing catering to their specific interests. There is value in giving consumers a little moment of joy, which is what EOS set out to do with our marketing strategies to introduce new products. If you have an audience that exists prior to changes in the marketing, it takes a lot longer for the change to get impacted in the existing audience. But if you launch something new, and you're reaching new audiences, you're starting from zero and that's a real test of how impactful it is. As far as we can see, number one, our body care business has been doing really well. And number two, it's over-penetrating specifically with Black women consumers. It's in our brand health numbers in terms of awareness, favorability, and purchase interest. Then, it's in our sales numbers, seeing triple digit growth.

We started with creator programs that showcased the level of diverse representation, but it eventually became a flywheel as the audiences of people who are in the communities with those diverse creators also have diverse audiences, which evolved into a virtuous cycle, as people started sharing things organically, with different types of consumers engaging with the EOS body care segment. You see the impact of the business growth, and of the brand affinity and it's cool to see all of that happening at once.

The Oxymoron of Responsible Marketing

When I first heard the term "responsible marketing," it sounded like an oxymoron. Marketing, in its worst form, represents the opposite of responsibility. At the lowest common denominator form, marketing is trying to get someone to believe something that they don't already believe, which you could argue is also a form of manipulation... a form of deceit. In its best iteration, marketing can be educational. It can also be entertaining, and there's value inherently in just being able to give people a little moment of joy and delight. It can also be influential, and in certain hands that influence can be really meaningful in promoting change more broadly.

I don't actually think that responsible marketing is an oxymoron. I see it as the best iteration of marketing, which is a conduit for influencing change, informing consumers, and giving something back to society, even if that contribution is as small as entertainment and as high on the food chain as societal change. According to Kang, giving something back in the form of marketing is something that we all aim to do as marketers.

On Repaying Societal Debt

At EOS, our marketing strategies are less about repaying a societal debt and more about rebalancing so that we are taking full advantage of the opportunities of a much more multifaceted marketplace than we had participated in before. Then, it kind of flips it out of being "We're doing this to do a good thing" and more of "We're doing this because it makes sense, it's good for growth, it's good for our brand. Now, we get to participate in 100 percent of the market, not 60 percent of the market."

As a smaller challenger brand, EOS does not have the scale and the resources to go everywhere and be everywhere in a "spend harder" kind of mode. We are sometimes forced to differentiate and be really thoughtful about how we market to our audiences, because we have to be smart about how we approach our marketing. We instituted a creative diversity guideline internally that had nothing to do with signaling to the outside world. It harkened back to the feeling that we had a deficit in our prior creator marketing, in terms of diversity, that we felt was, frankly, business limiting. Why would we only market to a segment of the available marketplace? We needed to change up how we were working with creators to show the level of representation, diversity, and breadth of different people that we believe our potential audience would have.

It Transcends the Performative

The last decade has brought about a shift in the consumer landscape, resulting in a pronounced desire for brands to reflect the diversity and identities of their customers. This evolution underscores the importance of authentic representation in marketing strategies. Modern consumers seek brands that resonate with their values, lifestyles, and identities, fostering a deeper sense of connection and loyalty. To meet these demands, brands must prioritize inclusivity in their messaging and imagery to ensure that consumers feel seen and heard. This celebration of diversity is the key to attracting and maintaining a loyal customer base in today's increasingly discerning market.

The biggest misconception about inclusive marketing is that it's some major disruptive change being thrust upon the industry. Inclusiveness isn't a divergence—it's a (long overdue) course correction. When we talk about inclusive marketing, we're talking about what it looks like to shape what brands offer and how they go to market to create meaningful and measurable social impact that also maximizes bottom-line business results. By including brand relevant cultural context brands make stronger emotional connections that unlock impact and deliver dollars and cents.

So, what's holding marketers back?

There is a perilous tendency to obsess over perceived downsides—return-on-investment (ROI) questions, risk of backlash, etc.—and it holds marketing leaders back from fully embracing and leaning into what is obviously the correct path forward. When done well and authentically, inclusive marketing practices lead to organizational impact across three key dimensions: revenue, social, and reputation. Three simple and perfectly reasonable changes in perspective can help facilitate better conversations about inclusivity in your marketing.

It's Actually Apolitical

An interesting thing I noticed a while back: many brands and teams that claimed to "not get political" were perfectly open to speaking out in support of Ukraine. Why is that? No one can argue that war isn't political. It seems like marketers felt comfortable speaking up about this because it was very obviously the right thing to do. How is that any different from taking a stand on inclusiveness in society?

Understandably, many brands tread carefully in areas of political sensitivity to avoid alienating segments of their audience, but we need to stop viewing matters of equality and human rights as political. These matters should transcend political divides, and by reframing these issues as fundamental moral imperatives rather than partisan debates, brands can foster a more inclusive and socially responsible approach to their messaging. Advocating for human rights isn't just a matter of political correctness; it's a reflection of core values that resonate with today's conscientious consumers. Brands that authentically champion equality and human rights can build stronger connections with their audience and position themselves as agents of positive change in society. The prioritization of inclusivity and social responsibility over political considerations helps brands contribute to a more equitable world.

Reframe Perceived Risk

What if we anger people in our audience who disagree? What if our message is misinterpreted even by those who agree? What if we flat-out miss the mark and get called out? While these are all reasonable concerns, marketers and business leaders can (and do) freeze themselves in place when they focus on these theoretical risk points when it comes to taking a firmly inclusive stance.

I encourage you to think about this from the other side. The biggest risk is standing still, and sticking to the status quo. Effective marketers understand that staying complacent and stagnant in a rapidly evolving industry can lead to irrelevance and lost opportunities. Innovation is the lifeblood of successful marketing strategies, driving growth, engagement, and competitive advantage. Brands that fail to adapt and innovate risk falling short of consumer expectations, which leads to falling behind competitors. Embracing a culture of continuous innovation and agility is essential for staying ahead in the ever-evolving marketing space.

If you're asking yourself whether this is some passing trend that's going to yo-yo back to the previous norm, let me assure you. There's no chance. Gen Z is the most diverse generation ever across a spectrum of identity traits. The demand for inclusive marketing is only going to grow. That's just reality. Are you going to take the lead or follow behind? Fortune favors the bold.

Don't Obsess So Much About Measurement

It seems like many marketers treat social impact as a specialized category, needing its own unique financial justification and rigorous measurement process. But this compartmentalization may obscure the fundamental principle that social impact should be integrated seamlessly into broader marketing strategies. Rather than separating social impact efforts, marketers should approach them with the same rigor and accountability they apply to any other campaign or initiative. Establish clear goals and objectives upfront, and subsequently assess their attainment through comprehensive measurement and evaluation frameworks. By treating social impact initiatives as integral components of marketing endeavors, brands can align their actions with their values while driving meaningful outcomes and fostering positive societal change.

While the bottom-line benefits of inclusive marketing have been broadly proven out, it is folly to focus too much on immediate revenue impact. That's only part of the equation, because the social impact and reputational impact are critical, and will pay dividends in the long term.

We can't truly embrace the principles of inclusive marketing if we're continually getting caught up in the "buts" and "what ifs." The truth is that if you're not adamantly leaning into inclusive marketing, you're already falling behind. The opportunity to be a part of the most important conversation in marketing is right in front of you, and taking it isn't just the right thing to do morally—it's also the right thing to do for your business.

The Risk of Inaction is the Real Risk

When you are sitting at your desk, evaluating responsible marketing ideas and setting annual plans, what makes you hesitant about taking advantage of this innovative approach? Are you concerned with how your employees may respond because your team's lack of diversity may still be an issue? Maybe your worries involve potential backlash from audiences or stakeholders who may perceive such efforts as insincere or opportunistic. Financial implications, regulatory scrutiny, and legal challenges may also be top of mind for you. You aren't alone in these hesitations. Not even the companies on the Fortune 500 have figured this out, but I ask you to consider the opportunity cost of waiting. As marketers, we have our own plans, budgets, and social impact opportunities that are different from any internal workforce issues. Shouldn't we add value when we can, even if there's more work to do internally?

Let's dissect the commonly perceived risk of "getting cancelled." What does it actually mean to be on this mythical cancel list? Maybe your concern is the possibility of alienating conservative customers? I grew up in a part of Pennsylvania in an area that a lot of people refer to as "Pennsyltucky." As part of a loud, boisterous Nigerian family, we were definitely out of our "natural habitat," surrounded by the conservative customers you fear alienating. But guess what? My parents made amazing friends. My siblings and I made amazing friends. And those friends happily learned about our culture. We saw one another as humans, despite our differences, and we supported one another for the betterment of the collective. (Sound familiar?) Though they aren't the loudest voices, the vast majority of conservative people do not believe that the transgender community should not exist, and they are not going to make purchasing decisions based on that hatred. So, why are you letting a few dictate your brand decisions? We have to ask ourselves is there really any more risk involved than the sensibilities of a "loud minority."

Let me give you one final perceived risk—the notion that management will fear that you are being distracted from bottom line priorities. This book will give you example after example debunking that risk, but let's briefly consider a familiar friend. Dove's Evolution campaign was launched by Unilever in 2006 in conjunction with the Campaign for Real Beauty to highlight the reasons behind our widely held distorted views of beauty. The campaign resulted in $150 million worth of media exposure, racking up millions of views on YouTube in months.[8] Within the first decade of the campaign, Dove sales increased from $2.5 to $4 billion, making it Unilever's top-selling product. Responsible marketing is a full circle that naturally leads back to bottom line priorities. I hope that you will walk away from this book with the understanding that the real fear is not taking advantage of this opportunity from a dollar and cents standpoint. Brand leaders who embrace the opportunity will increasingly outshine those who falsely perceive their power as a burden.

REAL TALK WITH RESPONSIBLE MARKETERS
Antonio Lucio

Executive Vice President and Chief Marketing and Corporate Affairs Officer at HP Inc., Cofounder and Advisor at Virtuosi LEAP, Executive Fellow at Yale School of Management, Hall of Fame Inductee at American Advertising Federation, American Marketing Association, and the Forbes Most Influential CMOs, Antonio is an experienced and successful Global Marketing Communications Officer whose mission in life is to build businesses, brands, and high-performing global teams that stand the test of time.

Enhancing Lives

Responsible marketing is marketing that drives business growth by enhancing the lives of people inside and outside the company and protects and rebuilds our planet. It is good for business, good for people, and good for the world. If marketing exists to build brands that stand the test of time, the only possible way is to build those brands responsibly.

In-House Diversity Makes a Financial Impact

The work done at HP outperformed business goals and made a measurable social impact when we created an invitation to the entire marketing ecosystem to increase the participation of women and people of color across the entire ecosystem; client, agency partners, media, and production. The two-year effort not only significantly increased the participation of women and people of color in leadership roles across the multiple dimensions of the ecosystem, but quantitative readership proved that the output delivered dramatically significant lifts in purchase intent.

Mindset shifts start at the top. HP had one of the more diverse boards in corporate America and a CEO truly committed to the business case for diversity as opposed to being just the very important values case. Any significant move in the responsible marketing space cannot be a "flavor of the month" effort. It requires strategic alignment with the overall business goals and a clear process of change management where objectives are set, strategies and plans developed and executed, and clear business metrics are in place to measure results. Leadership is also important. In the case of HP, I personally led the effort to provide the required focus, resource, processes, and measurements required.

Change isn't Always Easy, So Ease Into It

Making changes of this sort is really hard work. Sometimes it requires significant investment in capital, time, and change management, as companies like Unilever and HP, that are working hard to enhance the sustainability of their products and business, have proven. Sometimes these efforts take time to pay out and the pressures of short-term results set in. Importantly, sometimes these efforts require a very different set of skills that the companies may need to build, partner or acquire. These fundamental shifts are not for the faint at heart.

Every marketer should be committing to building the business case for responsible marketing in their companies and categories. Start small, with a real tangible project. Measure results, prove the case, build the storyline, and then transform more broadly.

In 2023, I partnered with sparks & honey on the Responsible Marketing Index, and I want to share three really interesting statistics that speak to the why.[9] First, 81 percent of surveyed consumers believe that brands have a role to play in addressing social issues that affect their customers. But here is where it gets really interesting; 71 percent of consumers responded that they would be likely to buy an inclusive alternative to a product, even if it did not specifically apply to them. We used the example of a lipstick with an accessible cap, and while this is the answer I hoped to hear, I was blown away by the high percentage. Lastly, 74 percent of surveyed consumers said it is important for brands to help audiences see beyond stereotypes. Consumers are placing the onus on us as marketers to actually take the opportunity to advance culture and make the world a better place. As marketers, we provide solutions that make lives better. We create brands as shortcuts to understanding what those solutions and emotional benefits are, but it is also about adding value. If you can tap into people's intrinsic belief that we, as a society, need each other to thrive, you have a powerful advantage.

Notes

1 M. Kramer, M. Sidibe, and G. Veda. Dove and Real Beauty: Building a brand with purpose, Harvard Business School Case Collection, 2021. www.hbs.edu/faculty/Pages/item.aspx?num=56459 (archived at https://perma.cc/Q6TR-BZ7V)

2 M. Taylor. The enduring power and impact of Dove's 'Real Beauty' campaign, Strixus, 2023. www.strixus.com/entry/the-enduring-power-and-impact-of-doves-real-beauty-campaign-18095 (archived at https://perma.cc/4WSK-PKA3)

3 Mastercard. Mastercard True Name feature expands across the globe supporting transgender and non-binary communities worldwide, Mastercard, 2021. www.mastercard.com/news/press/2021/june/mastercard-true-name-feature-expands-across-the-globe-supporting-transgender-and-non-binary-communities-worldwide/ (archived at https://perma.cc/3K5R-NENV)

4 AP News. Lyft teams up with CVS Health to support equitable access to the Covid-19 vaccine, AP News, February 19, 2021. www.apnews.com/article/business-public-health-race-and-ethnicity-human-welfare-transportation-and-shipping-55c7bcdfce3a8ac6206179d77ad15fb1 (archived at https://perma.cc/XZL5-SMT9); Dove. Racial equity: The CROWN Act, Dove, 2024. www.dove.com/us/en/stories/campaigns/the-crown-act.html (archived at https://perma.cc/8HLA-R5GB)

5 M. Kulkarni (2021) *Social Impact Marketing: The essential guide for changemakers*, Kendall Hunt Publishing, Dubuque

6 D. Petruzzi. Dollar sales share of the leading lip balm/treatment brands in the United States in 2019, Statista, February22, 2024. www.statista.com/statistics/463377/us-dollar-sales-share-of-leading-lip-balm-treatment-brands/ (archived at https://perma.cc/E2YV-UGJ8)

7 M. Schlossberg and A. Lutz. The top 50 brands that cool teenage girls love, Business Insider, June 10, 2016. www.businessinsider.com/goldman-sachs-coolest-teen-retail-brands-2016-6 (archived at https://perma.cc/67ZJ-R2EQ)

8 G. Kumari. Dove: The rise of a purpose led brand, The Strategy Story, May 4, 2021. www.thestrategystory.com/2021/05/04/dove-brand-purpose/ (archived at https://perma.cc/38NT-WTLJ)

9 L. Bakare, and D. Harris. Responsible Marketing Index 2023, proprietary research led by Leslie Rodrigues and conducted in partnership with Lola Bakare to inform this book.

02

Make It Authentic

Brand-Relevant Social Impact

It wasn't actually dreamed up by Don Draper, but the story behind Coke's classic "I'd Like to Teach the World to Sing" ad is still one worth telling.[1] Here's what most people don't know about the iconic jingle—its origin story took place during an unexpected moment while the brand was having a small but mighty, authentic social impact in real-time. For the purposes of this story, think of this in terms of the difference between its functional, thirst-quenching benefits and the less directly product-driven emotional ones.

Bill Backer, a creative director at McCann Erickson, was in the middle of one of those endless at-gate airport flight delay moments where one of two things always happens. People either sink into the collegial comfort of commiseration, or they devolve into *Lord of the Flies* style anarchy. Usually for the former to happen, some sort of bonding catalyst sparks a sense of unity. In this case, as Backer observed, it was a shared love and appreciation of Coca-Cola.

From that moment, the insight behind the creative was born: Coke has the power to unite all kinds of people in a shared experience of love and joy, no matter their current circumstances or individual backgrounds. It's a glorious example of how often brand success is grounded in social impact. It can be so subtle we barely even notice, but just as that jingle did and would go on to continue to do for decades, it invariably leads to outsized commercial impact when we get it right.

If you weren't expecting this chapter to start here, honestly neither was I... but a key takeaway from my research and observations is that just like there's no one perfect way to do this, there's also no one perfect why to do this. When the why is solution-oriented, the simplest way to sum it up is in terms of its impact, not its impetus. The impetus comes from lasering in on the societal problem most relevant to a brand or product's unique value proposition, or solution. As long as it betters the lived experience of an underserved group or meaningfully addresses an in-need aspect of society and a brand or product has a reason to align, the range of valid impetuses to do so is endlessly expansive.

The Triple Top-Line Starts Here (and it Always Has)

The Triple Top-Line Flywheel starts with measurable, authentic, and real social impact that does one or a few of these five things: fosters diversity, enables inclusion, advances equity, cultivates belonging, or supports sustainability. And there is probably a list of other things you can add. A momentum emerges from really doing something that matters to your audience or your customers, and that social impact is what sets the Flywheel in motion.

Social Impact Defined

To systematize the process of creating a responsible marketing strategy that meets our current societal moment, this book defines social impact a bit more narrowly than the above Coca-Cola insight would suggest. If that Coke jingle teaches us anything, it's that the possibilities of positively impacting society are incredibly expansive. In this book, we're going to focus on four key areas: solving real problems, telling real stories, creating real opportunities, and influencing real policies. But think of these as inspiration vs. limitations. I mean that! Inspiration, not limitations! Good marketing isn't about a straight sales pitch. It's about engaging with your customers, showing them that you have their back, and earning their business. What does that even mean? It means customers want to see a purpose, not just profits. They want to feel that their buying decisions align with their personal values. They don't just appreciate brand efforts to make meaningful social impact—research shows that they have come to expect it. As seen in Figure 2.2, 80.8 percent of respondents surveyed in the 2023 sparks & honey Responsible Marketing Index believe it's important for organizations and brands to play a role in addressing social issues.

Even further, according to the 2020 Edelman Trust Barometer, 80 percent of people said they want brands to solve society's problems.[2] Socially responsible brand and marketing choices provide consumers with an emotional comfort that turns into brand loyalty and ultimately spending.

FIGURE 2.1 The marketer's Triple Top-Line Flywheel—responsible marketing and social impact

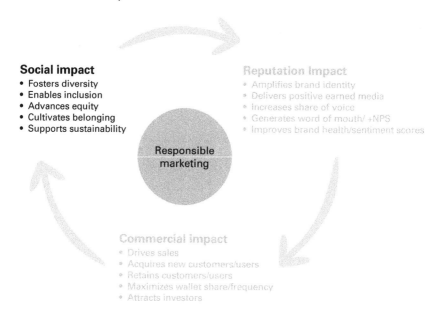

Social impact
- Fosters diversity
- Enables inclusion
- Advances equity
- Cultivates belonging
- Supports sustainability

Responsible marketing

Reputation Impact
- Amplifies brand identity
- Delivers positive earned media
- Increases share of voice
- Generates word of mouth/ +NPS
- Improves brand health/sentiment scores

Commercial Impact
- Drives sales
- Acquires new customers/users
- Retains customers/users
- Maximizes wallet share/frequency
- Attracts investors

FIGURE 2.2 Do brands and businesses have a role to play in addressing social issues?

% of respondents

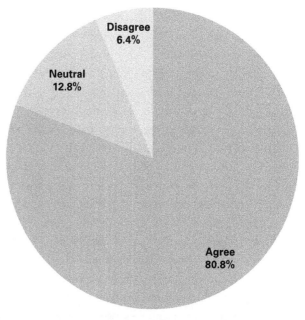

Disagree
6.4%

Neutral
12.8%

Agree
80.8%

SOURCE Based on data from the 2023 sparks & honey Responsible Marketing Index

I define social impact as meaningful, measurable, and enduring changes in conditions that positively affect a historically-excluded group or urgent cultural cause, and who exactly is historically-excluded is going to vary by brand. Categories of social impact include but are not limited to pay equity, economic equity, accessibility, gender equity, environmental sustainability, voting rights, and so many more. It's important for me to provide a clear understanding of what authentic social impact is and what it is not because we receive a lot of social impact messages from brands, but the vast majority of them are not backed by any social impact activity.

SUPERCHARGING THE FLYWHEEL

To supercharge your Flywheel, do one or more of these five in a way that aligns with your brand values and you will have DIEBS on taking a stand that also delivers results.

- Foster *diversity.*
- Enable *inclusion.*
- Advance *equity.*
- Cultivate *belonging.*
- Support *sustainability.*

When it comes to setting up your responsible marketing plans for success, intent shouldn't even be part of the conversation. What matters is what actually happens, not what we hoped might or hoped would. More often than not, you'll know social impact when you see it, but if I have to break it down to a defining attribute, it is positive output driven. A devastating weather event has a social impact on the communities it hits, but not the sort we hope for. For marketers, that goes a step farther because all positive social impact is not created equal.

Marketers Make the World Better

At the 2022 Cannes Lions Festival for Creativity, I had the pleasure of taking part in its annual "CMO Accelerator" program, a special learning track dedicated to elevating the skill sets and perspectives of brand marketing leaders (often referred to as those on the "client" or "brand" side of marketing), led by the ever-charismatic and insightful former CMO of Procter & Gamble and current host of the CMO Podcast, Jim Stengel. One of the many impressive guest speakers we enjoyed intimate conversations with was Keith Weed, a brilliant marketing leader who rose through the ranks at Unilever after joining in 1983, becoming the top marketer at the company as CMO from 2010 until he retired in 2019.

As Unilever is well known for its consistently stated commitment to the intersection of marketing, social impact, and sustainability, I was absolutely brimming with excitement to hear his take on the fallacy that marketers focusing on "greater good" initiatives were somehow distracted from their core business goals. Predictably, his response reinforced the argument I will make throughout this book—that nothing could be further from the truth. Keith reminded the group that Unilever itself was founded in 1929 to reinforce new hygiene standards and address growing public health challenges across the UK's urban centers, you could almost feel the wave of lightbulb moments sweeping the group. What could possibly be controversial about monetizing the solutions society actually needs?

The Covid-19 pandemic offered brands various opportunities to make a social impact. It shone a bright light on transportation insecurity as a major barrier to healthcare for millions of Americans. In 2020, Lyft Rideshare company began providing free transportation for riders getting the Covid-19 vaccine. Users received a code they could apply to rides requested in the Lyft app to and from a vaccination site near them. Ride codes covered up to $15 each for two rides, which was the calculated cost to cover most of the rider's fares based on previous vaccine access rides.

They solved a real problem by closing the travel gap for people who didn't have access to transportation. When these types of initiatives are done right, the brand starts to think of ways to do something similar, which led to the company offering free rides to interviews. Lyft solidified its identity as the kinder rideshare giant that cares about people; and I spoke about their efforts with Karin Onsager-Birch, former Vice President of Creative at Lyft.

REAL TALK WITH RESPONSIBLE MARKETERS
Karin Onsager-Birch

Karin Onsager-Birch is a Creative Leadership Consultant and Board Chair at Moonshoot Inc, formerly Vice President of Creative at Lyft, and CCO at various creative agencies. Throughout Karin's career she has come into brand organizations and agencies that were demoralized, stagnant, and unconscious of their own potential, and each time, within three to twelve months, led meaningful and material transformation, ultimately making people and organizations energized, inspired, and moving forward with direction and purpose.

What *Irresponsible* Marketing Looks Like

Like so many things, it all depends on your vantage point!

Big picture, I think responsible marketing is all about doing good in the world and not pushing products people don't need. Irresponsible marketing risks creating harmful desires. Think about ads that damage body image or that make kids want sugary foods that are really bad for them.

A tragic example of this at its worst was a formula brand I won't name looking to drive their Africa business during the 1970s. They put up these huge billboards in villages to spread the message that formula was healthier than breastmilk. The problematic nature of that claim aside, there was another big problem—clean water was sadly hard to find in many of those villages. When mothers stopped breastfeeding and used formula mixed with dirty water, their babies suffered from cholera and malnutrition as a result. Marketing doesn't get any more irresponsible than that.

Zoom in to my experience at Lyft where some of the executives thought any use of paid media was irresponsible because, as a technology-driven company, weren't we better off investing in product? So often in tech, the only marketing considered responsible is performance or product marketing, the kind that delivers measurable, near-term ROI on every single dollar spent. Of course, we know better than that! I might say that that thinking is irresponsible because it is so short-term. So it really depends on who's talking.

Kindness and Community as a Competitive Advantage

Lyft drew me in with its vibrancy and the founders' genuine desire to do right.

The company was founded on the idea of creating cities centered on people, not cars. One founder had studied hospitality and urban planning in college and wanted to make cities more friendly and connected. The other founder, an engineer, saw the environmental damage and waste in empty car seats during drives and wanted to solve for that.

As many of us remember from the early days, Lyft had passengers sit in the front seat with the driver, a true ridesharing experience vs. our competitor's focus on replicating the luxury limo service experience. Focusing on affordable, communal travel was friendly and fun, but it also had a serious financial upside.

Balancing Image and Impact

Today, many companies try to do the right thing, whether it's for genuine reasons or just to jump on the purpose bandwagon for image. Even if the motives are mixed, the positive impact still matters in my opinion. I get annoyed when people are cynical about companies doing good, and talking about it in their marketing, because the momentum it creates is beneficial for everyone.

During Covid-19, Lyft's Vaccine Access Program was the perfect example of responsible marketing that's also smart for business and makes a real social impact. The program wasn't a no-brainer. There were some concerns about alienating anti-vaccine customers, but the founders stuck to their values. Ultimately it was about doing what was right.

In the end, people got access to the vaccine, and Lyft gained precious market share at a time when people were otherwise staying indoors. Ride volume shrunk to half its normal size during the pandemic, so imagine what a powerful stimulant this program was.

Even though a lot of the team was thinking about it from a pure "good for the world" perspective, it was incredibly defensible on the finance side of things too. When a corporate entity is practicing really responsible marketing, the focus is finding that sweet spot at the intersection, and it's absolutely possible.

How Visibility and Creativity Power Responsibility

Responsible marketing is like everything else—if it's invisible, it won't work.

There are lots of companies out there who actually do very nice things, but nobody knows because they don't invest in telling those stories.

Take the Lego brand. Behind the scenes, they're investing in inventing fully sustainable plastic. Why don't we all know about that? Why aren't they shouting that story from the rooftops? Modern marketers have to think beyond "not wanting to brag" about the good things they do. To positively impact long-term brand building, these efforts need to get as much attention as, if not more than, the quick-turn acquisition and short-term sales tactics we're encouraged to focus on.

Responsible marketing is also a great opportunity for companies to get extra mileage out of their creative teams because talent gets turned on by projects that come from the heart. If your heart swells at the very thought of working on it, your friends are going to like it, your Mom is going to love it, and you'll bring more juice to the table. Those are the projects people can't stop thinking about, and the creativity that results only benefits the business.

The Importance of Finding the Fun

Responsible marketing doesn't have to be serious or morose.

That's what I think a lot of us are getting wrong. Creatives need to find a way to represent marketing ideas that still have the personality of the brand. It should tickle you as a consumer. We all want to be surprised and delighted.

What makes responsible marketing great isn't any different than what makes any marketing great. It has to start with the getting attention part, then the "Oh, it's for a really good cause!" part heightens the impact from there.

Identifying Impact Opportunities

A brand's commitment to improving the lived experience of a historically-excluded group or addressing a cultural or environmental cause like economic inequality or climate change has to be rooted in the essence of its core value proposition, like anything else. For a change in conditions to be meaningful, it has to be meaningful from the perspective of the beneficiary. This is a non-negotiable that comes with the upside of forcing the intended benefactor to decenter themselves. You might think that "meaningful" is a weird word to focus on, but it introduces the concept of the intended beneficiary.

Growth Audiences as Intended Beneficiaries

Who are the under-indexed audiences to whom you have a chance to market? A segment of your potential consumer base that has not been focused on, making a potential for growth. There is a risk of over-focusing causing a transformative effect, so it has to be as much about the opportunity to positively impact that audience as it is about the opportunity for the company to benefit from their dollars. People who haven't developed a responsible mindset often put this in terms of "tapping into an X market." We need to get away from the concept of tapping into. We are not tapping into; we are pouring into. That shift sets you up for thinking more about the growth audiences as your intended beneficiaries vs. people who are going to benefit the brand. When you do that, the brand still reaps more benefit than otherwise, but it requires authentically making that mindset shift to find the right ideas.

On the heels of Black square-mageddon during the summer of 2020, Uber showed us all the danger of focusing on intent vs. impact. All of a sudden, maybe around July, I saw my LinkedIn newsfeed become flooded with the company's employees sharing snapshots of billboards and bus shelters emblazoned with what was little more than a self-congratulatory sentiment:

"If you tolerate racism, delete Uber."

It sounded great, sure, but I had a few questions. What did it actually mean to "tolerate racism"? Wouldn't that include hearing a racial slur in conversation and saying nothing, laughing at a racially insensitive joke, or speaking at a conference with few or no Black speakers? What about knowing a racialized employee is paid under market and saying nothing because they seem happy enough? Even if a working definition of tolerating racism existed, was the company assessing who is doing so in any meaningful way? If a driver or rider is proven to "tolerate racism," are we really relying on that individual to self-report?

Furthermore, if we believe in the concept of systemic racism, which we all ought to, isn't the reality that racism isn't an "action" one chooses, but an attribute of the society in which we exist?

Here's what makes it even more interesting. When I researched this campaign in the days after seeing it, I discovered that the company had buried the actual authentic social impact of their effort by wrapping it in performative packaging. Behind the scenes and beyond the splashy billboards was a real program with the attributes we define as authentic social impact. A program about education of riders and drivers alike, focusing on providing actionable solutions for addressing the impacts of racism both experience. In trying to go for the splashy sexy moment, they kept themselves from fully realizing the impact of the great work that was already going on, as so often happens. Social impact as created and/or amplified by marketers to ultimately achieve desired commercial outcomes is different from CSR or philanthropy efforts, but those efforts can be the foundation of marketing storytelling. Instead of using real, ongoing work to their advantage, the rideshare company tried to fake it unnecessarily, and none of us were convinced.

Historically-Excluded Communities

There are exponentially infinite ways to define historically-excluded communities. There is no set list of what it means. Sometimes you understand that when you think about a brand's value proposition. If the value proposition (VP) is convenient fitness in your home that motivates you because of the way we created it and the attachment of the fitness instructors that are part and parcel of the equipment itself (that is part of what differentiates Peloton; it is not just the bike—it comes along with its own ecosystem), which solves the problem of people stopping their use after a while. From that VP, you start to consider the community that is being excluded. You need to be able to think more expansively than what a historically-excluded group is in the way that you have seen it defined elsewhere. You could develop a completely new set of historically-excluded consumers because of the way you define it, and doing that in a way that is novel is also a driver of authenticity versus performativity. People say we under-index for Black consumers, so we are going to do this for Black people, but let's get into the meat of it. "Black people" is not a category. But if you start to think of teens who are interested in makeup but they cannot find products for their skin that they can afford, that is a specific and novel historically-excluded audience that includes Black people but can also include South Asian or Latina teens. It starts to become a more real articulation of what the segment actually is and creates a less limited scope for the brand to make the impact it needs.

The Peloton. Anyone. Anywhere campaign centered around a short film that highlighted the brand's offerings for all ages, fitness levels, and abilities. It featured diverse individuals working out in their homes, gyms, or communities using the latest Peloton app. Through storytelling, Peloton made fitness more welcoming for all bodies and people at any stage in their health and wellness journey.

Another iconic campaign, We All Have Our Reasons, similarly focused on inclusivity by showcasing people of different body types, abilities, and those using prosthetics, emphasizing that fitness is for everyone. This approach effectively aligned Peloton's social impact with its value proposition of providing convenient, comfortable exercise options at home. By targeting those historically excluded from fitness spaces, Peloton fostered a sense of belonging and achieved significant social impact, reinforcing their commitment to user satisfaction and community building.

Peloton took an opportunity to pour into an audience that had not felt welcome in the fitness world. They highlighted people with different body types, people with different abilities, people who may be using prosthetics, and people who may feel embarrassed to work out in front of other people, and actually showed them using the product. Here the social impact outcomes include healthier people, belonging for all body types, and more—in a way that deeply aligns with the product's value proposition of exercising within the comfort of one's own home.

Solve New Problems, Unlock Incremental Growth

In *The Lean Startup*, Eric Ries continually drives home the point that solving unaddressed problems is the simplest pathway to incremental growth.[3] After all, what could be more logical? That principle is at the crux of the business sense behind focusing on historically-excluded groups. Who is more likely to have unmet needs and desires than those who have been historically excluded? As I stressed in the introduction, this book assumes its readers believe in the moral mandate of making the world a better place for more of the people in it. (If you got this far, that means thankfully, we're aligned there!) While the moral argument is the first reason to prioritize a focus on historically-excluded communities, the hybrid benefit of that focus leading us to fertile ground for product and marketing opportunities is at the crux of why triple top-line strategic planning is as foolproof as it is.

When I spoke with Google Senior Product Inclusion and Equity Program Manager Sydney Coleman, she explained how her team prioritizes inclusivity by putting identities first.

"Our approach is putting identities first. We use a framework on dimensions of identity and thinking about a number of different attributes like race, gender, age, ability, geography, language, so on so forth, and all of their intersections. When you're talking about building equitably or thinking of a new innovation, whether it's a new product, feature, or campaign, it's really about centering the most marginalized user throughout that entire design and development process. And we can't approach it like checking a box. We have to represent people in their most authentic sense. That requires that we think about their identities and how their identities stem from being a member of a larger community, then considering the intersections of those identities."

The takeaway for those of us learning how to think about this is that there's no wrong or finite answer when it comes to determining a brand's approach to identifying relevant historically-excluded groups. At Google, Coleman's team also uses another lens to determine their areas of focus, a brand or industry's historical responsibility. She shared how this led to

"RealTone" technology within Google Pixel phone cameras, a case study we will continue to come back to throughout this book. With RealTone, Google Pixel solved a real, brand relevant problem faced by a historically-excluded group and talked about that problem being solved at the top of the funnel to grow affinity for the brand at large.

"Historically, there's been a ton of inequity in terms of how camera technology works differently for people of color because of skin tone bias, so having that embedded into the technology historically was something that we were trying to change. We started by working directly with communities to inform how the technology was being built. We think we have the most inclusive camera today because we did this at the outset, rather than bringing people in at the end to end like an evaluative process."

Just imagine the potential across all categories of brands if more team's took this approach. Consider the Band-Aid brand, for one. I grew up in an era where the very notion that a Band-Aid be colored anything other than beige was beyond the scope of reality. I remember seeing the contrast of a calamine lotion colored bandage against my deep brown skin and registering a dull discomfort. The badge of honor feeling of pride that kids get when sporting a bandage was always tinged with a feeling of persistent alienation. Even without consciously thinking it, deep down I felt the reality that this thing I was kind of proud to be wearing wasn't actually made for me in the same way it was made for my white friends.

Addressing Societal Debts

In what ways, past or present, has your brand, category, or industry contributed to societal harm? What do you owe society based on the contributions to societal harm by your brand, your category, or the industry you are in? How can you address those harms in the way that you go to market? The concept of historical debt is one of the most powerful ideas I'll share with you in this book. Think of it as the lighthouse that beckons your brand toward identifying its most natural responsible marketing dance space. It's also one of the toughest to stomach when you're coming from a place of corporate fragility. The key is to shift your mindset from the fear of being associated with anything negative to the upside of proactive acknowledgment and atonement.

Impact Insights

What functional benefits and emotional promises can align to meaningfully address relevant social debts? This is the brand relevance piece, and it is often the part where, when we see a lot of performative activity, businesses get tripped up. It is not about supporting anyone and everything that matters. It's about the functional benefits and authentic emotional promises of the brand. That's how you find your impact insights, and when you act on those, you can choose ways that also deliver on your incremental commercial success.

Transcending the Performative

When it comes to influencing real policies, it's not just about throwing your brand's weight around. It must also be about authenticity and being true to who you are as a brand. People aren't fooled by empty gestures or hollow statements. They want to see genuine commitment, a reflection of values that align with their own. Trust is the cornerstone of any successful brand–consumer relationship, and nothing builds trust faster than showing you're not just in it for the bottom line. So how do you communicate this commitment to your audience and consumers at large? According to the sparks & honey 2023 Responsible Marketing Index, it isn't just one thing brands should be focused on but a combination of activities. As seen in Figure 2.3, consumers expect brands to engage in broad efforts, from product innovation to policy advocacy."

Advocating for policies that resonate with our brand reassures customers that your brand is here for more than just their wallets—you are here for their wellbeing and the betterment of society.

By aligning advocacy efforts with brand identity, brands can escape the profit-stealing trap of becoming just another faceless corporation. Instead, they can stand out as the brand that authentically contributes to long-term sustainability, both in terms of business success and the broader societal and environmental impacts of your operations. In a competitive market, brand relevance in policy advocacy can serve as a unique selling point that attracts consumers who prioritize social responsibility.

Taylor Morrison Homes is transcending the performative in a real way through its initiative to provide temporary housing for cancer patients and their families during times of treatment by building a custom home community

FIGURE 2.3 How consumers expect brands to address social issues (% of respondents viewing activity as important)

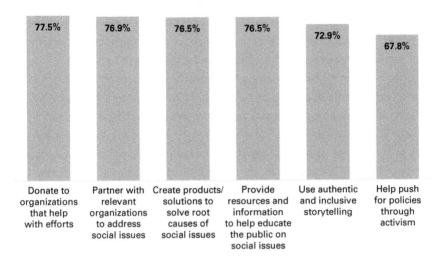

77.5%	76.9%	76.5%	76.5%	72.9%	67.8%
Donate to organizations that help with efforts	Partner with relevant organizations to address social issues	Create products/ solutions to solve root causes of social issues	Provide resources and information to help educate the public on social issues	Use authentic and inclusive storytelling	Help push for policies through activism

Brand and business activities

SOURCE Based on data from 2023 sparks & honey Responsible Marketing Index

near a cancer center close to the company's headquarters. The company showcases the value of their homes by putting them where there is an urgent need, such as a place for loved ones to stay while getting cancer treatments.

Yes, there is also a benefit for the company because it showcases their homes, but it is far from performative because it is actually solving a consumer problem. Even breaking it down in terms of functional benefit and emotional promise, the functional benefit of a home is shelter and protection. The emotional promise is that "you are going to feel better here" in these nice homes, which is what the people in this situation need. That creates a full circle connection where that emotional promise aligns with the functional benefit that anyone who buys a Taylor Morrison home gets.

REAL TALK WITH RESPONSIBLE MARKETERS
Stephanie McCarty

Chief Marketing Officer at Taylor Morrison, Board Member at Cecilian Partners, Inc., and Advisory Board Member at Zillow Group, Stephanie is a marketing and communications executive with an unrivaled passion for driving change, building culturally relevant brands from the inside out and fueling business growth.

Why Sales Should Be Secondary

I think responsible marketing is using your superpowers for good. It drives so much, the products and services and goods that we as consumers buy every day, and we can be very persuasive and influential. So how do you use those gifts and talents to sell goods and services and products that solve the world's problems?

I often compare my choice in career to those who amass tons of debt and undergo extensive training to become a doctor and to serve others. Marketing has the power to be used for good but it can seem so evil and manipulative. As we continue to evolve as marketers, our roles also continue to evolve. It's almost like stack ranking, where sales almost have to be the last thing instead of the first thing. Instead of doing all things for sales, it's doing all things for the good of humanity. It's for the world, the environment, the people, the brand first, and sales is secondary. I think as long as you focus on that first one, and you do that with as much thought and intentionality as you can, the second is an added layer that will just be an output and result of doing that first piece.

That is a huge shift in approach. Performance marketing, click-through rates, KPIs, and all of the jargon that I get asked when I go on marketing podcasts... yes, we track all of that stuff. I have tons of dashboards, but the things that I chase on a day-to-day basis sometimes are the ones that are more anecdotal, and it's the feeling that we create.

Communicating Directly With Your Consumers

When I think of all the insights that I garner from conversations with customers, it's fascinating how many consumers reach out to me wanting to know if all the stuff we put out there about our brand is true before they sign on the dotted line, because they don't want to invest a million dollars to build with just anybody. They want to make sure that they're working with good people, with honest people who might get it wrong sometimes, because people make mistakes, but are still going to do their best. And we're just a company, a good company doing good things, because there's a lot of companies that might be good, but they're chasing the wrong things. Yeah, I care about performance marketing, but I think that's table stakes. That's just how you do your job, but I don't get up every morning thinking about how many website visitors I got and converted.

Conversations are what CMOs should be concerned about, because those calls that I receive are the best use of my time here. They are the heart and the passion that I bring to the company. How we bring the brand forward in a meaningful way that we know at the end of the day will drive sales.

How a Small Initiative Caused Big Change

I think I'm in one of the most difficult sectors to get people. That's because it's a dog-eat-dog, old white men world. And that's just the mold that was created 100 years ago. My advice to those trying to get the more conservative execs onboard is to start small, and to bring them along. When I first got here, we started just talking about philanthropy, and how do you get people involved in doing good. We started a campaign that's been around now for, I think, almost seven years. We call it Build Joy and we do it every year. We send an email from our CEO to the whole company and we say "If you had $1,000 to build joy in your community, what would you do with it?" It's a question that comes from the heart. The submissions are personal. "My brother's daughter's undergoing treatment for this" or "I'm a former recovering alcoholic. I want to help more alcoholics recover. Here's how I would use that $1,000." We get hundreds of submissions across the company every year.

Then we pick 10 to 15 people every year for us to go out and build joy in their community. They bring their iPhone and they videotape it and they allow the organization to go on their journey with them. Then we have this three-week campaign internally where we release these videos. Sometimes the idea starts with one person internally, but they bring their whole team with them. They bring their whole division or their community office or the corporate office, and they all get behind this one person's idea to bring joy into the world.

That one initiative, which we started seven years ago, has just snowballed into all these fresh ideas coming from within the organization to feed the funnel of all these other great ideas. So then when an idea came in to plant butterfly gardens, they used the $1,000 to buy the milkweed to plant all these butterfly gardens. We thought, "We should put butterfly gardens in every single model home community that we build everywhere!" We got into contact with the National Wildlife Federation for assistance and now we have a huge partnership with them on preserving wildlife and groundskeeping in all of our communities. We create pathways and walkways, and we have children's play escapes built out of recycled material.

The original internal campaign created this ripple effect within the organization. In the role that we play to serve others, we create open spaces in all of our communities that serve the community and the broader one. A couple of years ago, we started involving homeowners to Build Joy. Then we gave them money to do it as well. Now stakeholders are telling us what causes matter to them, and it's $1,000. Instead of traditional market research, we can speak to them in ways that are not so direct or salesy, but meaningful. So that's where we make that social impact to our customers who purchased years ago. That's how we keep them engaged and hope that if they ever move again, they want to build Taylor Morrison again.

Building Partnerships For Good

The cause marketing aspect of what I do became very easy for me because of my CEO who had her own brain cancer scare 10 years ago. She's been very honest with the organization on whole health and mental health and prioritizing your wellbeing. So that's become kind of a pillar of our employee value proposition. We can leverage that outside because it is an authentic part of our brand.

Our partnership with Banner was an obvious choice. Banner has a program called Home Away from Home where they essentially fund cancer patients to stay in a hotel and receive transportation. But we all know that a hotel is not the most peaceful, serene environment when you're exhausted from hours and hours of treatment, whether that treatment lasts one week or six months. That's a hard living experience when you've got loved ones with you. There was an easy opportunity to say, "Hey, you have so much raw land on your campus and we're a land developer first and a homebuilder. We have the tools, the talents, and the experience to turn that land into a community development of homes that can be used within spitting distance of the hospital. It's a two-bedroom home where you can have as many people as you need to be with you for however long you need to stay. It allows more people access to the treatment that a lot of people can't get because they can't afford to travel to it. It made so much sense based on who we are and what we value as an organization.

We can swing hammers and bring trades together to build foundations of homes. We can address homelessness and build shelter for people who are in a rough patch through partnerships. So, why not use our talents and what we have at our disposal for good?

What's on the Horizon

The evolution of responsible marketing will be about disrupting the idea that there always needs to be a different way to talk to a Latine audience or a Black audience or a white audience. It's more about, "What are the mindset segments that you want to appeal to? And what stories are you telling to make an impact not necessarily based on what they believe today?"

Even from a product standpoint, we know that the most successful products aren't about giving people what they want. They're about giving people what they may have felt but didn't know they needed. Creating even a seemingly small sense of belonging where there was none before is still incremental. Like my Band-Aid example, experiencing discrimination in any form is experiencing death by 1,000 cuts. No one cut feels deadly, but each one chips away at your confidence until it crumbles entirely. As humans, why would we want that for each other, why wouldn't we fix it if we could? Well luckily, if you're reading this, you can. After all, marketers specialize in making the most of movements. We study our consumers. We listen to our customers. We look out for the cues that signal something new emerging. When those cues are subtle, we become activists. We spark belief and help our colleagues see things in a new light. When those cues are deafening, things get a little tougher. With alignment something must be done, it's on us to figure out what, how, and why.

This is your moment to be emboldened.

The global movement demanding that companies take action to elevate diversity, equity, and inclusion starts with HR and CSR, but it doesn't have to end there. Brands have the power to make an impact across multiple dimensions, for all stakeholders and the communities we all call home.

RESPONSIBLE RECAP

- Social impact is a meaningful, measurable, and enduring change that positively affects historically-excluded groups or urgent cultural causes. It emphasizes the importance of authentic, activity-backed impact over mere messaging and urges marketers to prioritize tangible outcomes aligned with their brand's values for successful responsible marketing.

- Brands have to be willing to stand up for their values as much as they're willing to deliver on their core value proposition, always staying true to their highest ideals and evolving how they interpret their core values to deliver on societal dynamics over time.

- Supercharging the Flywheel involves fostering diversity, enabling inclusion, advancing equity, cultivating belonging, and supporting sustainability.

- Responsible marketing goes beyond fulfilling existing desires, instead aiming to meet unacknowledged needs and foster a sense of belonging, recognizing the incremental impact of even small gestures and urging marketers to take proactive action in response to emerging societal cues.

Notes

1 The Coca-Cola Company. Creating "I'd Like to Buy the World a Coke," The Coca-Cola Company, 2024. www.cocacolacompany.com/about-us/history/creating-id-like-to-buy-the-world-a-coke (archived at https://perma.cc/8PKU-SWN6)

2 Edelman. Trust Barometer special report: Brand trust in 2020, Edelman, June 25, 2020. www.edelman.com/research/brand-trust-2020 (archived at https://perma.cc/4DGW-BX4H)

3 E. Ries (2011) *The Lean Startup: How constant innovation creates radically successful businesses*, Random House, New York

03

Make It Known

Reputation Impact

When Maya Angelou said that people don't remember what you said, but how you made them feel, she gave us a poignant insight about the way reputation shapes consumer behavior. Not only do people remember how you made them feel, how they feel also determines what they buy.

It's why employing stewards to influence and navigate the interactions between marketing choices and a brand's reputation is such a worthy investment. Managing the commercial impact of brand reputation is a succinct way to describe high-level goals of any and every marketing job. I challenge you to think of one that doesn't ultimately drill down to those seven words. From CMO to social media manager to SEO analyst to creative director, managing the commercial impact of brand reputation is the essence of what all the work is about. The reason why this is true sets us up to spend this chapter unpacking the role reputation impact plays in the practice of responsible marketing... for better when it's done right, and, unfortunately, for worse when it is not.

Why Reputation Impact Matters

Understanding this all goes back to the historical reasons why brands came to exist in the first place. For a brand to deliver on its promise of outsized value to the business, it must first gain, retain, and grow belief in the emotional value it promises to the people. Then, it must gain, retain, and grow the people's trust that the emotional value promised will continue to be delivered, no matter what functional value the brand they believe in offers next.

FIGURE 3.1 The marketer's Triple Top-Line Flywheel—responsible marketing and reputation impact

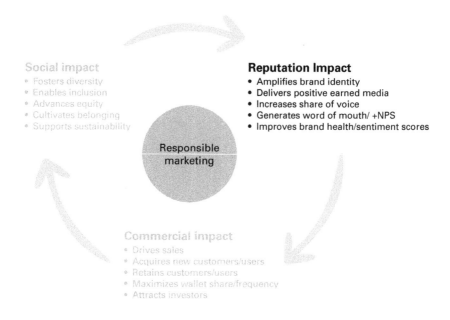

Social impact
- Fosters diversity
- Enables inclusion
- Advances equity
- Cultivates belonging
- Supports sustainability

Reputation Impact
- Amplifies brand identity
- Delivers positive earned media
- Increases share of voice
- Generates word of mouth/ +NPS
- Improves brand health/sentiment scores

Responsible marketing

Commercial impact
- Drives sales
- Acquires new customers/users
- Retains customers/users
- Maximizes wallet share/frequency
- Attracts investors

The concept of branding has been around for thousands of years, with some of the earliest examples dating back to ancient civilizations. For example, the ancient Egyptians used branding to identify and distinguish different types of goods, while the ancient Greeks used branding to indicate the origin of a product.

In terms of modern branding, the first commercial brands were established during the Industrial Revolution in the late 18th and early 19th centuries. As mass production became more and more possible, businesses began to use branding to differentiate their products from those of their competitors. Branding became increasingly important as businesses expanded their reach and began to sell products beyond local markets. It helped businesses to establish a reputation for quality and reliability, which in turn helped to build customer trust and loyalty.

Today, when consumers have more choices than ever before, branding and reputation are in a co-dependent relationship. They need each other, they shape each other, and when the integrity of one is compromised, the downfall of the other isn't far behind. If reputation is a brand's currency, brands with strong reputations have deep pockets. These brands don't just weather storms—they go one step further and thrive in them. They turn consumers into advocates that work on their behalf and crises into opportunities for growth. They naturally attract talent, partners, and investors. They transcend from being known to being beloved by everyone that matters, especially shareholders, for one simple reason. They are continually rewarded with the gift of free stuff.

The Triple Top-Line's Most Reliable Tool

When practiced effectively, responsible marketing is rewarding because it addresses real societal needs while creating real commercial impact. As the connective thread between social and commercial impact, it's also rewarding because, to say it plainly, it helps marketers get free stuff—the kind of stuff that's so elusive, you couldn't pay for it, even if you wanted to. Because this stuff is earned with influence, there's no way to force it—but responsible marketing is the most reliable tool there is for triggering the magic of growth-driving reputation impact.

Amplifying Brand Identity

As you identify opportunities for social impact as part of the Triple Top-Line Flywheel, I encourage you to answer this question: how can addressing an impact insight connect with consumer hearts and minds to elevate brand reputation? Understand that, as you make decisions about where to concentrate their social impact, you are also making decisions about your reputation impact.

In 2023, when I learned about Target's decision to scale back Pride Month activations in store, I was so disappointed that I went live in the moment. I happened to be in Minneapolis at the time, right across the street from Target's headquarters, attending the Brand-Led Culture Change Sustainable Brands conference. It hit too close to home for me to not immediately spread an extremely important message: we must not negotiate with terrorists. And the loud minority of people who do not want all of their fellow citizens to be free in the way that they want to be free, to love who they want to love, and live as who they truly are, that loud minority is getting way too much attention from the people at the top of corporations who have the power to actually change culture. Brand-led culture change is an interesting notion to consider through the lens of what is happening now, which is brand-led cultural regression. It will continue if we allow it to, and we must not allow it.

I know some amazing people at Target corporate who were also upset by the decision making. And I know that there were also some who were probably convinced by the company line that the decision was about protecting safety. But let's not get it twisted.

We will never be safe if we are not free. We will never be safe if we support hatred. Maybe in the short term, we will be more comfortable and protect ourselves from some uncomfortable situations but let's not get that confused with the idea of safety. Safety is a state of freedom and freedom has nothing to do with hatred. When schools were diversified in this country, there was a lot of upset, threats, and violence, but we still had to get it done. By choosing to step backwards in its social impact, Target negatively impacted its reputation as a people-centered organization, not just among members of the LGBTQIA+ community, but also among their allies and any consumer that valued the retailer's initial efforts.

The Halo Effect

If you're a Beyoncé fan like I am, you remember the themes of adoration and commitment in her 2009 song "Halo." Just like she sang about in the song, the reputation impact of responsible marketing has the power to make consumers feel secure in your brand values, keeping your brand not only top of mind, but at the top of their purchase consideration list long after your direct interactions with them. Also, as Beyoncé experienced, this halo effect can even replace any mindshare occupied by near-term past failures with an immersive sense of positive sentiment. An emotional connection does this most powerfully, and that emotional connection is often best tapped into by acts that make an impact beyond the individual who feels more connected because of them. Emotions motivate your target audience, having even more influence over a person's intent and decision to buy than the actual content of the marketing material. Out of 1,400 successful advertising campaigns, those with purely emotional content performed about twice as well (31 percent vs. 16 percent) as those with only rational content.[1]

Beyoncé was willing to forgive Jay-Z because she could feel his halo, and consumers are willing to forgive brands that have messed up when they're given a real reason to do so. Volkswagen's "Dieselgate" shows how brands can use social impact to successfully rehabilitate a bad reputation. In 2015, the United States Environmental Protection Agency (EPA) issued a notice of violation of the Clean Air Act to the Volkswagen Group. The agency determined that Volkswagen intentionally circumvented EPA emissions tests in diesel-powered vehicles by programming diesel engines to only activate emissions controls during laboratory testing, thereby hiding the fact that their vehicles emissions output did not meet US environmental standards. The discovery led to a major product recall, internal shakeups, and consumer distrust. The company's deliberate intention to break the law created reputation damage that was seemingly irreparable.

This is how the Triple Top-Line Flywheel comes to life. Responsible marketing can create a halo effect that protects the narrative on how a brand is perceived, even when mistakes are made. Once your brand becomes known as purpose driven, sustainable, ethical, conscious, or a changemaker (whichever word of the marketing lexicon you prefer), you have more freedom and leeway to take risks, drive change, and solve real problems.

RESPONSIBLE MARKETING WIN
The Halo Effect of Hellmann's Mayonnaise Food Conservation

As part of Unilever's larger commitment to helping achieve the UN's Sustainable Development Goal 12.3 (reducing food waste by 50 percent by 2030), Hellmann's set out to inspire and enable 100 million people around the world every year to be more resourceful and less wasteful with their food.[2] Hellmann's became a messenger, though some found their reliance on unhealthy products an inappropriate platform for delivering this important point.

Triple top-line score: 3/3

✓ **Social impact**

✓ **Reputation impact**

✓ **Commercial impact**

Approximately 40 percent of all food in the U.S. is wasted and approximately 43 percent of that food waste happens at home.[3] The first segment of the initiative was launching the Fridge Night Mission, a four-week program where participants only consume the food they already have in their kitchens one night a week. According to Hellmann's, the program reduces household food waste by up to 33 percent.[4] To make it easier for consumers to get on board, Hellmann's created a recipe app where users can list the foods they have on hand to find meal and recipe ideas.

In 2021, the company began leveraging the massive audience of the Super Bowl to spread its message. The food waste awareness ad featured celebrities in humorous situations with the tagline of tackling leftovers to "Make taste, not waste." The *Animal Crossing: New horizon* Nintendo video game also helped bring the message to younger consumers. Hellmann's Island was integrated into the game, so players could drop off their spoiled turnips. For each turnip dropped off, Hellmann's made a financial donation to distribute the equivalent of two nutritious meals to food-vulnerable populations.

Hellmann's has created a long-running corporate social responsibility program that incorporates a central part of its core product. It has taken the negative reputation of mayonnaise as an unhealthy food option and transformed its reputation into one of social impact that also drives its market share. But not everyone has gotten on board with Unilever's vision.

In 2023, Terry Smith, a Unilever activist investor made the following statement: "A company which feels it has to define the purpose of Hellmann's mayonnaise has in our view clearly lost the plot."[5] But the truth is that the only person who had lost the plot was HIM. Hellmann's championed a response to food waste by encouraging the use of mayo to jazz up leftovers. These new occasions increase usage frequency and deepen market penetration, as people who already buy mayo use more, then buy more often; and new people start buying mayo because they've now been convinced of a reason to do so. If there's a world where that isn't a commercially-driven strategy, it's not the one we live in. And the fact that this commercially-driven strategy also addresses a real social problem is net positive upside, not a distraction.

What would Terry Smith prefer? Discounts? Coupons? Downweighting? Price gouging? Google search ads or some other type of short-termist low-value marketing detritus that is far from in the best interest of shareholders... assuming they've invested for the long term vs. Vegas-style Wall Street arbitrage games? (And shouldn't we be focusing on the interests of our committed investors as responsible stewards of a brand?)

I could go on, but here's the takeaway: don't let people who are irrationally resistant to change stop you from seeing when it's actually good for everyone. People who would rather leave money on the table than make the world a better place are inherently dangerous, and we spend way too much time listening to them.

Improving Brand Health

Making the Most of Making it Known

When it comes to driving reputation, brands have to keep it real because transparency has never mattered more. Consumers trust brands who are willing to say what is going wrong, what went wrong, or what is unclear instead. Stop trying to obfuscate. Just like there's something enduring about people who are willing to admit when they're wrong, brands willing to do the same can actually turn mistakes into wins.

In 2015, Airbnb faced some very public backlash after Harvard researchers released a working paper indicating that travelers with "distinctively African American names are 16 percent less likely to be accepted relative to identical guests with distinctively White names." With the report, widescale social media reporting by travelers who experienced discrimination, and a lawsuit over the allegations, Airbnb had much to contend with.

CEO and cofounder Brian Chesky released a statement that began with an acknowledgment, followed by an apology. It read in part,

> Discrimination is the opposite of belonging, and its existence on our platform jeopardizes this core mission. Bias and discrimination have no place on Airbnb, and we have zero tolerance for them. Unfortunately, we have been slow to address these problems, and for this I am sorry. I take responsibility for any pain or frustration this has caused members of our community. We will not only make this right; we will work to set an example that other companies can follow.[6]

The company subsequently took several measures to address and prevent discrimination on the platform, including a 32-page report documenting an extensive audit and the resulting measures that were implemented. Airbnb also strengthened their campaign for inclusion, punctuated by an ad during the 2017 Super Bowl.

When Working With Agencies, Don't Give Up Your Agency

When brands are faced with reputation setbacks, they often rely on external public relations (PR) agencies to change the narrative and redirect the public eye. While these partnerships can help brands elevate their reputation, even the best PR firm gets it wrong sometimes, especially when faced with an urgent crisis. Take the PR rep who avoids conversations about negative outcomes, for instance. Of course, these aren't comfortable or enjoyable conversations, but they are necessary, and if your PR agency isn't talking about it, consider it a red flag. Ignoring a crisis in hopes that it quietly goes away is the quickest route to letting people outside of your brand attack your reputation. Don't let a PR firm silence you. Craft a message that centers transparency and builds stakeholder trust and go forward with it.

REAL TALK WITH RESPONSIBLE MARKETERS
Nate Nichols

Founder and Creative Director at Palette Group, Co-Founder at Allyship and Action, Adweek YoungInfluentials 2020 Winner, Nate is committed to championing diversity and inclusion in the advertising and creative industries.

Telling Real Stories

At Palette we work in all different categories. We love playing in sports, gaming, fashion, footwear, education, tourism. Brands who want authentic stories come to us. It's about building a body of work that says something real. We work very hard to craft stories that center the community's true voices.

Sometimes Responsibility is Saying "No"

I think there's always the challenge of saying no. Sometimes you have to say no to people, no matter how much you want the project. Those are when it's the most difficult. When you feel the red flag, you have to protect your team and yourself because we're on this journey and we have to keep healing. If we don't prioritize healing, then I can't create a safe space for others.

The Commercial Impact of Soul

We have been doing that work, and now when we do our capability sessions, it's just gratifying because it's very clear, whether it's with Netflix or Puma or Newark Public Schools. We just tapped into the emotion of it. We were able to capture the emotion of that experience and it was dope. Now we're working on projects that are the largest we've ever worked on.

The people see us very clearly and that feels wonderful. We're not a multicultural creative agency. You don't come to us for that. What even is that? You come to us because you came for that bottle of emotion that we're able to like tap into. Palette group is putting the *soul* back in advertising.

Delivering Positive Earned Media

We've all heard the theory that "all press is good press," but allow me to qualify that with a very important nuance. All impressions are not built equally—the more it costs, the less it's worth. Paid media and earned media are two sides of the same coin with very different reputation impacts.

The earned media that social impact delivers is the responsible marketing equivalent of having your cake and eating it too. Yes, value lies in the purpose behind the goal itself, but an unsolicited and very public pat on the back can go far in driving reputation impact. Regardless of the source or platform, all earned media is valuable for creating a growth-driven reputation impact. It's a sad realization, but we still live in a society where doing the right thing is often the exception and not the rule, so when brands champion real change in a transparent and purposeful way, it feels like a novelty, and people talk about it. They share their positive experiences on social media. Magazines write glowing articles. Thought leaders analyze the brand and its initiatives on LinkedIn. Suddenly, the brand is trending, not because of a purchased hashtag, but because it earned the reputation impact by driving societal change.

WHAT EARNED MEDIA LOOKS LIKE

- press mentions (traditional/citizen or peer to peer)
- press features (traditional/citizen or peer to peer)
- organic social media mentions
- stakeholder reviews/ratings
- industry awards and recognitions

Paid media is exactly what it sounds like, and while it may not carry the weight of earned media coverage, it can have its benefits for brands seeking to craft, maintain, or fix their reputations. By controlling the placement and timing of messages, brands can strategically reach the specific demographics, interests, and behaviors that they need to push a desired reputation impact. It's instant visibility, and as long as there's transparency and purpose behind it, the effort may pay off.

But paid media also presents challenges, especially when it comes to its trustworthiness in the eyes of stakeholders. When weighing the value of earned and paid media, I consider three categories: high-trust impressions, high-worth impressions, and high-value impressions.

A high-trust impression increases the likelihood that recipients of the message will view the brand as credible and authentic, necessities for brands looking to build up their reputation.

High-worth media impressions occur on the highly regarded or prestigious platforms that audiences deem extra worthy of consideration: mentions in the primo publications, inclusion in exclusive celebrity events, or recognition by industry leaders. It's the glow up for brands seeking to elevate their image and reputation.

Thirdly, the high-value media impressions come through media channels that offer a considerable ROI. Partnerships with influential social media accounts or partnerships with highly reputable and trusted organizations create high-value media impressions because the brand benefits from the audience demographics and established engagement levels of the media channel. It's like instant credibility by association.

As I said before, there may be some good in all of these media types, and it's not the worst idea in the world for brands to dabble in more than one option when working to establish or improve brand reputation.

REAL TALK WITH RESPONSIBLE MARKETERS
Margaret Molloy

Founder at Molloy Marketing Advisory, Board Member at CIE Tours International, Creator/ Founder at WearingIrish, formerly Global Chief Marketing Officer at Siegel+Gale, and formerly Host of the How CMOs Commit podcast, Margaret is a strategic, business-minded business-to-business marketer who drives innovative strategies that grow company profit, profile, and pride.

The Responsibility of Longevity

I think about managing diverse stakeholders over time. I think about legacy, and I think about the opportunity to balance short term with long term. That's my perspective on responsible marketing. I think that's a very robust area of exploration, and this idea that responsibility when it comes to building a brand is building an enduring brand. Enduring means transcending time, transcending my role as CMO. So when I think of responsible branding, responsible marketing, I think about aligning diversity quarters over the long term. I think about it as greater than my tenure in a company.

The Struggle to Maintain Long-Term Goals

I think many are struggling with, from a tactical perspective, balancing investment or expenditure in performance: marketing versus branding. There are three main challenges that companies face regarding this issue. At a very operational level, they have finite resources, energy, human hours and budget agencies, etc. So that's the day-to-day level district. The second component is about strategic intent, and is a little more philosophical, involving questions like, "Are we brand building for the long term? Or are we just responding to quarterly earnings for Wall Street in the capital markets?"

The third component is audience alignment. There is quite a significant misalignment right now, between what employees are asking of marketers, what Wall Street's asking of marketers, and what the community, observers and commentators are asking of brands. In my study of marketing over the many decades of my career, I've never seen it so out of whack.

That's a very strategic burden, not just a responsibility, but a burden marketers have to navigate. Quite frankly, many of them have had training that doesn't equip them well for this, because they came up the communications route, or generally demand generation route or in some categories in event planning. These decisions are super strategic, and you need the frameworks.

I would argue, one mechanism is to look at how many senior marketers have an MBA, and it might not be so many. A business degree provides the kind of skill set that employs a lot of muscles that you get with that training. That's the challenge for marketers without an MBA. They need to employ many different skill sets and the ones that got them where they are aren't necessarily the skills that may get them out of this conversation to a piece of action. The risk that creates is paralysis.

Mayonnaise Makes Moves to Save the Planet

One company worth noting is Hellmann's Mayonnaise, a Unilever brand. There was an article in the *Financial Times* where the investor community complained, "Wait a second, you're about making sandwiches tasteful. You're not about solving for the planet." I oversimplify to make the point.

I argue that every brand needs a purpose. Surely, every brand needs to lead with their societal purpose. They might have a purpose that is: make your leftover sandwiches taste great, and do so in an ecologically appropriate way.

I mention that because brands need to command a price premium. If I go to the store right now, and I've got the white label, generic mayonnaise on one shelf, and I've got the Hellmann's on another, there's a significant price difference. The question on the table is, how many people will extend the hand for the Hellmann's? Is it because of that climate meeting? Or is it because it's a better mayonnaise? And how do you get that balance right? I think that's a super interesting conversation.

The reality is consumers can only process so much. So it's a question of, *where's the emphasis?* For some brands, we should absolutely be leading with societal purpose, but I think people have over simplified it.

A Company with a Big Mission

A great example of a purpose-driven company is One Ten. It's a really good, interesting entity. They started out immediately after George Floyd. Siegel+Gale actually named the company and developed their identity.

They are a direct connection for companies, and their mission is to create one million well-paying, family-living jobs for people of color who don't have a college degree, and to accomplish that goal within the next decade. They have some big connections, including IBM. We did the work to come up with their brand and their platform, and it's a genuinely good organization.

I think the brand has a really interesting mission because they are targeting a significant percentage of the population that doesn't have a college degree, yet many job opportunities require one. This means there are a lot of people left out of the conversation and not earning a living wage.

Margaret Shares Her Mistake

At the risk of being vulnerable, I will tell a personal story where I made a mistake, and I learned from it, I hope. About five years ago, I was in Boston, hosting events. This particular event was a roundtable conversation around brand-building CMOs from top companies, and CMOs were on panels and other CMOs would guest. It was a lunch, not large. I was delighted with myself. I felt the conversation was really robust. I had female and male speakers and different types of industry representation. There was lots of great conversation.

When I got back to my desk, I had a note from one of my guests. The gentleman I didn't know very well, but I knew him through the Harvard Business School Network and I invited him, a CMO of a local company. Essentially the note said, "Margaret, thank you very much for inviting me to your branding event. The hospitality was wonderful, and you did a great job of moderating the session. However, if you think you had the future of branding on that panel, you were very mistaken. I hope you do better when you go to Atlanta and other cities."

He was a Black man, and immediately I knew what the mistake was that I had made. I was so focused on gender, and that component, that I wasn't focused on racial representation. Instead I saw diversity in *gender* perspectives. I also saw diversity in industry perspectives, but I didn't understand that I had to go beyond being colorblind to being color aware, focus on representation, go that extra mile. I didn't appreciate that I was so focused on the disadvantage women have that I compensated by being really thoughtful about recruiting them. I wasn't focused on other groups.

So I share the story because it's very honest, and it was eye-opening for me. I took my team into the room afterwards, and they were asking me why I seemed upset by this and I said, "No, this gentleman has given me the best gift I've ever received. He's given me constructive feedback. I commit, and you can all bear witness to this," I said to my team. "I will never do a panel without at least one colleague of color on that panel."

A coworker then told me, "Margaret, you know how we get these panels. Your network is how we get these panels. You personally invite people." They continued, "We want to respect you, but don't you know that your network isn't so diverse?" I thought, *challenge accepted*. So ever since I've been trying harder. I'm not going to claim victory. There is no victory to be had. But I am working so much harder to make sure that all my invitees are professionals from different backgrounds that I can fully invite into the conversation.

Diversity in Practice

It was a huge revelation for me, personally. And honestly, it makes me a better host and a better colleague, because even if it doesn't get the bottom line directly, I'm better and more educated. I'm more informed in the conversations. Make no mistake, it's been work, because I grew up super modestly, but I moved in circles over time, and they became less and less diverse. As I went up and up, they got less and less diverse. So I took on the challenge. I am humbled by the generosity of our colleague who gave me the feedback.

The following year, I was back in Boston, and I was invited by an organization to host their event. They invited me and they said to bring someone, so the first person I reached out to was my friend who had written me the note. I asked him to please do me the grace and honor of being on my panel. He said "Thank you, I'd be delighted." At the event, he was unsurprisingly fabulous, and I asked to speak with him afterwards.

I asked, "Why would you bother telling me this? That was a very big investment you made in me." And he said, "Well, there are two reasons. One, because I know you really mean well. And you would be open to the message. The second reason is, I had a blind spot, and someone had to tell me." He said, "I've been doing events for a while, too, and I was told I had neglected LGBTQ people. I was so sad. I was so focused on race that I forgot that community." He said, "I was just paying it forward." I thought, *wow, how cool is that?*

Performative vs. Purposeful Marketing

As companies do the work of reputation building, one of the things that comes up quite often is the line between performative and purposeful marketing. Since the ramp up of responsible marketing initiatives after the murder of George Floyd, the question of "Should you do it if it's performative?" grew louder. The word performative has come to represent a company doing something they don't really mean. It's not genuine, not authentic. And a key metric that a lot of people have been using to identify what qualifies as performative is what the company is doing in other areas of the business. But when we think about it this way, we are essentially disqualifying who can play a role in making the world a better place. We need to challenge and reframe the idea that just because there might be something going on in another department or area of a company when it comes to things outside the purview of a marketer, it doesn't mean that they can't do real authentic and non-performative responsible marketing to address issues that may not be properly addressed in other areas of the company.

A more productive way to think about what's performative versus purposeful is the careful examination of a particular action in terms of its own merit. We must give marketers more of a chance to play a positive role in society, regardless of what might be going on, or not, in areas of the company where they have no control. This book offers a definition of what it means to transcend the performative for marketers, but we do well when we think about every sort of action that is being done by a marketer or a company on its own merits. Perfection seeking can limit progress from happening at all, leading us to overthink ourselves out of doing something that might benefit people.

Imagine there's a brand that wants to advocate for women, but it is revealed that somewhere in the business the brand is financially supporting a politician who has been criticized for operating in anti-feminist policies. That doesn't mean that the brand still can't do something positive in its advocacy for women through solving a real problem, creating a real opportunity to advocate for real policy, or telling real stories relevant to the brand that center their stakeholders who are women. As long as they do that in a way that honors the intended beneficiary, that is the metric for making it purposeful versus performative. It is not the other company operations that are happening outside of marketing.

RESPONSIBLE REFRAME

If you want to address a systemic inequity without being performative, don't create work for those affected by it as your means of contribution.

Reputation Killers

The momentum of the Triple Top-Line Flywheel slows when brands fail to move past the performative in their social impact, but even when they do, communication of the work to consumers and stakeholders must be carefully tailored to avoid over- or underselling.

Wokewashing and Greenwashing

Wokewashing and greenwashing are akin to the corporate world's version of "faking it until you make it," and truthfully, some brands don't plan to even try. They simply place a rainbow flag on their products once a year, with no intention of making a social impact for the LGBTQIA+ community. But for the brands that do place the goal of doing good at their core, overselling or exaggerating their efforts can be a costly mistake that interrupts the Triple Top-Line Flywheel before reputation impact is reached.

If your beautifully shot commercials claim that buying your product is the equivalent of planting a tree, then the trees had better be planted. If your campaigns include people of every ethnicity, gender identity, and body type, then your board representation can't resemble a 1950s country club. Consumers have a discerning eye and an even more discerning nose for the garbage that can underlie a campaign filled with oversold promises. And the savviest among them will peel back the layers of glitter to research what is truly underneath. When they broadcast that truth from the pedestals of every social media platform, your brand's reputation takes the hit.

Woke Hushing and Green Hushing

Woke hushing and green hushing can also be damaging to a brand's reputation, even though they both take a "less is more" type of approach. They happen when companies choose to keep their social impact efforts away from the public eye by either downplaying them or not disclosing them at all, like some type of covert operation. Brand leaders may choose this route because they view the publicity as bragging and prefer to take the humble route. Alternatively, the reason may stem from that fear of risk that we discussed in Chapter 1. They worry about being accused of greenwashing, so instead of being open and transparent about their actions, they choose to stay silent. After all, why risk being wrongly accused of hypocrisy when you can avoid the conversation altogether?

Underselling tactics are essentially non-strategies that hinder the momentum of the Triple Top-Line Flywheel. Brands cannot fully benefit from growth driven reputation impact if they do not share the stories of their social impact. And when the reputation impact is hindered, it can't fuel the economic impact of responsible marketing.

Responsible marketing and brand reputation are mutually reinforcing aspects with a symbiotic relationship where a benefit to one also benefits the other. The prioritization of ethical, transparent, and socially responsible practices engrained in responsible marketing plays a critical role in shaping and maintaining a brand's reputation. Consumers are more likely to engage with and support brands that they perceive as ethical and socially responsible, leading to positive word-of-mouth, brand advocacy, and loyalty. Conversely, responsible marketing helps brands to better mitigate reputation risks and crises. Consumers are more likely to give the benefit of the doubt to brands with a strong reputation, making them more receptive to messages about corporate social responsibility, sustainability, and ethical business practices. Brand reputation isn't much different than a human reputation. It's the proof in the pudding. It's the space between what you aimed to do, how it went, and how people perceived it.

RESPONSIBLE RECAP

- The function of a brand is and has always been to benefit from a reputation that precedes and exceeds a consumer's experience with any given product, offering or service. Responsible marketing naturally exploits this by tapping into the heightened emotional connections humans have with unmet societal needs.

- Reputation impact creates a halo effect that accelerates growth beyond the Flywheel. We've all heard the saying "A rising tide lifts all boats." It applies here!

- Being an upstander (like Mastercard does for the Trans community with True Name) is a great way to maximize the halo effect of reputation impact.

- The Triple Top-Line Flywheel demonstrates the five ways reputation impact directly relates to more efficient marketing budgets. By amplifying brand identity, delivering positive earned media, increasing share of voice, generating word of mouth, and improving brand health, responsible marketing creates commercial impact on both sides of the coin. (Higher revenue, lower costs).

- Transcending the performative is key to keeping the momentum going— even if the social impact piece transcends the performative, the work still needs to be talked about in a way that doesn't oversell or undersell, leading to reputation killers like wokewashing and greenwashing (overselling) and wokehushing and greenhushing (underselling).

- As Chapter 4 will cover in detail, reputation impact directly influences commercial impact. The sparks & honey Responsible Marketing Index indicates, almost 3 out of 4 consumers would buy a product that fills a societal need (like a low mobility friendly lipstick cap) because of the good will solving a societal need for someone else garners.

Notes

1   R. Dooley. Emotional ads work best, Neuroscience Marketing, 2009. www.neurosciencemarketing.com/blog/articles/emotional-ads-work-best.htm (archived at https://perma.cc/SV7P-MEEZ)

2   U.S. Food and Drug Administration (2024) Food loss and waste, FDA, March 5, 2024. www.fda.gov/food/consumers/food-loss-and-waste (archived at https://perma.cc/CE75-EHLP)

3   U.S. Food and Drug Administration (2024) Food loss and waste, FDA, March 5, 2024. www.fda.gov/food/consumers/food-loss-and-waste (archived at https://perma.cc/CE75-EHLP)

4   Hellmann's. Our initiative: Fridge Night, Hellmann's, 2024. www.hellmanns. com/us/en/fridgenight.html (archived at https://perma.cc/SL76-HLRR)

5   Financial Times. Terry Smith vs Unilever: Which is guilty of mayo madness? *Financial Times*, January 14, 2022. www.ft.com/content/d7109e75-04be-4106-9e3f-85cb1b485ae6 (archived at https://perma.cc/4WBK-ZNK8)

6   MarketingWeek. Airbnb CEO: Brand's advertising is about 'education' not sales, Marketing Week, 2024. www.marketingweek.com/airbnb-advertising-is-about-education-not-sales/ (archived at https://perma.cc/9NR2-VU3C)

04

Make It Count

Commercial Impact

Responsible marketing and philanthropy are not the same thing.

I repeat.

Responsible marketing and philanthropy are not the same thing.

The founder of Patagonia, Yvon Choinard, expressed that, "Every time I do the right thing, I make money."[1] Contrary to some popular belief, non-profit organizations aren't the only entities that exist to make a meaningful social impact. I'll go so far as to challenge you to name any company with a degree of long-term success that at some level (theoretically if not defensibly) didn't start out with the goal of adding authentic societal value in some way. And yet, somewhere along the way, perhaps as we have been forced to understand and evaluate the role companies play in an increasingly polarized societal landscape, the false binary between making money and adding societal value took root in the popular imagination. And it hasn't let go.

Unlearning this false binary is key to the journey to adopting a more responsible marketing mindset. Allow yourself to imagine what becomes possible when we stop seeing social impact as an alternative to commercial impact and start cultivating a causal relationship between the two. Think of it as the difference between a singular objective and a catalytic objective. Unlike philanthropy, responsible marketing isn't single-mindedly about making a difference that really matters to the world. It's about taking action to make a difference that really matters to the world, which in turn leads to the results that really matter to a business. One of the most harmful myths holding us back from fully committing to responsible marketing is the absurd notion that focusing on making a positive social impact is inherently at odds with focusing on bottom-line business objectives. As seen in Figure 4.1, the responsible marketing Flywheel details tangible commercial

FIGURE 4.1 The marketer's Triple Top-Line Flywheel—responsible marketing and commercial impact

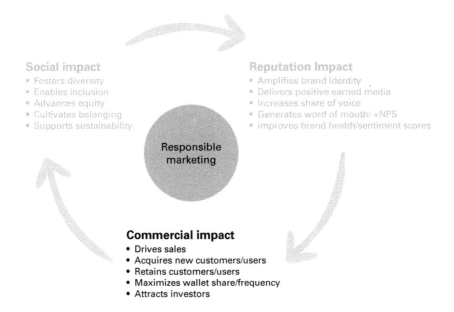

Social impact
* Fosters diversity
* Enables inclusion
* Advances equity
* Cultivates belonging
* Supports sustainability

Reputation Impact
* Amplifies brand identity
* Delivers positive earned media
* Increases share of voice
* Generates word of mouth/ +NPS
* Improves brand health/sentiment scores

Responsible marketing

Commercial impact
* Drives sales
* Acquires new customers/users
* Retains customers/users
* Maximizes wallet share/frequency
* Attracts investors

impact areas, some or all of which are goals that can and should be directly linked to any social impact efforts.

e.l.f. Beauty's growth proves how far this is from the truth.

In 2024, e.l.f. announced a collaboration with tennis star Billie Jean King to highlight the facts around gender equality in corporate board-rooms.[2] An extension of the brand's Change the Board Game initiative, the Serving Facts campaign features King serving fact-filled tennis balls during an in-progress board meeting. Among the hard facts included on the balls are statistics like "Women make up only 27 percent of U.S. corporate boards" and "The average U.S. corporate board is 88 percent white." Another ball states that e.l.f. Beauty is one of only four of the 4,200 U.S. traded U.S. companies with a board of directors composed of two-thirds women and one-third diverse representation. In 2024, Kory Marchisotto, CMO of e.l.f. Beauty, posted about the campaign on Linked In, pointing out that diverse boards are more likely to outperform financially and experience enhanced profitability. She put the definitive period on the end when she stated, e.l.f. Beauty can prove it with their 20 consecutive quarters of growth.[3]

The Prototype: Regenerative Business

Regenerative business represents a paradigm shift in our economic model, one that is increasingly being recognized as "the prototype" of our future economy. This approach goes beyond sustainability—it's about creating systems that actively regenerate and add value to the environment and society. In a regenerative business model, the focus is on holistic wellbeing and long-term resilience, not just short-term profits. This model envisions businesses that work in harmony with natural ecosystems, contribute positively to communities, and create economic systems where the output of one process becomes the input for another, thus mimicking natural cycles.

By shifting the narrative and focus of consumerism, responsible marketing helps bring the vision of a regenerative economy to life. Traditional marketing often encourages consumption for consumption's sake, leading to wasteful practices and a depletion of natural resources. Responsible marketing promotes awareness and appreciation of regenerative practices, educating consumers about the long-term benefits of supporting businesses that prioritize ecological restoration, social equity, and economic inclusivity. It can steer consumers towards choices that support a more sustainable and regenerative economy while also acting as a catalyst for innovation. As consumer demand shifts towards regenerative products and services, companies are incentivized to innovate in this direction, creating a regenerative cycle of new, more sustainable products, and business models that align with both social and commercial principles.

In 2022, Timberland announced plans for its products to have a net positive impact on nature by the year 2030 with the measurable goals of 100 percent of its products circulatory designed for zero waste, and 100 percent of natural materials sourced from regenerative agriculture, with the objective of giving back to the environment more than it has taken out.[4]

While we often hear conversations around regenerative business in relation to environmental policies, there is no limit to the possibilities of regeneration for brands that seek to make a social and commercial impact. If you have ever experienced one of Ben & Jerry's chocolate fudge brownie ice cream treats, you have likely tasted the baking talents of Greyston Bakery, a Colorado-based socially conscious business that practices regenerative hiring policies through its Open Hiring policy.[5] The no-questions-asked form of recruitment has gain significant notoriety for breaking down employment barriers for demographics of the population that are often labeled as 'unemployable' to include the formerly incarcerated, unhoused individuals, and recovering addicts.

As the world grapples with environmental and social challenges, the regenerative business model emerges as a necessary evolution of our economy. Responsible marketing is instrumental in this transition—it not only informs and persuades consumers but also inspires businesses to adopt regenerative practices. By aligning consumer desires with the health of the planet and society, responsible marketing can help usher in an era of economic activity that restores, renews, and revitalizes our world.

RESPONSIBLE INSIGHT

Lyft always cared about doing the right thing. The more unethical our competitor became, the more Lyft wanted to show they were the good guys, like the Ben & Jerry's of transportation. 'Rolls to the Polls' was a fantastic example of this. That program offered $15 off rides to vote, which helped people who couldn't otherwise get to polling stations. This was also great for customer acquisition—the best kind of win–win! Soon our competitor followed with a similar program, so it grew into a bigger win for democracy as a whole.

SOURCE Karin Onsager-Birch, Creative Leadership Consultant and Board Chair at Moonshoot Inc., formerly Vice President of Creative at Lyft, and CCO of various creative agencies

---

Reframing Short-Termism

Short-termism has never been a friend to business growth. Since the very first entrepreneur set out to sell their goods or services, the temptation of prioritizing immediate results and quick wins has stunted the potential for strategic long-term goals. This hyper-vigilant focus on such short-term metrics as quarterly sales targets or immediate ROI happens at the expense of building sustainable brand equity and fostering long-term customer relationships. Short-term focused marketing often neglects investments in brand-building activities such as product innovation, customer experience enhancement, or market research, which are critical for a sustainable commercial impact.

When brands lack stakeholder loyalty, they are forced to constantly seek out new customers as replacements for those that choose to look elsewhere due to dissatisfaction or feeling unheard. It becomes a game of diminishing returns with higher customer acquisition costs, decreased customer lifetime value, and reduced profitability over time.

Reframing the pitfalls of short-termism requires a balanced and strategic approach to brand marketing that prioritizes long-term value creation and sustainability. It's brand-building activities, cultivating customer relationships, listening to stakeholders, and adopting metrics that measure success beyond immediate sales metrics. With a more holistic and responsible view of marketing, brands can experience the commercial benefits that come along with a long-term mindset to drive lasting growth and profitability.

FCLTGlobal is a not-for-profit organization that encourages long-term behaviors in business and investment. According to the 2022 Forbes article "Short-termism is hurting companies and costing lives," FCLTGlobal found that long-term-oriented companies perform at superior levels in terms of revenue and earnings, as well as job creation.[6] As referenced in the same article, firms operating with a long-term mindset cumulatively grew their revenue on average 47 percent more than other firms, and their earnings grew 36 percent more.

RESPONSIBLE INSIGHT

If you're incapable of looking at your P&L and your financial objectives, and tying your commitment to your culture internally to that goal, then you just simply don't get it. You will probably make it for a few more years, but it's going to be really hard, and the opportunity cost is like there's money coming out everywhere. It's an attrition, like the succession planning that doesn't exist because you don't care about your culture.

I still feel like you can make a lot of money and do the right thing. I don't feel like the opportunity cost is you have to choose one or the other. It's about finding a better way of doing things. I'm here to say that you can do both, and it's been quite successful. You don't have to completely sell your soul or put your values to the side to build a successful and healthy business.

SOURCE Lauren Lotka, Global Talent Partner focused on cultural and transformational change

---

Why We Are Wired To Resist

Consumer culture is a necessarily skeptical one. We've all heard a version of "They just did that to make money" said with disdain when a brand claims to be doing something for the greater good. And who can blame the skeptics? We've all been burned before. But the unintended consequence of letting the fear of being called a fake hold us back is the same fate met by Holden Caulfield in *The Catcher in the Rye*. Like the novel's protagonist, we become too busy calling out all the phonies to achieve our full potential. With the principles of responsible marketing, we're armed with the tools needed to overcome our fear.

Raising the bar is what responsible brands do, and their resistance to the resistance gets rewarded in a variety of ways, including commercial impact. Why wouldn't you want to be the brand that took a risk and got it right? And, to be clear, getting it right may include getting some things wrong along the way, but the long game is sustainable commercial impact, not a short-term win that gets celebrated today and forgotten tomorrow.

Trader Joe's is widely recognized as one of the grocery store chains that generally get it right. In 2022, the MBLM marketing agency ranked it number one in brand intimacy within the retail space.[7] Through analysis of more than a billion words used in consumer discussions about retail brands, the agency found that almost half of all consumers who write about Trader Joe's have an emotional bond to the brand. The grocery chain is credited as being the first to provide reusable bags, and that was in the 1970s.[8] Today, their artistic totes have become a staple, with loyal customers anticipating the newest designs. Trader Joe's uses compostable bags in the produce department and has done extensive work in its food security effort, providing more than 100 million pounds of food to those in need. All of these components have worked together to make Trader Joe's a company that provides a social impact and receives a commercial impact, generating almost twice the average revenue per square foot of its rival grocery stores.[9]

But Trader Joe's is not perfect, and it has experienced some bumps along the way. In 2020, in response to a grassroots petition, the grocer accepted responsibility for the racial stereotyping perpetuated in some of its product names and immediately made the necessary changes.[10] The specialty chain has also faced a number of unfair labor practice allegations.[11] But even as Trader Joe's navigates these challenges, it continues to experience the commercial impact of raising the bar and doing the work.

Optimizing Social Impact For Earning Potential

How can addressing an impact insight deliver incremental commercial success for your brand? This is a question that I pose as part of the Triple

Top-Line Flywheel to help brands discover their impact opportunities, because remember, this is not about non-profit thinking. The responsible marketing thought process includes both social impact and commercial impact, and if done right, in equal measure.

Responsible marketing can actually exist in harmony with the principles of free market capitalism. In a free market system, maximizing profit and shareholder value is the driving force behind business. Responsible marketing broadens that perspective beyond short-term financial gains to encompass long-term societal health, so that brands recognize the link that exists between sustainable success and the wellbeing of the customers, communities, and environments in which they operate.

Consumers have become increasingly value-conscious, seeking brands that align with their ethical and social beliefs. Companies that commit to the responsible marketing framework attract these consumers, who will eventually evolve into a loyal customer base, an intrinsic part of long-term profitability.

According to research undertaken by consulting firm McKinsey, Hollywood leaves about $30 billion on the table annually by continually undervaluing the commercial impact of representing historically-excluded communities.[12] McKinsey found that by adopting a more culturally impactful business model, the movie industry could potentially gain $12 billion to $18 billion each year from Latin film consumers, $10 billion annually from Black movie goers, and $2 billion to $4.4 billion from the Asian and Pacific Islander market.

These findings underscore my distinction between responsible marketing and philanthropy. It would not be an act of selfless sacrifice for these Hollywood execs to move in a deliberately inclusive manner. There is a $30 billion pay-off being thrown away every year, not to mention the far-reaching impact their actions could have on the sustainability of the industry as a whole. As the world becomes more Black and Brown, consumers will increasingly demand to see themselves represented in a real way on the big screen. If these top decision makers don't turn from short-term gains to the long run picture, the negative commercial impact of their shortsightedness will continue to grow.

REAL TALK WITH RESPONSIBLE MARKETERS
Annie Jean-Baptiste

Founder/Director of Product Inclusion and Equity at Google, Member at Black Angel Group, Founder at Equity Army, Board of Mentors Member at Monday Night Mentorships, and author of Building for Everyone, *Annie is a business-disrupting tech executive who balances the business and human cases for inclusion. She transforms companies into human-centered, authentic brands that can tap into unlocked growth opportunities. She has brought her forward-looking, data-driven approach to game-changing products serving over a billion users each and inspired other industries to follow suit.*

Reflecting on Our Beautifully Diverse World

We all deserve and yearn to feel seen. That is a core human need. Responsible marketing is a key part of having a holistic, end-to-end process that builds products that work for the world.

The research shows that consumers and users want to see the beautiful diversity of the world reflected back at them in marketing and storytelling. In fact, consumers are more likely to take the action businesses want them to take when there is representative marketing collateral. The myth that focusing on historically-marginalized groups takes away focus from the bottom line is simply not true. Demographics are shifting and shifting rapidly, and for businesses to be successful they need to make sure that they build for everyone.

Responsible Marketing Makes Business Sense

Establishing diverse and inclusive organizations is an economic imperative for every industry. Any business that isn't reaching a diverse market is missing out on enormous revenue potential and the opportunity to build products that suit their users' core needs.

Diversity and inclusion isn't just the right thing to do. It also makes business sense and should be part of core strategy. Inspire your workforce, earn the love of your customers, and build your business. You can do well and do good as long as you continue to center those you are serving—you don't have to have all the answers.

Asking the Important Questions at the Outset

The truth is, this work doesn't slow down the process—it's about being intentional from the onset. When planning your strategies for the year, what agencies are you partnering with? How can you get perspectives from groups that have been historically marginalized? How do you allow real consumers to tell their stories authentically? Planning up front leads to successful campaigns at launch.

Conscious Capitalism

Relearning Self-Interest

Known as the Father of Capitalism, 18th century economist Adam Smith popularized the idea that the pursuit of self-interest is the fuel that powers a thriving economy, and, I would add, the creation of social benefit. Now, I'm not referring to Donald Trump holding a charity golf event on his own golf course and charging full price for everything. I'm talking about unapologetically embracing and maximizing the impact of responsible marketing on core business goals. I highly doubt that I need to teach you what it means for something to positively impact a business on the backend. As marketers, once we utilize that word, we are always talking about money. We are always talking about business results. We are always talking about something that can be characterized as self-serving. But if you are really thinking about what is in the interest of your consumers, you cannot help but have social impact, and that becomes a powerful lever to fuel the productivity of the business, leading to dollar and sense outcomes. It is possible to do both and there is intrinsic value in examining the reasons why it is OK for social impact and cause-related campaigns to also have a commercial impact. For you to have responsible marketing, it needs to become OK for you to think about commercial impacts as an integral part of the picture. It is a win–win situation that benefits brands in a variety of ways, and that includes commercially.

The Invisible Hand

The Invisible Hand theory, proposed by economist Adam Smith in the 1700s, suggests that in a free market economy social good can result from individuals acting in their self-interest. In relation to the business world, the theory implies that the pursuit of profit maximization indirectly benefits society through the creation of wealth, which in turn generates greater employment opportunities, drives innovation, and fosters a stronger economy for all. Though mostly referenced in relation to direct bottom line decisions, it is also relevant to the commercial impact of the Triple Top-Line Flywheel. As modern business leaders increasingly recognize that their actions have broader social and environmental impacts beyond financial profit, they embrace initiatives to address societal challenges, which indirectly leads to benefits like enhanced brand reputation, increased customer loyalty, and profit maximization. This is how businesses making a social impact can be seen as a manifestation of the Invisible Hand at work.

I am on a journey of reminding people that capitalism isn't the problem, our bastardization of it is. What do I mean by our bastardization of it? Think of all the ways we interfere with the Invisible Hand to help those at the top maintain their unfair advantage. Not true capitalism. Think of the inherent lack of equitable, meritocratic access to funding that determines what new businesses come to life. Not true capitalism. When your gender, race, who you love, level of physical mobility, the particular way your brain works, how and where you grew up, what your parents did and who they know… when any of those things directly determine the likely "success" of your endeavors, a system is not true capitalism.

Take compete clauses, for instance. In a free market economy, workers must be free too, not just those who control the means of production. Non-competes get in the way of equitable value exchange by enabling something one click short of indentured servitude. Not ideal. Why pay a competitive wage when your employees are legally disincentivized to seek better compensation elsewhere? And as an employee, why do your best work if you know your employer has little incentive to compensate you fairly for it?

The trickle-down effects of non-competes and other mechanisms that get in the way of a truly free market may serve the short-term interest of those who have amassed the most power, but they hurt us all more in the long run!

Late-stage capitalism is the term often used to describe the phase of capitalist economies characterized by economic inequality, corporate dominance, and the erosion of social safety nets. It represents the cumulative effects of intensified contradictions and unsustainable practices on capitalism, driving concerns about social justice and environmental degradation. In a nutshell, the idea is that late-stage capitalism is fundamentally flawed because the interests of mediocre yet powerful people are protected to an extent that doesn't allow the best ideas to rise to the top. A level playing field, one enabled by diversity, equity and inclusion, is necessary for the Invisible Hand to do its thing. In what I call "true capitalism" winners and losers are determined purely on merit, and that can't happen if whole segments of the population never have the chance to win. Per the Flywheel framework, real social impact is an efficient starting point to real commercial impact.

RESPONSIBLE MARKETING WIN
Telfar Turned an Inclusive Mission into Fashion and Fortune

Fashion designer Telfar Clemens has become a household name with his signature bags gracing the arms of the most fashionable people in the world. But his rise to global recognition started with a mission to make the fashion industry that refused to open the door more inclusive.

Triple top-line score: 3/3

✓ **Social impact**

✓ **Reputation impact**

✓ **Commercial impact**

As a young college student, Clemens noticed the gender fluidity in the clothing he and his friends wore and built a fashion label to reflect what he saw as a missing offering within the fashion industry.[13] A self-taught designer, Clemens launched the Telfar label of unisex pieces in 2005 with a commitment to being inclusive for all. He took no money from investors and did very little marketing, chiefly relying on customer loyalty and reputation impact to grow the brand.

For more than a decade, the Telfar brand was ignored by the fashion giants, yet Clemens stayed true, not only to the goal of making fashion more inclusive, but also making a social impact through support of a cause with far-reaching implications within the New York City community. In 2017, Clemens designed uniforms for the White Castle hamburger franchises, donating all proceeds from the partnership to a Riker's Island bail fund for teenagers who were forced to remain at the prison due to their inability to post bail. Later that year, Clemens was awarded $400,000 from the CDFA/Vogue Fashion Fund, providing the working capital needed to produce a larger inventory of the increasingly popular Telfar bag along with additional product offerings.

In 2020, with a public nod from major fashion icons like Beyoncé, Oprah, and Selena Gomez, Telfar became a household name. But he continually stayed true to the brand's original mission of making fashion inclusive and creating a space where individuals from all walks of life feel welcome. As the popularity of Telfar bags grew, supplies became limited. In response, Clemens expressed his disappointment at the air of exclusivity around the bags and announced the Telfar Security Bag Program, an event for all consumers to pre-order any bag of any color with a guaranteed delivery date.

Telfar is an example of outsized commercial impact resulting from a commitment to doing the good work. But this story also exemplifies the power of the Council of

Fashion Designers of America Vogue Fashion Fund's responsible marketing initiative. The program created a real opportunity that ignited a chain of societal and economic impacts. The Fashion Fund provided Telfar with the capital to grow while also spreading the message of inclusivity. Nothing about that storyline is performative, and the fashion powerhouse that Telfar has become adds the extra seasoning to make this a Triple Top-Line win.

Creating Commercial Impact For Historically-Underrepresented Groups

There's much more work to do to create supportive ecosystems for Black entrepreneurs, who continue to face tremendous hurdles when it comes to accessing capital to grow and thrive. They must continually climb uphill to secure a viable network of partners, including banks, investors, foundations, and corporations. Black entrepreneurs start their business with about $35,000 of capital, while white entrepreneurs start with 3x more.[14] As a result, Black-owned businesses report higher levels of debt; and only 4 percent of Black-owned businesses are still in operation after three and a half years, compared with an average of 55 percent for all businesses. In May 2020, Aurora James, founder of the 15 Percent Pledge, took to Instagram with a message for the world's largest retail brands, asking them for equitable Black representation on their store shelves. She targeted retailers who consistently count on Black consumers to stay in business year after year. In response to the post, over 28 of the world's most recognized retailers accepted the pledge, redirecting $14 billion in revenue to Black brands.

Speaking with NPR's All Things Considered, James talked about the growth of Black consumer dollars, which is expected to reach over a trillion dollars by 2030. She said that these consumers want to see themselves represented in retail spaces, offering them the same level of options given to other shoppers. James made it clear that one-time donations don't cut it. Retailers need to step up and commit to the diversity, maintaining a more diversified product assortment.[15]

James is not alone in this line of thinking; 75.7 percent of respondents surveyed in the sparks & honey Responsible Marketing Index believe it is important to "create programs to directly benefit underrepresented or impacted communities" and 76.4 percent of respondents believe it is important to "run a program to make resources and/or products accessible to an impacted community." A slightly smaller number, 73.6 percent, believe that it is important to "create an innovative solution that is not a product but helps a community or a relevant cause," while 71.1 percent believe it is important to "provide inclusive alternatives to current products." Similarly, 74.1 percent of respondents believe it is important to "partner with brands or businesses owned by underserved, underrepresented, historically-excluded, or impacted individuals."

RESPONSIBLE INSIGHT

75.7 percent of respondents surveyed in the sparks & honey Responsible Marketing Index believe it is important to "create programs to directly benefit underrepresented or impacted communities."

Support from major retailers amplifies the visibility of products targeted towards Black women, addressing consumer demand for inclusivity and meeting specific needs. Support for these brands provides a larger platform for them to showcase their products to a wider audience, leading not only to increased sales but also to the elevation of awareness for all Black-owned businesses in this space, contributing to greater representation and diversity within the retail landscape. Demand is a function of unmet need, whether or not that need is something consumers are conscious of or not. For generations, Black people have moved through the world with a misguided belief that sunscreen was not necessary for our skin. When the medical messaging around skin cancer finally got around to debunking this myth, Black women found the market saturated with products that left our melanated skin looking chalky. There was an unmet need in the sunscreen space for tinted sunscreen that blended into darker skin complexions, but consumers did not recognize that need until Black-owned companies like Black Girl Sunscreen and tennis star Naomi Osaka's Kinlo Skin recognized the opportunity for social impact and stepped in to to fill the void.

Moreover, there is a growing consumer demand for companies to support Black-owned brands, suppliers, and vendors; 80.8 percent of respondents in the sparks & honey Responsible Marketing Index agreed that "It is important for brands and businesses today to play a role in addressing social issues impacting their consumers and audiences." Consumers increasingly seek to align their purchasing decisions with brands that recognize the value in Black-owned businesses and the power of the Black dollar.

The existing gap in meeting the specific needs of historically-excluded groups is not exclusive to the beauty industry. There is much work to be done in all retail and service areas, including financial services, healthcare, and food. Many of the products and services currently do not adequately consider the unique preferences and requirements of these consumers, fueling the exhausting sense of exclusion and dissatisfaction that has existed for decades. In response to this, Black consumers have demonstrated a willingness to shift a substantial portion of their annual spending—estimated at around $260 billion—to companies that demonstrate an authentic commitment to addressing their needs and preferences, representing an outsized commercial impact opportunity for businesses that prioritize diversity, inclusivity, and cultural literacy in their product offerings and marketing strategies.

According to the 15 Percent Pledge organization, 29 companies have signed multi-year contractual commitments to help shift more than $14 billion to Black businesses.[16] That includes retail heavyweights like Nordstrom, Bloomingdales, and Macy's, as well as more niche retailers like Sephora, Crate & Barrel, and Athletica.

RESPONSIBLE MARKETING WIN
How Ulta Beauty's 15 Percent Pledge Helped Black-Owned Brands Scale Their Business

Recognizing the value of elevating, celebrating, and consistently supporting the influence that underrepresented voices bring to the beauty industry, Ulta Beauty signed on to the 15 Percent Pledge.

Triple top-line score: 3/3

✓ **Social impact**

✓ **Reputation impact**

✓ **Commercial impact**

Ulta joined the 15 Percent Pledge in May 2021 with a commitment to responsible marketing in a variety of opportunity-generating ways. The beauty retailer dedicated $25 million in media investments on multicultural platforms to nurture relationships with beauty enthusiasts representing historically-excluded groups. Ten percent of this investment was directly spent with Black and Latin owned media outlets.

Its MUSE Accelerator program is also breathing life into Ulta's stated commitments by providing diverse business with education, support, resources, and mentorship for retail readiness. Speaking with Vanity Fair about joining the 15 Percent Pledge, Monica Arnaudo, Ulta Beauty chief merchandising officer, reiterated that simply launching the program was nowhere near adequate. She said that the company was also committed to creating an ecosystem of support for the brands, towards the goals of driving equity, guest acquisition, and ultimately wealth generation. Grassroots activism can create commercial impact.

This is an incredible example of how the Triple Top-Line Flywheel works—how grassroots activism can create significant commercial impact. The 15 Percent Pledge started with the identification of a real problem among Black businesses and a willingness by major retailers to create real opportunities. Ulta Beauty acknowledged the historical biases that have contributed to the obstacles for growth for impacted groups and acted to make a social impact, ultimately moving the Flywheel towards outsized commercial impact, not just for itself, but for the brands it served as well.

Woke and Profitable

In 2022, Rolling Stone published an article entitled "Companies that get 'woke' aren't going broke—they're more profitable than ever."[17] The writer debunks the right-wing rallying cry that when brands align themselves with liberal or progressive values, their bottom lines suffer. The article mentions the Keurig debacle of 2017 as the start of this sentiment. Reporting about sexual misconduct allegations against a US Senate candidate, a Fox News host expressed doubt over the veracity of the accusations. In response, Keurig pulled advertisements for their coffee makers from his show. Fans of the talk show host called for a boycott, with videos of them smashing Keurig coffee makers going viral across social media. The tantrums did little to affect Keurig's bottom line. In 2018, its parent company acquired Dr Pepper Snapple Group and experienced a roughly five percent increase in profits over the previous year. The company's decision to stand up for the safety of women brought about a positive economic impact.

In 2021, Kellogg Co. took a stand in partnership with the Gay & Lesbian Alliance Against Defamation (GLAAD) by releasing a limited-edition "Together with Pride" cereal and donating $3 from every box sold to GLAAD. The American Family Association, a Christian fundamentalist and anti-LGBTQ group, demanded a boycott of Kellogg's based on allegations that the campaign was pushing homosexuality on children. These efforts were also fruitless in the long run with Kellogg Co. outperforming market predictions with an increase of almost 12 percent in the fourth quarter of 2022. A commercial impact resulted when Kellogg stood up to make an impact, ultimately benefiting the brand, its businesses, and society.

When executed effectively, responsible marketing has the power to generate significant commercial impact for businesses. Marketing efforts that align with ethical and social values resonate with modern consumers, ultimately driving the Triple Top-Line Flywheel towards long-term profitability. Responsible marketing not only contributes to the greater good of society as a whole, but also delivers tangible benefits to businesses, reinforcing the notion that doing good is not only the right thing to do but also the business-savvy thing to do.

RESPONSIBLE RECAP

- By creating systems that actively regenerate and add value to the environment and society, businesses can contribute positively to communities and ecosystems, mimicking natural cycles for sustainable growth.

- Responsible marketing plays a pivotal role in advancing the vision of a regenerative economy by shifting consumer narratives and encouraging support for businesses that prioritize ecological restoration, social equity, and economic inclusivity.

- Short-termism often undermines strategic long-term goals, hindering sustainable brand growth and customer relationships.

- Brands that raise the bar by embracing responsible marketing principles are rewarded with sustainable commercial impact and consumer loyalty.

- Responsible marketing aligns with the principles of free market capitalism by broadening the perspective beyond short-term financial gains to encompass long-term societal wellbeing.

- Deviations from true capitalism, such as non-compete clauses and economic inequality, hinder the equitable functioning of the market and have led to late-stage capitalism characterized by corporate dominance and social injustices.

Notes

1 V. Stanley. What can other companies learn from Patagonia's model? Yale School of Management, August 28, 2023. insights.som.yale.edu/insights/ what-can-other-companies-learn-from-patagonias-model (archived at https:// perma.cc/S5J2-XFQW)

2 e.l.f. Beauty. Billie Jean King serving facts for e.l.f. Beauty to change the board game to support inclusivity, e.l.f. Beauty, May 2, 2024. investor.elfbeauty.com/ news-and-events/press-releases/landing-news/2024/05-02-2024-110139809 (archived at https://perma.cc/LX8G-MH7C)

3 e.l.f. Beauty. Billie Jean King serving facts for e.l.f. Beauty to change the board game to support inclusivity, e.l.f. Beauty, May 2, 2024. investor.elfbeauty.com/ news-and-events/press-releases/landing-news/2024/05-02-2024-110139809 (archived at https://perma.cc/T9CJ-9FVS)

4 Sustainable Brands. Trending: Brands continue work to build traceable, regenerative ag supply chains, Sustainable Brands, 2021. www.sustainablebrands.com/ read/supply-chain/trending-brands-building-traceable-regenerative-ag-supply-chains (archived at https://perma.cc/2P7N-X9B5)

5 Greyston Bakery. Our story: A pioneering social enterprise that changes lives with brownies, Greyston Bakery, 2024. shop.greyston.org/pages/about-greyston (archived at https://perma.cc/EEQ5-FG94)

6 M. Murphy. Short-termism is hurting companies and costing lives, Forbes, September, 12, 2022. www.forbes.com/sites/markmurphy/2022/09/12/ short-termism-is-hurting-companies-and-costing-lives (archived at https:// perma.cc/UYM5-85KN)

7 MBLM. Brand intimacy: Trader Joe's brand ranking, MBLM, 2021. www.mblm.com/lab/brandintimacy-study/brand/?code=2022-12-0003-00890&groupId=1 (archived at https://perma.cc/TTA9-MZEL)

8 L. Petrak (2021) Trader Joe's charts its course for affordable sustainability, Progressive Grocer, February 12, 2024. www.progressivegrocer.com/trader-joes-charts-its-course-affordable-sustainability (archived at https://perma.cc/ SS8Y-93X2)

9 M. DiLallo. Buying Trader Joe's stock: Is it public? The Motley Fool, February 3, 2024. www.fool.com/investing/how-to-invest/stocks/how-to-invest-in-trader-joes-stock/ (archived at https://perma.cc/Q87S-5ZM4)

10 B. Hutchinson. Trader Joe's to change product branding after petition calls it 'racist', ABC News, July 19, 2020. abcnews.go.com/US/trader-joes-change-product-branding-petition-calls-racist/story?id=71868367 (archived at https://perma.cc/28MU-B2ME)

11 M. Sainato. Trader Joe's broke labor laws in effort to stop stores unionizing, workers say, Guardian, September 4, 2022. www.theguardian.com/ us-news/2022/sep/04/trader-joes-union-workers-labor-law (archived at https://perma.cc/8BX2-GSKF)

12 R. Sun. Hollywood forfeits up to $30b every year because of racial inequality, The Hollywood Reporter, April 24, 2024. www.hollywoodreporter.com/ movies/movie-news/mckinsey-report-hollywood-representation-1235880126/ (archived at https://perma.cc/MP48-UGLP)

13 S. Roberson. 7 reasons Telfar Clemens is a high fashion star, Revolt, February 2, 2021. www.revolt.tv/article/2021-02-02/60793/7-reasons-telfar-clemens-is-a-high-fashion-star (archived at https://perma.cc/UK7S-LX3H)

14 D. Baboolall, K. Cook, N. Noel, S. Stewart, and N. Yancy. Building supportive ecosystems for Black-owned US businesses, McKinsey, October 29, 2020. www.mckinsey.com/industries/public-sector/our-insights/ building-supportive-ecosystems-for-black-owned-us-businesses (archived at https://perma.cc/6HA7-H75M)

15 M. Martin. Update on retailers' "15 percent pledge," NPR, June 5, 2021. www.npr.org/2021/06/05/1003639671/update-on-retailers-15-percent-pledge (archived at https://perma.cc/4KDK-7Y7P)

16 Fifteen Percent Pledge. Dream Makers Founder Grant, Fifteen Percent Pledge, 2022. www.15percentpledge.org/grant-dream-makers (archived at https://perma.cc/L7ER-LZ4S)

17 M. Klee. Companies that get 'woke' aren't going broke—they're more profitable than ever, Rolling Stone, April 8, 2023. www.rollingstone.com/ culture/culture-features/woke-companies-broke-profits-1234710724/ (archived at https://perma.cc/JUX3-A9R5)

PART TWO

The Moves

Keep It Real

05

Solving Real Problems

With the Triple Top-Line Flywheel as our foundational framework, we're ready to talk about making moves. After analyzing scores of responsible marketing case studies, I've found that each success story does one or more of these four simple things—solves real problems, creates real opportunities, tells real stories, and/or influences real policies. I call these the four responsible marketing moves. Master them and you'll be well on your way to transcending the performative—starting with solving real problems.

In today's marketplace, responsible businesses recognize that actions speak louder than words. Instead of merely making statements about their commitment to social and environmental causes, they prioritize tangible service and impactful initiatives that drive meaningful change. This shift towards action-oriented responsible business practices reflects a growing consumer demand for authenticity, transparency, and accountability.

Solving problems in this context of marketing involves really creating solutions for urgent and meaningful challenges or missed opportunities that a historically-excluded group is experiencing, whether or not they are conscious of it; or a living, breathing cultural cause that needs to be addressed. Don't make the mistake of thinking of this as a zero-sum game. Moving towards solving problems, as long as it is meaningful, measurable, and long term, is often what this is going to look and feel like, but there is that movement and that is what we need.

It is very easy to not make the distinction between discussing problems and solving them. It often feels safer as a brand leader to stop at the discussion aspect, but that limits us from actually creating a solution to the problem. Going a step further is what creates the most success and honing in on something more specific than a discussion could. Uber's campaign following George Floyd's murder exemplified this missed opportunity. They did this billboard campaign saying, "If you tolerate racism, delete Uber."

The subline was: "Black people have the right to move without fear." Thanks, but what are you doing about it? It felt performative and appeared more of a pat on the back for making a public statement than actually taking action. It doesn't tell any stories about influencing behavior or create any mechanism to ensure that the Uber network does not include racist people. At best, it's a business limiting move because you are telling people not to use your product. But if you truly understood the issue, you would understand that if you live in the U.S. and you go to a job and exist as a human, you are at some level tolerating racism. How did they come up with the idea that some people are not tolerating racism? We all are. It shows a lack of nuance and understanding of what the concept of racism is. Yes, we want to move in practice to anti-racism, which can never be perfect in a systemically racist society, so it is a great example of discussing the problem, but not even educating about it, and certainly not solving it.

Service always wins out over statements. In today's world of highly entuned stakeholders, brands cannot take the easy route of making a well-crafted statement with no intention of putting action behind it. Service-oriented approaches command engagement with communities to identify and solve real problems. Service means action and the prioritization of collaboration with stakeholders. By contrast, businesses that focus solely on making statements without taking meaningful action risk being perceived as performative or accused of "greenwashing" their brand image. While public declarations in support of social and environmental causes may generate positive publicity in the short term, they lack substance if not backed up by concrete efforts to solve real problems in a meaningful way.

RESPONSIBLE MARKETING WIN
MAC Viva Glam: Solving Real Problems

In 1994, MAC Cosmetics launched a bright blue lipstick campaign named Viva Glam with a commitment to donate 100 percent of sales to the MAC AIDS Fund and raise awareness about the AIDS epidemic.

Triple top-line score: 3/3

✓ **Social impact**

✓ **Reputation impact**

✓ **Commercial impact**

The MAC Viva Glam campaign stands as a pioneering beacon in the realm of responsible marketing. Launched in 1994 at the height of the AIDS epidemic, the campaign swung open the door to social impact within the beauty industry, as well as society as a whole.[1] It was about much more than just selling lipstick. The campaign raised awareness about individuals affected by HIV/AIDS, raising awareness and challenging stigma. MAC leveraged star power to amplify the campaign's message by partnering with celebrities like RuPaul and Mary J. Blige. Including high profile endorsements was a strategic move on the part of MAC, further destigmatizing mainstream discussions about HIV/AIDS.[2]

One of the most significant aspects of the Viva Glam campaign was its direct financial support for HIV/AIDS organizations. MAC chose to donate 100 percent of the lipstick proceeds to communities and individuals affected by HIV/AIDS. It was a bold brand move, especially for the 1990s, and it demonstrated MAC's authentic commitment to setting a new standard for giving back within the beauty industry. But the iconic beauty brand did not stop there in its problem-solving initiatives. Viva Glam also broke ground as the most inclusive and representative marketing campaign of its time. MAC gave the spotlight to diverse models and celebrities of various genders, races, and sexual orientations, challenging traditional beauty standards and celebrating all forms of diversity. It was a powerful message that resonated with a wide audience and symbolized solidarity with the LGBTQ+ community, which had been disproportionately impacted by the AIDS epidemic.

From the Triple Top-Line Flywheel perspective, Viva Glam checks all the boxes, providing a social impact, a reputational impact, and an economic impact. The 100 percent philanthropic aspect of the campaign earned significant media attention, which enhanced MAC's reputation and drove sales across the brand. At the outset of the campaign, MAC was only sold in three countries. It is now available in countries around the world. Fashion designers like Marc Jacobs and Vivienne Westwood created entire collections around Viva Glam to stand in partnership with the brand. As a result, MAC evolved into one of high-fashion's most sought-after luxury cosmetics brands.

The ongoing Viva Glam campaign is one of the longest running social impact marketing campaigns. These positive outcomes extended far beyond the beauty products space. By maximizing its platform to advocate for real problem solving, MAC demonstrated the transformative power of brands to drive positive social impact. Through its bold commitment, MAC inspired other companies to follow suit, paving the way for future collaborations between brands and charitable organizations. A lasting legacy was established within the beauty industry, one that exemplified the social responsibility these platforms have to build relationships with stakeholders and help cultivate solutions for their challenges. The Viva Glam lipstick cemented its place in marketing history as a symbol of prioritizing purpose.

Identifying the Right Intended Beneficiary

With so many real problems in this world, brands must be thoughtful when determining where to place their responsible marketing efforts. They must choose between multiple needs to determine which beneficiary best aligns with their values and long-term goals, carefully considering and prioritizing specific individuals, groups, or communities who stand to benefit from the brand's social impact decisions. In responsible marketing, intended beneficiaries are much more than passive recipients of the message. They are actively engaged in pinpointing the real problems impacting their communities and empowered by the brand to participate in crafting a solution to those problems. By focusing on intentional beneficiaries, responsible marketers take meaningful actions that go beyond superficial gestures or tokenism. They seek to build genuine connections with their audience, understand their unique challenges, and tailor their efforts to deliver value and impact where it is needed most.

In 2021, Band-Aid launched OURTONE strips.[3] The product line offers Band-Aids in various shades of brown, providing more bandage options for communities of color, along with financial support for Black nursing students. After one hundred years of offering adhesive bandages, the Band-Aid brand provided a solution to the absence of color options among bandages in the first aid aisle. Recognizing this as a need among people of color, Johnson & Johnson hosted a series of focus groups to gather data from Black consumers about their insight, their expectations, packaging, and bandage shades. Jordan Mojka, Associate Brand Manager of Wound Care at Johnson & Johnson Consumer Inc., acknowledged that the country had allowed for a major product gap that needed to be solved quickly, with the goal of truly reflecting the communities that buy from them. Along with the OURTONE launch, Band-Aid partnered with the National Black Nurses Association (NBNA), which handed out samples of the new bandages at a health-related event, and the National Association for Community Health Centers, which distributed free samples to local community health centers.

The OURTONE story exemplifies the power of the Triple Top-Line Flywheel. The brand's problem solving created new products that expanded their footprint massively in a stagnant category. That is the ultimate goal of every consumer goods company's innovation team and the ultimate unlock of massive commercial growth.

REAL TALK WITH RESPONSIBLE MARKETERS
Ato Micah

Chief Executive Officer at Maverick Research, Board Member at Freezelink, Board Member at Credit Mall Limited, and Board Member at Norwalk Soap Company, Ato is a classically-trained brand marketing executive turned global entrepreneur and a passionate servant leader with 20+ years of experience delivering exceptional results for Procter & Gamble, Nielsen, and Millward Brown in the United States, Ghana, and Nigeria.

Bringing Market Research to Africa

Before Maverick existed, if you wanted to know what Africans bought, all the data sources were literally foreign brands. Nielsen, Ipsos, these billion-dollar behemoths, would essentially get the data collected by some local data collection folks, and then ship it off wherever in the world they actually held any African data.

How the data that was collected and how the models were created wasn't from an indigenous point of view. Even the talent to model all the retail data wasn't something that was available locally.

The answer, with regards to retail, is to have data scientists and analysts who actually live and breathe and experience that local environment in which the measuring is taking place. It brings the cultural elements to the table, really bringing that African context to it.

Building Local Talent

Another important aspect of Maverick's mission was building that talent, building the local expertise around retail audit analytics. We helped to teach and then build capacity and capability with local data scientists that we recruited over the past four years. It has been another way to lead and bring to bear the vision that we have, in terms of meeting and bringing the cultural resilience aspects to the market research.

We have an approach that brings relevance and a more realistic perspective to the data. And the data is, in itself, quite encouraging. We are calibrating the real risk, as compared to the perceived risk of entering the marketplace in Africa. The construct out there is that people cannot afford things, and I'm not saying that doesn't exist, but it's grossly overestimated. What the reality is, is that the market itself can take on a lot of premium products.

Look at the penetration of mobile telephony and all the services that have come along with that. Look at the adoption of things like feminine care and baby care by consumers. The average person from the West may not perceive that there's a huge market and a huge need. We continually challenge those myths and showcase the reality of the opportunity. There are ways to really engage the African consumer, and to bring meaningful products that actually solve problems to market. Local manufacturers are emerging to take advantage of this opportunity and drive the African economy even further.

Africa Rising

Let me share an example of how looking at the marketplace from an indigenous perspective can offer real opportunity. Years ago in the 1980s, the corner shop or the local retailers in neighborhoods and villages usually would buy in bulk and then turn those products into single-serving sachets (I mean as small as one spoon of sugar tied in clear plastic).

It took until the early 2000s for anyone to realize that there was a whole long tail of consumers that would buy these single-serving sachets as consumer-packaged goods. The single-serving options actually met a need and gave people access to products. That was one of the game changers. It helped to cause the rapid economic growth now termed "Africa Rising." It brings to bear, in terms of return, for operators and marketers to actually understand the marketplace and how it functions. Indigenous players like us bring this kind of new, local context to the data, which helps to improve the overall ecosystem.

Marketers like Ato understand the incredible depth of connection that brands can develop with target audiences. This intended beneficiary intimacy goes beyond surface-level interactions to cultivate a meaningful relationship based on the level of trust and mutual respect only gained through truly knowing and empathizing with the needs, preferences, and aspirations of those beneficiaries. It involves listening actively to their voices and identifying the real problems that they face in their lives. Intended beneficiary intimacy gives brands a deeper perspective into the problems that challenge their stakeholders, which is a key aspect of developing impactful campaigns that feel personal, relevant, and impactful to their audience.

RESPONSIBLE INSIGHT

We steep ourselves in the behaviors and desires of specific communities, and create the cultural relevance between their unique needs, and a brand's unique story, to create a lasting bond.

Why? Not because of DEI, although that's a beautiful and necessary byproduct of our work, but because these audiences influence and define broader culture and offer inarguable and extensive bottom line value to brands, and business longevity ultimately depends on their buy-in.

SOURCE Myles Worthington, The WORTHI Way, Company Culture & Values

Classic prioritization framework is a method that many businesses use to rank tasks based on importance and urgency. It involves categorizing items into different buckets for decision-making and resource allocation. Typically, those buckets are labeled as follows:

- Urgent and important: Requires immediate attention with significant consequences.

- Important but not urgent: Essential for long-term goals, but not requiring immediate action.

- Urgent but not important: Demands immediate attention but it will not contribute significantly to long-term goals.

- Not urgent and not important: Neither urgent nor important and may even be considered a distraction.

Software giant Intuit classified childhood education as an urgent and important matter in crafting their Intuit for Education initiative. With more than 50 million students as the intended beneficiaries, the program aims to turn Gen Z and Gen Alpha high-school students into the most financially literate generations in history.[4] According to Intuit, only 25 percent of all high school students are required to take a personal finance course as part of their curriculum. Unsurprisingly, that percentage is even lower within low-income school districts. That lack of a solid financial foundation can lead to lasting financial challenges in adult years, exemplified by the disturbing fact that only about 30 percent of individuals of all ages living in the United States can successfully pass a basic financial literacy quiz.

Intuit for Education is solving this real societal problem by evolving the teaching of personal finances through a unique approach that includes real world educational tools related to both personal and entrepreneurial finance, a highly flexible curriculum that can be self-paced and accessed from virtually anywhere, and interactive financial literacy games to keep students engaged. Intuit is maximizing the Triple Top-Line Flywheel by addressing the wealth disparity that exists among its intended beneficiaries and creating solutions that truly meet their immediate needs, intricacies that can only be garnered through real engagement with these stakeholders.

REAL TALK WITH RESPONSIBLE MARKETERS
Kenny Mitchell

Global Chief Marketing Officer at Levi Strauss & Co., Independent Board Director at e.l.f. Beauty, Advisor at Overtime, formerly Chief Marketing Officer at Snap Inc, Member at Black Executive CMO Alliance (BECA), and Advisory Board Member at The Tuck School of Business at Dartmouth, Kenny strongly believes in the old adage that leaders have the responsibility to "lift as they climb."

The Civic Initiative to Get Snapchatters to Vote

We believed that we had a bit of a duty and an opportunity to help drive civic engagement with young people and get them to own some of the outcome that was happening both nationally and statewide, so we had a pretty big campaign and a lot of activities around the app. The different surface areas of the app were intended to drive voter registration, education around candidates, education around the polling locations, and getting the vote out based on the state that you are in.

We ended up with about a million and a half first-time voters that registered through our platform. Which is pretty impressive. And we had millions upon millions of uses of different features. We had a lot of these amazing tools that would tell you how to register to vote and ensure that once you did, you knew when to vote, you knew where your polling location was and you could find information out about your candidate. That actually drove further engagement within our app, which was the commercial component of it. Very proudly, we were able to do something positive for society and in a pretty nonpartisan way.

I really benefit by working at a founder-led company with a founder who has a bit of a moral compass. We have a civics and public policy team. And we've got some passionate and creative folks that are like, *let's make this an election to remember on our platform.* And he was supportive as a leader. Some of my other executive counterparts were supportive and, ultimately, our boss or cofounder was supportive as well.

Let Your Brand Live Out its Values

One of the things that I've always found throughout my career as a marketer is that living out your values as a brand actually tends to deliver outsized impact because it's connected to things that people already care about. A lot of times as a marketer, you're trying to tell somebody about a new flavor, or a new item and they have to be really engaged in your category. You have to spend a ton on media to make that really resonate.

But if you're living out your values in connection to things that are relevant and that people are naturally passionate about, it actually won't cost you that much. You have an outsized impact, so that's another little secret sauce. The comps and community engagement involved in sharing might happen more naturally and more organically when you're living out your brand's values. So it is actually a bit of a force multiplier in that way.

Three Ways Snapchat Has Been Working to Help Youth

I think we feel a bit of obligation or responsibility or opportunity, whatever you want to call it, because we touch so many younger audiences. We have 90 percent penetration with people that are 13 to 24. We feel like there are some things that we can and should be doing that can have a positive impact for them during their formative years. It is also the right thing for us to do because it actually protects us as a business long term.

For example, last year, we had a big effort connected to fentanyl and education around fentanyl. We did it on platform and in conjunction with the Ad Council. Our platform is ephemeral by nature, so messages disappear. It gives a tremendous amount of freedom to communicate and connect with people, but it also attracts bad actors because you don't have a foot. We really redoubled our efforts around being able to detect message in a privacy-safe way.

The year before we had a big focus area on mental health. The thing about the pandemic era was just how difficult it was for young people, feeling so lonely and whatnot. We did something called Club Unity, with five or six different decently known folks that talked about their mental health challenges and offered up some of the things that they've been doing to deal with it. We hosted this virtual panel in session with some leading-edge mental health advocates that left people with tools and some things that you could find within our app and service.

A bit of a trend that we're seeing is actually around sexual exploitation, bullying as it relates to photos and videos and stuff like that. There's this term that young people use where they say, "Do you send?" and basically it means that you send nudes or provide pictures. We see that behavior cresting right now as something problematic, particularly since people were pretty suppressed coming out of the pandemic. People are rage living and this is a byproduct of that. So, it's a big focus area for this year.

Keeping Your Finger on the Pulse

As a marketer, I'm super curious. I recall sitting at a sushi bar next to a young woman who started using Snap right next to me, so I just struck up a conversation. I'm infinitely curious like that and I'm always doing my own personal, first-party research.

We also have a whole insights and analytics team who's dedicated to keeping us fully pulsed on what's happening, whether it be through on-the-ground user research, bigger focus groups, or even larger, longitudinal and quantitative studies. One of our unique positions is, "No one knows Josie better than Snapchat." So we have to keep a pulse on what they know, their values, what's important to them, what trends are forthcoming, because they will eventually serve us on our app. We want to make sure we're best positioned to be supportive in that way.

Kenny's Advice to Marketers

I want them to commit to something in the vein of empathy. They should have empathy for their consumer and express that in a way that delivers good for society.

To me, it's tying together two ideas. One is knowing your consumer really well and speaking in a way that's meaningful and relevant to them and around things that are important to them. Those typically will tie back to things that are important for the broader product world. It means you also have to get your brand strategy out of the way. You can't necessarily lead exclusively with your business objectives. You actually can get there by doing things through a consumer lens.

A Framework For Solutions

SMART goals is a framework that helps people and businesses solve problems in a strategic way. The acronym stands for:

- Specific: Well-defined, clear, and unambiguous, addressing what needs to be accomplished and what steps need to be taken to achieve it.
- Measurable: Specific criteria for measuring progress toward the goal.
- Achievable: Resources and time needed to attain the goal are available.
- Relevant: Realistic and relevant to the brand's goals.
- Time-bound: A clearly defined timeframe for achievement.

The type of specificity that evolves from the evaluation that goes into this type of framework becomes a key component for recognizing when real problem solving is truly occurring. By incorporating these specific criteria for success, brands can move forward with goals that are well-defined and aligned with broader objectives. That clarity and focus increases both internal and external motivation, ultimately leading to more successful outcomes.

RESPONSIBLE MARKETING WIN
How Mastercard is Leading the Way in Solving Societal Problems Within the Bankcard Industry

Mastercard identified and addressed real problems within the bankcard industry by implementing initiatives to expand inclusivity for the LGBTQIA+ community and improve accessibility for the visually impaired.

Triple top-line score: 3/3

✓ **Social impact**

✓ **Reputation impact**

✓ **Commercial impact**

The systematic difficulties around name changes create a huge problem for the transgender community. There is a lot of bureaucracy time involved that creates an inherent lag between you making that decision, your identity changing, and being able to represent that to the world with the basic things you need to use to live your everyday life, such as your credit card. A lot of data around the point of sale documents the risk of violence that we know is inherent in how transgender people experience the world. If you really start to consider the fear and the emotional weight experienced by a historically-excluded consumer and what they face in the world, you understand that you can relieve a lot of that by changing the way that your brand interacts with them.

True Name was introduced in 2019 during Pride Month through an informative video with real people sharing their challenges with using debit or credit cards that misrepresent their true identities. It also featured transgender and nonbinary actors explaining the value of True Name for their communities. Mastercard created a card that does not require the customer to have their birth certificate name listed on their credit card. It allows trans individuals, nonbinary individuals, and people who have changed their names for whatever reason to have a card that aligns with their desired identity. The brand moved far beyond the cheerleading phase of rainbow-colored credit and debit cards into the champion phase of making it easier for people who are transgender, which offers an amazing example of what it means to find the right social impact.

While most banks did not support True Name in the beginning, the success of the program eventually garnered a lot of interest from other banking institutions and card companies. Mastercard is encouraging the banking industry to step up and make this feature widely available. According to Mastercard, True Name has expanded with steady momentum. It actually changed an unjust system that had gone unnoticed by titans of the industry for too many years. Mastercard asked the question, "When it comes to the credit card industry, what are the societal debts that the industry has and how do they relate particularly to the most historically-excluded community?" They then identified those debts and implemented an impactful response.

The Mastercard Touch Card feature also exemplifies the power of a brand to provide real solutions to real problems. As payment cards continue to move forward by adopting modern, flat designs without embossed names and numbers, they're inadvertently setting back those who need to identify and differentiate their cards without the use of sight. This technology creates an accessible system of payment cards with unique, tactile notches—rounded for debit, squared for credit and triangular for prepaid—so visually impaired individuals can identify their cards with just a touch.

The company is also launching a signature melody as an audio cue for successful transactions. At checkout counters worldwide, visually impaired customers will have audible confirmation that their bank card purchase is completed. The Touch Card by Mastercard was designed with accessibility in mind to bring security, inclusivity and independence to blind and partially sighted cardholders around the world. The company identified an unmet need not being met in an inclusive way and created a solution that alleviated resulting pain points.

The LGBTQIA+ and differently abled communities have trillions of dollars in annual spending power. Failing to acknowledge their contributions to the economy, as well as their specific needs, is simply bad for business and bad for society as a whole. Mastercard is changing the entire bankcard industry with the innovative True Name and Touch Card features.

Solving Real Problems With a Side of Laughter

With the seriousness of real problems, it naturally follows that marketers tend to see the role of problem solving in a earnest way. We assume that our messaging must be soaked in seriousness, from the images to the tone of the written content. But this idea is a misconception that leads us to miss out on opportunities to engage with our stakeholders in a lighthearted but engaging way, while still solving for a serious problem. Bobbie is an infant formula company seeking to elevate the quality of baby formula by offering an original organic recipe from grass-fed cows. It contains no corn syrup, filler, palm oil, or soy. With a goal of supporting every parent, Bobbie offers safe and reliable options for moms who choose the breast, bottle, or both.[5]

On April 1, 2024, Bobbie shocked its LinkedIn followers by announcing its organic chocolate infant formula, complete with 100 percent dark cocoa and organic grass fed milk.[6] The initial responses ranged from applause over the "genius" of the idea to confusion about the dietary appropriateness of introducing chocolate to infants. With four simple words—Happy April Fool's Day—Bobbie revealed the humor of the post, giving its loyal customers something to smile about, while also attracting the attention of new consumers and using that time in the light to further their social impact.

When did marketing become a binary drive-through concept where you can only order either "purpose, or humor"… no fries with that either? It's laugh or cry only! Are we that lazy? Are we that uninspired? Are we that unable to walk and chew gum? Does keeping it light and fun as Rome burns around us really feel "sooooo refreshing" to the few who know, at least for now, they and theirs are the only ones truly safe from its flames? Are all other lives so meaningless, we truly miss the days we could laugh comfortably while they burned? Do we hear ourselves? Do we get that even in junior positions, not to talk of C-level ones, our choices in a single day can easily have more lasting influence on more humans than the average human will ever have in a lifetime?

I find it refreshing to have the opportunity to work and lead in ways that prioritize real commercial impact and real social impact beyond the performative—making both outcomes bigger and better than the sum of their parts (and surely any slapstick moment imaginable). I find it hilarious that some folks think their proud "anti-wokeness" makes them look "pro-business" (I know it's very confusing), yet the only thing anti-wokeness smacks of is a self-indulgent sense of personal nostalgia… the ultimate distraction and one no business that will endure tolerates from its stewards for very long. How even more hilarious it is that the purpose/humor drive-through franchisees are so focused on their irrational feelings, they've lost sight of what they once believed in—that lasting emotional connections are the point, not what those emotional connections are best nurtured with at a point in time, humor, purpose, otherwise. The darlings of the Aquarius age are taking over because they understand the assignment is about so much more than "make it funny" (even when it does). And those beloved Etsy holiday spots, with no vanity, and such deftness of hand, show those consumed with unhelpful nostalgia how, duh, being hilarious and socially impactful aren't at cross purposes at all.

In April of 2023, Mrs. Meyer's Clean Day stepped into the lane of impactful and lighthearted when it enlisted the help of Emmy-winning actor Tyler James Williams to launch the Lots of Compassion program.[7] Williams plays Mr. Eddie on the ABC sitcom Abbott Elementary, a first-grade teacher who puts his green thumb to work by creating a school community garden. With his help and some references to his television character, the Mrs. Meyer's brand transforms vacant lots into thriving gardens in historically-excluded communities across the country. Local communities receive $20,000 grants to plant gardens. In this "art imitates life" ad campaign, the brand used the lightness of a popular sitcom to draw audience attention and spotlight this important social and environmental initiative.

RESPONSIBLE REFRAME

Just a reminder of how deeply misunderstood the power of responsible marketing is:

- Since when were "purpose" and "entertainment" two different categories?
- Since when was entertainment any more about selling than purpose is?
- No matter what kind of marketing it is, selling is always the point.
- When brands miss the mark on that, it means *their* work was ineffective, not that an entire category of work is ineffective.
- My question is why certain pockets of the marketing and advertising industry feel so invested in making a case against the practice of taking a stand for society and making it count for the business.
- If a win–win can generate the same or better returns, what kind of illogical person just wants a win?

When brands prioritize the goal of solving real problems, the Triple Top-Line Flywheel essentially moves on its own. The proof becomes the message as they just tell people how they are solving real problems and that becomes the marketing.

RESPONSIBLE RECAP

- The essence of problem-solving in marketing lies in addressing urgent and meaningful challenges faced by historically-excluded groups or cultural causes in need of attention, even if they are not consciously aware of them.

- It's crucial to distinguish between merely discussing a problem and actively solving it, as the latter involves meaningful, measurable, and long-term solutions.

- In responsible marketing, brands must carefully select beneficiaries whose needs align with their values and long-term goals.

- Intended beneficiaries are actively engaged in identifying and solving real problems, empowered by brands to participate in crafting solutions.

- Marketing is not a binary concept requiring either purpose or humor.

Notes

1 MAC Cosmetics. Viva Glam 27: Timeline, MAC Cosmetics, 2024. www.maccosmetics.com/vivaglam-timeline (archived at https://perma.cc/B2N2-DRMA)

2 K. Intner. A brief history of MAC's iconic Viva Glam campaign, Harpers Bazaar, December 23, 2021. www.harpersbazaar.com/beauty/makeup/a38573019/john-demsey-mac-viva-glam-interview/ (archived at https://perma.cc/Z2XK-UUZE)

3 B. Royall. The story behind BAND-AID brand OURTONE adhesive bandages, Johnson & Johnson, June 15, 2021. www.jnj.com/caring-and-giving/the-story-behind-band-aid-brand-ourtone-adhesive-bandages (archived at https://perma.cc/9UZK-JC24)

4 D. Zasada. Intuit for education: Helping the next generation become financially literate, Intuit, September 25, 2023. www.intuit.com/blog/social-responsibility/intuit-for-education-helping-the-next-generation-become-financially-literate/ (archived at https://perma.cc/W2ED-XSWQ)

5 Bobbie. Our story: Feeding is a journey, Bobbie, 2024. www.hibobbie.com/pages/our-story (archived at https://perma.cc/A7VH-PGY3)

6 Bobbie. Introducing our latest innovation, LinkedIn, 2024. www.linkedin.com/feed/update/urn:li:activity:7180622989204279296/ (archived at https://perma.cc/BM4C-3SQM)

7 D. Directo-Meston. Emmy-winning actor Tyler James Williams on growing his green thumb beyond "Abbott Elementary," The Hollywood Reporter, April 14, 2023. www.hollywoodreporter.com/lifestyle/lifestyle-news/tyler-james-williams-mrs-meyers-clean-day-lots-of-compassion-1235368563/ (archived at https://perma.cc/CA77-YRHD)

06

Telling Real Stories

they say:
"sticks and stones can break bones
– but words can never hurt"
yet, I've seen stones and sticks
break lips and bones in hips
after words commanded such action
or seen violence in metaphor
or pushed in minds before children were four years or four months old
now
tell me—what are words worth?
children learn about subject, object, and predicate
symbolically constructing sentences
in American classrooms
where white students are taught as subjects
while Black students are treated like objects
destined to be subjected to life sentences
because of semantic switch-ups that set statutory precedence
now
tell me—what are words worth?
"Words worth," Carlos Andrés Gómez[1]

The imperative to tell real stories shouldn't surprise any experienced
marketer, but a responsible marketing context makes the expected more
challenging to achieve. Why? We're up against a pervasive and systemic lack
of culturally literate infrastructure across the entire marketing ecosystem.
Said plainly, we're only good at telling the real stories we're most familiar
with when it's the untold ones that inherently set us up for outsized impact.

Storytelling dates back to the beginning of brand marketing when brands used visual stories in their print ads to connect with consumers through pictures. In 1948, De Beers launched its A Diamond is Forever campaign, becoming the first jewelry brand to associate diamonds with love and marriage, and influencing the widespread custom of giving diamond engagement rings.[2] At a time when luxury purchases were overshadowed by the financial devastation of World War II, DeBeers used storytelling to create an emotional connection to diamonds, moving lovelorn consumers to spend, even when it meant spending beyond their means.

As advertising expanded into radio ads, marketers had to evolve their storytelling methods from images to attention-grabbing verbal narratives. Many brands embedded their messaging within radio dramas, which reached their height of popularity in the 1940s. These shows used dialogue, music, and sound effects to tell their audiences compelling stories, and with no visual elements, so advertisers were forced to rely on words and audio effects to fully develop their narratives. The introduction of radio dramas offered household product brands an opportunity to reach captivated home-makers as they listened to the 30-minute dramatic stories. Procter & Gamble maximized these story telling opportunities to turn products like Ivory soap into household staples and rename the generational phenomenon that we now know as "soap operas."[3]

Though some marketers also used motion pictures as an advertisement platform during the 1940s, television brought visuals to a much broader audience. Watchmaker Bulova aired the first televised advertisement in 1941, right before the start of a Brooklyn Dodgers and Philadelphia Phillies baseball game.[4] The 10-second ad featured a picture of a Bulova watch face on top of an outline of the United States, as the announcer declared, "America runs on Bulova time." While far from the definition of impactful storytelling by today's standards, this grainy marketing campaign opened the door for the visual enhancement of turning a catchy slogan into successful storytelling.

Nike mastered the art of storytelling with its Just Do It television campaign. Debuting in 1988, the ad featured an 80-year-old athlete jogging across the Golden Gate Bridge as he informed the audience that he runs 17 miles each morning.[5] The narrative of the simple ad evoked feelings of determination and personal commitment, a message that became synonymous with the Nike brand. The Just Do It commercials that followed kept with the same messaging and simple storytelling. Nike featured prominent sports stars like Michael Jordan and Bo Jackson, along with everyday fitness enthu-siasts and high-school athletes. Within the first year of the campaign's launch, Nike's sales increased by over 40 percent.[6] But beyond the economic impact, it cemented Nike's reputation as a leading brand storyteller, a designation that no other athletic wear has been able to quite replicate.

The digital revolution of the internet moved marketing campaigns into utilizing websites and blogs for storytelling. Content marketing arose as an essential part of sharing narratives to a wide audience. This new form of marketing further expanded as brands began establishing their social media presence. The free-flowing exchange of communications and ideas brought on by social media made relatability and authenticity more vital than ever before. Rather than persuading consumers, like the goal of articles or arguments, stories reveal. They replace the burden of proof with something more powerful—the steadfastness of belief.

RESPONSIBLE INSIGHT

The way you instill confidence in people is with great stories, showing them "Here's what it looks like." What we're trying to do is create prosociality: behaviors that are intended to benefit others. I've been using that term a lot lately because I love it. It's this concept that "I am willing to do what's good for the many."

I think, especially in a capitalistic society, and especially in America, that we need more prosociality now than ever. But you are dealing with really good storytelling in the opposite direction. America's sense of exceptionalism and frontierism and the individual ruggedly pulling themselves up by the bootstraps is ingrained, not just as a story, but also in the structural racism that we live in.

SOURCE Anthony Veneziale, Co-creator of Freestyle Love Supreme

---

What Makes a Story Compelling?

In the book *The Storytelling Edge: How to Transform your business, stop screaming into the void, and make people love you*, Shane Snow and Joe Lazauskas explore the impact of effective storytelling on businesses.[7] It explains that good storytelling has an effect on the consumer's heart and mind, and with this understanding, brands can maximize the effectiveness of utilizing compelling narratives in their marketing campaigns. The book lays out four pillars of great storytelling:

- Relatability: When audiences connect with the experiences of a story, it can resonate and expand into commercial impact.

- Novelty: Stories are more memorable when they contain some unusual or unexpected element.
- Tension: Readers stay engaged when stories include conflict and suspense.
- Fluency: The most effectively crafted stories have a seamless flow that makes them easy for readers to take in.

These pillars and methodologies help brands cultivate marketing content that engages and builds lasting customer relationships. The sparks & honey Responsible Marketing Index found that 72.9 percent of respondents agreed that businesses should use authentic and inclusive storytelling, underscoring the responsibility of brands to offer real narratives.[8] But in the context of responsible marketing, there are some things that stories must include to earn the designation of "real." First and foremost, brands should go to the source, which are the people the campaign is actually about. Far too often, marketers try to replicate stories instead of amplifying them, resulting in a pathetically inauthentic representation that consumers see right through. Give sources the mic and let them tell their own stories. Providing a space for real narratives from real people creates the type of relatability that translates into commercial impact.

REAL TALK WITH RESPONSIBLE MARKETERS
Sara McCord

Founder and CEO at Sara McCord Communications, Power Coach: Strategy at Powerful Professionals, and Member at We are the Board, Sara helps thought leaders, businesses, and brands become known by creating viral marketing campaigns and meaningful content.

Start With Intention, Then Follow Through

For me, there are two key components that are absolutely fundamental. I don't think that something can qualify as responsible marketing without these two key components: intention and outcome. If either one of those don't exist, you're not going to have a responsible marketing campaign.

I think intention is important because you're not just going to fall into responsible marketing, and, candidly, that's where a lot of people get it wrong. They don't set out with the intention to have a responsible marketing campaign. They might set out with an intention not to do anything wrong. Or they might set out with an intention not to be a bad person. Or they might set out with an intention just to make a lot of money. First of all, there are people still today for whom responsible or inclusive marketing is not even in their value set. And if it's not even in your value set, the likelihood that you're going to land on an actual responsible marketing campaign is so slim, even if you're a good person. Intention is important.

The second part of it is the outcome. We have to include that because that holds accountable the camp of people who say, "I had the right intentions..." But then they didn't go through and hire the right people or do the right things or have a thoughtful campaign. So you tell them, "That's lovely, and you're halfway there, but it's still not a responsible marketing campaign because you didn't actually land on the target."

Sara Defines Upstanding Behavior

I am not a bystander. I don't have that bone in my body, and I think that that's another thing that builds your credibility. If you see something, say something. Stand up for people. When it's the appropriate thing to do, go stand up for them.

When you genuinely care about people, go extend yourself, be generous with your network, with your opportunities, with your time. I do think that marginalized communities in particular need people who look like myself to stand and lock arms with them when the time calls for it. I think that that's part of upholding someone else. It's not just that you celebrate them when everyone's celebrating them. It's on the days that somebody's treating them like crap that you still need to celebrate them. We all recognize when people do that in our lives.

What Does Upstanding Marketing Look Like?

I don't think it's actually what it looks like. I think it's what it feels like. I think about the commercials that make me cry, or in the campaigns that make me cry because I'm so touched. A marketer reached in and touched my heart. I'll give you an example. It was Oreo about two years ago that did an ad about a dad who originally was not accepting of the fact that his child was gay. He was really struggling with it, and then at the end of the commercial, he painted his fence with a rainbow.

I just remember watching that video and crying, and one of the things I thought was so beautiful, so powerful, was that the brand was being brave showing someone who had to go through a learning process. I thought that it was reflective of our times. Sadly, it didn't surprise me that a father would be hesitant, but then in the course of this rather short commercial, this father became welcoming and made his daughter feel seen and feel significant. It was beautiful to me, because, going back to the idea of being an upstander, we know that there are going to be people who are going to boycott Oreo because they're taking a stance like this, but Oreo is saying: "We don't care. We want to show that humans can learn and love and grow."

The other impressive thing about the Oreo campaign is that it was more meaningful than performative. I think one of the reasons why I find it more compelling is that the brand took the time to "reach one, teach one" as opposed to just saying, "We're going to put one of everyone in our ad and call it inclusive." Not that that isn't important, because representation absolutely matters. But I think, for me, maybe that's why this ad stands out. It made me feel something. I think when a brand takes a risk and does something that no one else is doing in the name of inclusion that can also make you feel something, I think that's brave.

As Sara's example illustrates, authentic storytelling must come from the person experiencing it, otherwise brands run the risk of alienating that person and minimizing the impact of the experiences, which misses a valuable opportunity to accomplish the four aspects of the storytelling edge. Responsible marketing is marketing that works, and if the narrative doesn't feel real, it's not going to work. This is about effectiveness and driving a business impact. Those are all ways that we measure our success. So going to the source, yes, it's the right thing to do, but for us as marketers, it's also the right thing to do to ensure it's going to work. Questions may arise about what sort of diamond will be mined from someone's story, but it can be a costly mistake to rely on a prediction. Marketers must get in the field and find out.

GREAT STORYTELLING IMPACTS RESPONSIBLE MARKETING STORIES

1 **Diverse perspectives enhance authenticity**
   A range of perspectives makes narratives more authentic and relatable. That authenticity resonates with audiences, allowing them to reflect on real-world experiences beyond the confines of a marketing team's direct knowledge.

2 **Community engagement increases relevance**
   By involving communities and stakeholders in the storytelling process, marketers can ensure that their narratives are relevant and genuinely

reflective of the people they aim to represent or engage. This collaborative approach can uncover insights and nuances that a more controlled, internal process might miss.

3 Building trust through transparency
Releasing control and embracing openness builds trust with audiences. Today's consumers have a detection meter for messages that are overly manufactured or not genuinely representative. Transparency mitigates skepticism and fosters a stronger connection between brands and their audiences.

4 Empowerment leads to advocacy
Allowing those directly impacted by the stories to have a say or even lead the narrative can empower individuals and communities, turning them into brand advocates. When people see their own voices and stories reflected authentically, they're more likely to amplify the message.

5 Adapting to cultural sensitivities
In an increasingly global market, understanding and respecting cultural nuances is crucial. Releasing control and engaging with cultural consultants or community members ensures marketing efforts are sensitive and not inadvertently perpetuating stereotypes or cultural appropriation.

6 Innovation through co-creation
Collaborative storytelling can lead to innovative marketing strategies that stand out in a crowded market. Co-creation with diverse communities brings fresh ideas that a more insular process might not achieve.

7 Meeting the demand for social responsibility
Consumers increasingly expect brands to contribute positively to society. Authentic responsible marketing stories that involve real people and address real issues demonstrate a brand's commitment to these values, enhancing reputation and appeal.

8 Long-term relationships over transactions
Responsible storytelling is part of a broader strategic shift from transactional marketing to building long-term relationships with audiences; authentic stories that genuinely engage and reflect the audience foster loyalty over time, beyond any single purchase.

But handing over the microphone is not enough if it doesn't come with some level of autonomy and authority for sources to tell their stories with transparency. Marketers have to also respect the source for these narratives to work. I equate it to the mediocrity of colonialism, where a group of people think they've come up with this great idea, when in reality they went to the source and then took it from them. Establish clear objectives that not only center the source, but also benefit the groups that the source represented as the intended beneficiaries of the storytelling in every way. This mutual understanding prevents misrepresentation between the source and brand, while also fostering trust between the brand and its audience.

When aiming to tell authentic and responsible marketing stories, one of the most important components is also one of the most difficult to adopt—the practice of releasing control. Marketers must let go and give their sources the reins. It isn't about relinquishing quality or brand consistency; it's about embracing authenticity, diversity and engagement to create more impactful and meaningful connections across consumer stakeholders.

RESPONSIBLE MARKETING WIN
How Essity's #wombstories Campaign Gets Source Centered Storytelling Right

Essity, the creators of Bodyform feminine care products, released control of its marketing narrative to consumers when it launched the #wombstories campaign. The powerful story is an animated and real-life look at the many conditions of the female womb, with the goal of dispelling the stigma surrounding women's health by highlighting the vast experiences of women's bodies throughout their lifetimes. Essity let the message go where it wanted, regardless of the risk or distaste that may result.

Triple top-line score: 3/3

- ✓ **Social impact**
- ✓ **Reputation impact**
- ✓ **Commercial impact**

As Tanja Grubner, FemCare Global Marketing and Communications Director at Essity, explained, "With #wombstories we are starting a movement. We want to boldly go where no other brand has been before; inside women's bodies and emotions to truly represent their sensations and feelings that we believe are not only invisible but ignored, overlooked or denied. #wombstories reveals a woman's narrative inside and out and we hope to put these topics on the table for all to talk about. We believe that only once we understand women and everything they go through, can we care for them with our period and daily intimate care products."[9] #wombstories challenge traditional narratives about women's bodies with compelling stories around the pain and challenges associated with menstruation, the extreme pain of endometriosis, the emotional impact of experiencing miscarriages and infertility, the miracle of birth, the demystification of menopause, and the validation of personal child-birthing decisions.

Through its groundbreaking social impact, #wombstories empowered women to share their experiences and struggles within a safe space while calling attention to the women's health issues that are often left out of general health discussions around policy. It also boldly breaks down the societal norms that make women and girls feel shame around the natural processes of their bodies. Corporate Knights recognized the power of the #wombstories campaign, including Essity in its Global 100 list, which represents the top 1 percent of companies worldwide in terms of sustainability performance based on 25 quantitative key performance indicators, including sustainable revenue and racial and gender diversity.[10] Magnus Groth, President and CEO of Essity, called the recognition a demonstration of the company's dedication to responsible business practices. Essity also received the "Platinum Medal" in the 2023 Ecovadis CSR Rating and was included in S&P's Global Sustainability Yearbook in 2022.[11] In 2023, the company experienced its most profitable year ever, with a net sales increase of 12.1 percent compared to the previous year.[12] Essity's earnings per share from continuing operations also increased while its operating cash flow experienced a 130 percent uptick.

Essity identified the impact opportunities of its industry by recognizing the societal debts that had been maintained in part by the traditional marketing campaigns of female products. The company then found the functional benefits and emotional promises that it could provide women by enhancing conversations and telling authentic stories around women's health, stories that had been largely avoided in public settings. This strategy has helped Essity build a lasting reputation as a proponent of women's health, and has also resulted in significant commercial impact.

The Pitfalls of Misaligned Narratives

Brands descend into the peril of misaligned narratives when they fail to establish clear objectives that encompass the priorities of those represented. The potential dangers are vividly illustrated in the realm of reality television where subjects often find their stories manipulated, edited, and repackaged to serve a narrative arc that prioritizes drama and scandal over truth. This manipulation, while perhaps beneficial for short-term viewership gains, can lead to a profound sense of betrayal and frustration among subjects. It underscores the risk of narratives that deviate from the source's understanding and the ethical imperative of aligning story objectives with those being represented.

For responsible marketing stories to maintain their integrity, the reasons for their telling must be transparent and straightforward to ensure that all parties involved—especially the subjects—have a clear understanding of the narrative's purpose and the message it intends to convey. When subjects are fully informed and their insights are integrated into the storytelling process, the resulting narrative is not only more authentic but also more impactful.

Consider a marketing campaign focused on highlighting the resilience of small business owners in a particular community during challenging times. For this story to be responsibly told, the objectives—perhaps to inspire, inform, and drive support for these businesses—must be clearly communicated to these owners, along with an identification of the target audience. With the owner's understanding and agreement on these objectives, the campaign narrative will remain true and free from sensationalism or misrepresentation. The level of clarity refines the story's purpose and the manner in which it is told so that it resonates in a way that fosters a connection that is both meaningful and relevant. A fully aligned narrative not only honors the subjects' stories but also enhances the audience's trust in the brand's commitment to genuine, respectful storytelling.

In 2014, the president of a popular online dating site used the company blog to tell a story about his manipulation of data provided by site users to conduct his own sociological experiment around dating habits and race. He analyzed raw data about users and turned those numbers into a narrative that Black women and Asian men are the least desirable demographics on dating sites. While the data may have supported the outcome, there was much critique around his clumsy method of storytelling. The narrative was shared widely and loudly without any support or corrective measures, and critics argued that the site was not only highlighting existing prejudices but essentially reinforcing them. The backlash against the platform's insensitivity was intense, underlying the responsibility that accompanies the art of storytelling and the mindfulness that brands should exercise when presenting narratives that touch on deeply personal and societal issues.

In the journey towards more responsible marketing, the onus is on brands to cultivate an environment where stories are not just told but shared—with objectives that are clear, transparent, and understood by all involved. When done right, responsible marketing stories have the power to do more than just sell products or services—they have the capacity to enlighten, to connect and to drive positive change. In essence, the art of telling real stories provides a profound opportunity for brands, a chance to engage with audiences on a deeper level and tell stories that matter with integrity. By sharing the storytelling process with the subjects of these stories, brands can set a new standard for how marketing stories are told, and why they matter.

REAL TALK WITH RESPONSIBLE MARKETERS
Jose "Pepe" Gorbea

Global Head of Brands, Agencies and Sustainability Innovation at HP, Impact Council Member, D&AD, Professor of Marketing for Social Impact at ESADE Business School, and keynote speaker, Pepe is an impassioned marketing leader and speaker with a proven track record of revitalizing brands strategically by inspiring teams to deliver breakthrough, consumer-centric campaigns and sustainable innovations for over 23 years at Kraft Foods, Nestlé, Mondelēz, Grupo Bimbo, and HP Graphic Arts across global, regional, and local roles.

Improving on the Education of Future Marketers

I got an invitation to become a marketing teacher at a university in Barcelona. I met the Dean of the university and he showed me some numbers, and they are the number nine marketing school in the world. Wow. Number nine. Because I thought the top 10 were mostly US-based universities. But this one is among them.

He told me that what I'm doing on co-creation for good was an element that was missing in their program. He invited me to help them, along with another 20 people who they invited to reinvent the marketing program of the future. So we went really deep with an agency that did marvelous work on organizing content in arcs, which I've never done before, which was a learning experience. You have a big thought and a big purpose, which is a straight line on a graph. But then there's an overarching theme to your story. Let's call this story the marketing program of this university.

And underneath that story are sub-stories that connect. The way you organized content based on that thinking gives you a lot of clarity in terms of the flow of the story, and the priority and the right sequence of the story. It was really cool to do that. Through that process, I wrote my own arc on what marketing should be doing, and I gave it to the Dean. I had a call with him and said, "This is what I think you should be doing."

What Do You Want Your Legacy to Be?

It started a whole snowball effect, a positive effect on my career and what I want to do with my life in the next few years. I want to activate purpose. HP gave me a platform to start that journey six to seven years ago. But now I think I have a much bigger one for myself, that I can clearly touch marketers earlier in their career, while they're still at university. So when they get into corporate or doing their own startup, their brains are already wired. You touch them when they're at the beginning of that journey. It's like the *Inception* movie with Leonardo DiCaprio. It's like I'm introducing co-creation for good into their brains, so whenever they go out there in the world, they have a better toolkit to tell stories.

My first teaching experience was so rewarding. I was super nervous. I had never talked to so many people. Once I started going, though, it became very natural and the conversation even became more fluid than with senior teachers. They wanted to ask me, Why are you doing this? Why do you believe in this? What's the purpose? Not the purpose of the brand or the marketing campaign, but more my purpose behind enabling it. I told them that for me, the biggest purpose, in a way, is to leave a legacy that I created a better way to do marketing. If I can achieve that, I'll die a happy man.

As an entry point, what I was telling the classes was, "You need to think: what is your personal purpose, as a marketer? Where do you want to be 20 or 30 years down the road? How do you want to be seen and remembered? What's your contribution to society and the planet?"

Marketing Takes Courage

I think responsible marketing is about common sense, using common sense to do the right thing. Also, at the same time, having the *courage* to do the right thing. It's a lot about creative courage.

Marketing can take courage, especially in the U.S. after what we saw happen to Bud Light, and then Hershey in Canada. My point is that it takes creative courage. I think it's a superpower. You have to have the balls to do it, to say the right thing in the right moment. The chameleon in the logo of my company is adapting to context in the moment, but also having the balls to do it. I think the message that they have sent out to the world after the Bud Light disaster, to any other marketers, regardless of where they are on the planet, is, "Don't take chances. Don't take risks. Because you're going to be punished. You're going to lose your career. You're going to be outside on the street." I think people are just going to be playing it safe. I think that's what is going to start happening, that many businesses that have great stories to tell are going to say, "You know what, I'm not going to take a chance." It's scary.

I hope that by educating marketers at universities, I keep the spirit alive. I can also give them guardrails on how to do it well, and avoid disasters, because disasters will continue to happen. I think the thing with Anheuser is that the company didn't have their back and didn't hold hands with the marketing team. I think you need to work with a team that is conscious of the fact that sometimes things might go wrong.

Taking Action to Help Emigrants from a War Zone

One of the highlights of my career will always be the CMO Accelerator, where I just wanted to activate purpose. When I was looking at what was happening in Ukraine, my first question was, how do I take action? In the position at HP, how do I start taking action against this war with my grain of salt, which is not about sending these people food, or clothing. We tend to think that giving a donation is going to fix the problem, but I don't think it's going to fix the problem. So if you look at the drama of the Ukrainian problem, it's about all the people that have fled the country. What do they need?

More than food or clothing, they need an opportunity for a job. That's the best gift that you can give. My thinking then became, *how do I connect CMO leaders from the Cannes Lions to meet all of these Ukrainian creative talents?* That whole thing has become a little bit of my thesis on how to do co-creation for good. Even from a B2B point of view, which is not the classic campaign with the big brands, it's just people working B2B or age-to-age, or human-to-human, you need to take action and to build a platform that invites you to make a decision. If you want to take action, you get all the framework in place to do that. That has become my model and my M.O., in a way, in terms of building this out.

Making Stories by Starting with the Community

Story-making is about listening to your community. It's about *deeply* listening to your community, understanding across the value chain of marketing where the problems are, as you're trying to deliver a product or a service, how the product gets sourced, created, produced, distributed, consumed. The concept I'm talking about is called "integrative marketing." Marketing is about teaching the marketers of the future how to think across the value chain to build stories.

So what does story-making for good mean? First of all, remember the old benefit ladder of attributes all the way up to emotional benefit? The problem with that way of thinking in marketing is that it only focuses on the person that is in the act of consumption. It doesn't focus on the person in the act of problem solving in communities. When you look at value chain marketing transversally, you start looking at your end-to-end value chain as a product or a service, and then you can make the decision as to "Can I make a positive impact in the community to bring that to life?"

One of the case studies that I presented last year was Nescafé. They told the stories of the coffee farmers for Nescafé, all 20,000 of them individually. It was looking exactly at the value chain, an awareness that the value chain has a really powerful story to tell, and it was not "buy more coffee" at the point of buying. It was about the community, and the impact, and how Nescafé gives them financial prosperity, education, jobs, and many, many other things. This is the thesis behind story-making: you invite the community to be the story-makers. The story-makers in the Nescafé example are the farmers.

Let Go and Let the Consumer Drive

I always say, the brand has to build the road for the consumer to drive the car on. The problem with marketers today is that they want to build the road *and* drive the car at the same time, while the consumer just sits on the sideline. It has to evolve so that we give the consumer the keys to the car. We build the road, but they drive. Letting go of control is one of the hardest things to teach marketers how to do.

The Power of Responsible Investment

Telling Real Stories Takes Long-Term Thinking

Like anything else, responsible marketing storytelling follows the adage of getting what you pay for. Successful companies invest in a variety of tangibles, from improvements to products and services to more efficient operating equipment. Business leaders prefer these investments because the return is typically observed relatively quickly, but this type of narrow foresight undermines the value of responsible brand investment. For storytelling to be genuinely responsible, brands must be willing to invest in their sources. This investment goes beyond mere financial remuneration, encompassing a commitment to ensuring that the sources—the people and communities whose stories are being told—are the primary beneficiaries of the narrative in multiple ways.

The ethical framework of responsible storytelling posits that the sources of these narratives should not merely serve as fodder for brand campaigns but should be active participants and beneficiaries of the storytelling process. This principle challenges the traditional marketing paradigm, which often sees brands leveraging stories for their gain, sometimes at the expense of the sources. In contrast, responsible storytelling advocates for a model where the welfare, dignity and enrichment of the source are paramount.

Investing in sources means recognizing their intrinsic value and compensating them accordingly. Financial remuneration is a critical aspect of this investment, because it is important to acknowledge the value of their time, insights, and contributions of those whose stories are being shared. Brands can get into legal and reputational trouble when they use the relatability of their sources without adequate recompense. We see this far too often as brands champion the unauthorized use of sources' social media content for their storytelling purposes. That story or reel stood apart because it was compelling and impactful. As marketers, we receive bonuses, recognition, and awards for our efforts in creating exceptional campaigns. Why would we not compensate these content creators for their attention-grabbing stories?

For storytelling to be authentically responsible, the source, or the group they represent, must be the intended beneficiary in all respects. This paradigm shift requires brands to engage with sources as partners rather than mere subjects, involving them in the storytelling process from inception to execution. Such collaboration ensures that narratives are not only authentic and respectful but also that they serve the interests and needs of the sources themselves.

This beneficiary-focused approach also mandates that brands invest in initiatives that provide tangible benefits to sources and their communities long after a campaign has run its course. This holistic approach ensures that storytelling does more than exploit; it enriches, empowers and elevates the source. Whether through direct financial support, development programs, or platforms that amplify their voices and stories, the goal is to ensure that the storytelling process contributes positively to the source's well-being and prosperity.

RESPONSIBLE MARKETING WIN
Heetch Rideshare's Investment in Amplifying a Community's Voice

In 2023, Parisian ridesharing app Heetch used visual storytelling to push back against the bias and negative stereotypes produced by a generative AI tool.[13] The brand's investment of time and resources centered the intended beneficiary in a way that elevated an entire community through genuine stories that will continually shape its representation to the world.

Triple top-line score: 3/3

✓ **Social impact**

✓ **Reputation impact**

✓ **Commercial impact**

Heetch is a ridesharing agency largely operating within the suburbs of Paris, an area also referred to as "La Banlieue." When the company's leadership discovered biases in AI-generated images of the community, they used real stories to take a stand and craft a data source of more honest representation. Heetch alleged that when the descriptor "banlieue" was included in a prompt for 'French weddings', the AI technology generated images of two unhappy people on a dirty street with rundown buildings on either side. Yet, when the word "banlieue" was left out of the prompt, the system generated images of happy couples in attractive, well-kept French settings.

To provide a more balanced and representative data set of the Paris suburbs, Heetch invested in the creation of thousands of postcards, each with its own photograph of the community and its residents, along with the headline, "Greetings From La Banlieue." The company distributed the cards to stores, laundromats, sporting venues, restaurants, and barbershops throughout the neighborhoods, as well as placing them in all their rideshare vehicles. Each card was pre-addressed to the AI company's headquarters and included a QR code link to a banlieue image database with the hope that the AI company would receive the influx of postcards and make changes to its technology.

In the company's announcement of the initiative, Heetch CMO Renaud Berthe spoke about the dangers of propagated stereotypes and how they led to the biases depicted in the AI-generated representations of La Banlieue. He said the company's large presence within the community and relationships with community members necessitated a call to action. Heetch let real images of the community tell the story and champion diversity while also fighting against the false narratives being spread by the AI-generated images. This very public stance also provides a lesson in the reputation impact of the Triple Top-Line Flywheel. In making its social impact, Heetch included its stakeholders. They had them take pictures of the community. They empowered them to send the postcards to the AI company. They gave them a collective voice in telling their story.

Ensuring Everybody Wins

Investing in sources is not solely a moral obligation; it presents a strategic economic advantage for brands. The discerning consumer supports brands that align with their values and demonstrate a commitment to ethical practices. Brands can showcase that commitment by telling stories with integrity and creating genuine partnerships that foster trust, loyalty, and engagement. Responsible investment in sources can be the catalyst for a brand's impact on positive social change, aligning brand narratives with broader movements for equity, sustainability, and justice. This is the path for brands to position themselves as leaders in the corporate responsibility arena and benefit economically by attracting partners, collaborators, and talents who share these commitments.

Consider a brand that partners with artisans from marginalized communities to bring their stories and crafts to a global audience. By investing in these artisans—not just through fair compensation but by providing resources for skill development, business acumen, and market access—the brand ensures that the storytelling process directly contributes to the artisans' economic empowerment and cultural preservation. The resulting narrative is one of mutual growth and respect, illustrating the profound impact of responsible investment. Similarly, a campaign focused on environmental conservation may leverage stories from indigenous communities deeply connected to the land. By allocating resources to support these communities' conservation efforts and legal battles, the brand does more than tell a story; it becomes an active participant in the cause, with the sources as the primary beneficiaries.

For brands committed to responsible storytelling, the willingness to invest in their sources is non-negotiable, though it may require a shift in perspective. Sources are much more than a means to an end. They must be respected as partners deserving of respect, compensation, and empowerment. By embracing this approach, brands can transcend traditional marketing tactics, delivering stories that are not only compelling but also ethically sound and socially beneficial. Responsible investment leaves exploitation out of the corporate equation to foster a marketing ecosystem where authenticity, respect, and mutual benefit are consistently at the forefront. As brands navigate the complexities of modern storytelling, those who choose to invest responsibly in their sources will undoubtedly lead the way and establish new standards for what it means to tell stories in an interconnected, conscious world.

REAL TALK WITH RESPONSIBLE MARKETERS
Lisa Hurley

Founder at The Great Exhale, award-winning activist, entrepreneur, writer, Top 10 LinkedIn Creator in Inclusion and Diversity, Judge at The Anthem Awards, Member at Forbes BLK, and Cofounder of The Introvert Sisters podcast, Lisa's work centers on Black women, and encompasses self-care, community care, and Black joy.

Responsibility is the Foundation

I think responsible marketing is about doing good, and not in a performative sense. I write about the performative versus the real, the actual, the concrete. It's about doing good, and not necessarily for brownie points, just doing good because it is the right thing to do. The bottom line result follows as a consequence. The brand or the company also has to be OK with the bottom line results not being a fast follow.

If you're doing XYZ campaign and expect results within a quarter, are you doing it for the right reasons? Because that thinking is 100 percent profit-driven as opposed to being cause-driven. If it is genuinely cause-driven, you have to give the cause a chance to blossom and expand and grow, prove its worth, and do its work.

Responsible marketing might not always be the cool, "jazz hands" side of things. It is the deep, foundational part of a building that you don't see. It is actually holding everything up and nothing else can really authentically exist without that foundation, without the responsibility at its base. Belonging there means playing the long game.

Creating Content Responsibly

When I started this journey as a "content creator," I hadn't thought of myself in that sense at the time. I felt a sense of responsibility. I hold the weight of being Black. Being a woman. Let's add being a woman with natural hair. Being a medium Brown woman. A woman of a certain age with my accent. I try to bring as many of those layers as possible to the fore. All of that informs everything that I write.

I also feel the responsibility of representing Barbados, which I don't mean in an egotistical way. As Black people, everything we do affects the community. If you do something untoward, it is viewed as damaging to the entire community. As somebody from a tiny island, I'm aware that anything I do, people will assume all Barbadians do, for better or for worse, and so I try to make sure that it's for better.

Being your Unapologetic Self

In today's world, we are constantly ingesting, processing, observing, and then finding creative ways to express all of it. For me, as a copywriter, whether it is in a subject line, in an email, or in an entire broader campaign, all of that comes through everything that I am exposed to. The intersectionalities of life inform everything and you can't help but for that to happen.

When I first started writing content seriously on LinkedIn, I made a conscious decision. It was 2020, and there was so much going on. I felt called to start talking about it. I decided I was going to show up as my most unapologetic self. No masking. No self-censoring. I was just going to show up as me and people were going to have to receive it. Period. I wasn't making any compromises on it.

I write about everything. It might be a Rihanna song or the meme of the day that tickled me, but I absolutely fearlessly dive into deeper topics as well. It goes back to the responsibility part of it.

I started from a very pure place, and If you have purity of intention at the foundation, I think that makes a big difference, because it is going to affect how you show up.

The Ethical Imperative? Tell the Whole Truth and Nothing But the Truth

To understand the depth required in responsible marketing stories, one need only look at the old-school process of investigative journalism. Not to be confused with the current phenomenon of social media journalism, true investigative journalism has earned a reputation for its unwavering dedication to uncovering the truth. It requires journalists to dig deep, corroborate their findings, and present a narrative grounded in facts and comprehensive analysis. Investigative journalism does not seek to unethically persuade with half-truths or one-sided stories. It aims to reveal all sides and enlighten the audience with meticulously researched and verified information.

This same dedication to accuracy and comprehensiveness is what sets responsible marketing stories apart. Like investigative journalists, marketers aiming to tell these stories must allocate ample time and resources to the process of storytelling, ensuring that every claim is substantiated, every source is vetted, and every narrative is as complete as possible. An ethical imperative exists for marketers to cause no harm to the subjects and themes they explore. This requires a rigorous process of discovery and engagement with the subjects of marketing campaigns. There needs to be an understanding of their contexts, challenges, and perspectives. To do this, marketers must listen more than they speak, give some control over the narrative, and approach their subjects with humility and a genuine desire to learn. This comprehensive approach ensures that the storytelling is accurate and resonates on a deeper level with audiences.

Brands can't fail to allocate the adequate time and resources necessary to tell authentic stories and then expect to reach their audiences in a truly relatable way because these investments are crucial for the creation of responsible marketing stories. Just as investigative journalists devote weeks, months, or even years into uncovering a story, marketers must be willing to demonstrate an elevated level of dedication to crafting narratives. That may look like funding extensive research, engaging with multiple sources, and revisiting the narrative several times to ensure its integrity. Nobody said it would be easy, but brands invest in meticulous processes all the time when it comes to internal processes and product development. The willingness to do the same in the furtherance of responsible marketing signals a commitment to values beyond profit. It demonstrates a willingness to contribute positively, prioritizing the impact of storytelling on people and communities over mere commercial gains.

For a brand story to champion responsible marketing, every aspect of the narrative, from the language used to the visuals presented, must be carefully considered and chosen to accurately represent the source and the community they represent. This attention to detail ensures that the stories are not only engaging but also respectful and true to the experiences of those they depict. In practice, this means going beyond surface-level engagement to explore the nuances and complexities of the sources represented. It requires a commitment to understanding the broader context in which these stories exist, including the socio-political and economic factors that influence them.

In short, that means no shortcuts. No skirting around the hard work or opting for convenience and speed over the value of thorough research. That is the type of half-stepping that creates inaccurate narratives, not only misrepresentative of the subjects but also potentially harmful. The allure of shortcuts is a siren song that beckons brands away from authenticity and integrity. We exist in a culture where speed is prioritized over thoroughness. But responsible marketing stories, much like the tried-and-true tenets of investigative journalism, demand a commitment to precision and depth, and a steadfast avoidance of shortcuts. Relying on stereotypes, failing to engage with represented communities, and using sensationalism undermines the credibility of the brand.

Responsible marketing stories have the power to effect real change by challenging perceptions and inspiring action. They contribute to a more informed and empathetic society while enhancing the brand's reputation, building trust and loyalty. In the pursuit of responsible marketing stories, the avoidance of shortcuts is not just a matter of ethical importance but a strategic imperative and the analogy of investigative journalism serves as a powerful reminder of the impact that meticulous and comprehensive story-telling can have. By dedicating the necessary time, resources, and attention to detail, brands can transcend the transactional nature of traditional marketing by crafting narratives that truly resonate, inform, and inspire. This commitment to responsible storytelling is a testament to a brand's values, demonstrating a profound understanding of the role businesses can play in shaping a more equitable and truthful world.

RESPONSIBLE RECAP

- The most compelling stories come directly from the source.

- For stories to be truly authentic, brands must be willing to relinquish control and allow the stories to unfold naturally, guided by those who have lived them.

- Clear, shared objectives between the brand and the sources of stories are essential for ensuring narratives are aligned and beneficial for all involved.

- Responsible storytelling requires a commitment to thoroughness and accuracy. Shortcuts can lead to misrepresented or incomplete narratives, undermining the integrity of the marketing effort.

- Brands should not only compensate their sources but also invest in their well-being and communities.

- Like investigative journalism, responsible marketing stories should be underpinned by meticulous research and a deep understanding of the subject matter.

- Authentic stories must be effectively shared and consumed. A real story can't realize its intended impact if it isn't seen.

Notes

1 C. Gomez. Carlos Andres Gomez: Videos and Poems, Tumblr, 2024. carlosandresgomez.tumblr.com/poems (archived at https://perma.cc/4JE3-PLRC)

2 DeBeers Group. About us: A diamond is forever, DeBeers Group, 2024. www.debeersgroup.com/about-us/a-diamond-is-forever (archived at https://perma.cc/LC5Q-F7CR)

3 J. Suess. Our history: P&G put the "soap" in "soap opera," Cincinnati, October 4, 2017. www.cincinnati.com/story/news/2017/10/04/our-history-p-g-put-soap-soap-opera/732149001/ (archived at https://perma.cc/AU8B-WN84)

4 D. Choi. The first television commercial ever aired 75 years ago today, Business Insider, January 1, 2016. www.businessinsider.com/first-television-commercial-ever-2016-6 (archived at https://perma.cc/3LX5-AHWX)

5 Business Insider India. 25 Nike ads that shaped the brand's history, Business Insider, July 26, 2021. www.businessinsider.in/advertising/madison-avenue/25-nike-ads-that-shaped-the-brands-history/slidelist/22213093.cms (archived at https://perma.cc/YP3W-B42T)

6 N. Maheshwari. The power of "Just Do It": A comprehensive analysis of Nike's Iconic marketing campaign, Medium, February 20, 2023. www.medium.com/@nehalmaheshwarie/the-power-of-just-do-it-a-comprehensive-analysis-of-nike-s-iconic-marketing-campaign-8e4adf4a4d0d (archived at https://perma.cc/EX43-RGWN)

7 S. Snow and J. Lazauskas (2018) *The Storytelling Edge: How to transform your business, stop screaming into the void, and make people love you*, Wiley, Hoboken

8 L. Rodrigues. The sparks & honey Responsible Marketing Index [proprietary research], 2023

9 Glamour (2020) Bodyform chronicles 'womb stories' in all their emotional complexities, Campaign Live, 2020. https://www.campaignlive.co.uk/article/bodyform-chronicles-womb-stories-emotional-complexities/1688134 (archived at https://perma.cc/A9ZP-THAC)

10 Essity. Essity ranked one of the world's most sustainable companies, Essity, January 18, 2023. www.essity.com/media/press-release/essity-ranked-one-of-the-world-s-most-sustainable-companies/7cb1f2813f57846c/ (archived at https://perma.cc/LAR5-47S8)

11 Essity USA. Essity has been awarded a Platinum Ecovadis Medal, Essity, 2024. www.essityusa.com/media/global-news-features/platinumecovadismedal/ (archived at https://perma.cc/T5GX-A8PJ); Essity. Essity included in Sustainability Yearbook 2022, Essity, February 2, 2022. www.essity.com/media/press-release/essity-included-in-sustainability-yearbook-2022/fdd281e58d4c47f2/ (archived at https://perma.cc/DXH9-44JM)

12 Essity. Year-end report 2023, Essity, January 25, 2024. www.essity.com/media/press-release/year-end-report-2023/9260e7e008099708/ (archived at https://perma.cc/4JHV-ZZ5D)

13 P. O'Connell. Ride-hailing app Heetch celebrates the Paris suburbs in campaign highlighting bias in generative AI, Contagious, November 21, 2023. www.contagious.com/news-and-views/ride-hailing-app-heetch-celebrates-the-paris-suburbs-in-campaign-highlighting-bias-in-generative-ai (archived at https://perma.cc/6DK6-HDC2)

07

Creating Real Opportunities

I was raised with one foot planted in the ideals of Western individualism and the other firmly rooted in West African collectivism. The latter is grounded in a steadfast belief that paying it forward always pays off in the long run. This belief is so deeply rooted that Yoruba people consider it taboo to even think about the "return on investment" of caring for others. Ever so nuanced and not at all transactional in nature, the value exchange we believe in can only be described as spiritual. It's a cultural norm to expansively invest in the success of those in our family and community who need it without at all considering what we might get in return beyond the joy of being useful. Similarly, creating real opportunities for the intended beneficiaries of responsible marketing initiatives is an investment that offers brands far more value than is possible to directly quantify.

Applying Triple Top-Line Flywheel Thinking

Responsible Marketers Create Opportunity Every Day

When seeking to create opportunities, brands have countless options for showcasing their commitments, including educational and employment opportunities or collaborations with social impact agencies. Training and skill-building programs tailored to underrepresented communities can include internships, apprenticeships, mentorship programs, or job-training workshops. By investing in the professional development of diverse talent, brands not only contribute to greater diversity within their own workforce but also empower individuals from marginalized backgrounds to access opportunities for economic advancement and upward mobility. Brands can also network to collaborate with social impact agencies and non-profit organizations to support initiatives like workforce development programs, scholarship funds, and community outreach efforts aimed at addressing systemic barriers to opportunity and promoting social equity. These initiatives not only benefit individuals from underrepresented backgrounds but also strengthen the brand's reputation, foster goodwill among consumers and stakeholders, and ultimately drive long-term business success.

LinkedIn's Plus One Pledge provides a platform for business professionals to mentor individuals from underrepresented groups and assist them with career opportunities. LinkedIn is leveraging its foundational objectives to facilitate valuable business connections that might not otherwise occur, helping to break down barriers to employment and professional advancement. This is the type of commitment that resonates with consumers and earns their trust.

When brands collaborate with organizations, communities, and stakeholders to identify opportunities for amplified impact, they can develop comprehensive and effective marketing campaigns that address social issues from a broader perspective. These are the types of partnerships that enhance cultural literacy and create a broader social impact that represents a more diverse range of voices and experiences. Diverse perspectives are included in the decision-making process, further enhanced with open lines of communication for feedback. When team members feel empowered to voice their opinions and perspectives related to social impact, the resulting opportunity offerings can champion both inclusivity and a more expansive impact.

Optimizing For Brand Relevancy

McNees Wallace & Nurick LLC is a full-service legal practice that represents corporations, small businesses, and individuals. In 2020, the firm launched the Legal Equity Advancement Program (LEAP) with the goal of helping Black-controlled businesses in southcentral Pennsylvania overcome systemic barriers to entry. Chosen businesses receive a year's worth of free legal services to handle issues around business organization, taxes, employment, intellectual property, MBE certification, and contract review. LEAP also offers seminars and opportunities for businesses within the program to network. In 2023, recognizing the successful impact of the program, McNees expanded it to include additional regions of Pennsylvania, Ohio, and Maryland.[1] "We are thrilled to again offer this service to our community, and even more excited that we are expanding LEAP so significantly," said Adeolu Bakare, LEAP co-chair at McNees.

"Black-owned and Black-controlled businesses too often face high hurdles to getting started and staying operational over time. Our goal is to help break down these barriers and provide tools for sustainable growth and long-term success." In establishing this much needed service, McNees analyzed a real need facing Black businesses and looked within to evaluate how their existing services could meet that need, meet the moment, and cultivate early relationships with businesses that could grow to become top clients—with the likelihood of that being much more so because of the high-end legal guidance they received early on that set them up for outsized success. Everybody wins!

This type of opportunity evaluation and creation requires a comprehensive understanding of the needs and challenges faced by all stakeholders and then assessing the feasibility of options that meet the moment. The chosen strategies are not to be rushed into without a thorough understanding of their alignment with the brand's core values and capabilities. It's a systematic approach that incorporates research, goal setting, and strategy development before moving into the implementation phase.

In 2022, digital food and travel network Tastemade and Blavity, a Black-focused digital media company, evaluated an opportunity to create Sauce, a food vertical aimed at young Black foodies.[2] With tailored content ranging from recipes to food sustainability, Sauce celebrates all things related to Black dining and celebration. As of 2024, the collaboration had evolved into a long-form series and co-developed sponsored content for brands. They also introduced Churned in Culture, a first-to-market collaboration with Ben & Jerry's.

In creating this opportunity, these two brands evaluated their individual cultures and goals to find an intersection that would uplift the experiences of their collective stakeholders. The collaboration provided Blavity with access to Tastemade's significantly larger audience, along with an opportunity to evolve its content into a food focus that drives greater views and engagement.[3] For Tastemade, the partnership provided the credibility and authenticity the brand needed to expand into the space of telling Black stories.

Regenerative Impact is Authentic Impact

Authenticity must lie at the core of any effective social impact initiative. Brands that create real opportunities alleviate the burden of trying to appear authentic because when responsible marketing creates real opportunity, the work's authenticity speaks for itself. Creating opportunity demonstrates a willingness to move beyond the ease of writing a check or making performative gestures. It shows consumers that the brand stands behind its words, going beyond the easiest options to open the doors for long-term impact. When companies set out to create real opportunities, authentic social impact naturally follows. The two become intertwined when companies genuinely commit to making a positive difference.

Social impact cannot be treated as an add-on, separate from the fabric of a brand's internal operations and marketing strategies. By identifying the social impact opportunities, companies can create opportunities that naturally align with their specific industry. Yelp did a masterful job of intertwining social impact with opportunity creation when the company introduced its Black-Owned Business attribute in 2020. In partnership with My Black Receipt, a movement galvanizing consumers to spend $5 million at Black-owned businesses between Juneteenth and Independence Day, Yelp created a free searchable Black-owned business resource.[4] Kezia M. Williams, Lead Organizer for My Black Receipt and CEO of the Black upStart, said the digital initiative is the first of its kind, initiating a challenge for consumers to buy from Black-owned businesses and publicly share their purchases on a platform. She explained that collective impact drives the recirculation of dollars into Black businesses and communities.[5]

As of January 2022, over 45,000 businesses had self-identified as Black-owned by voluntarily adding the attribute to their Yelp business pages.[6] In February of 2022, Yelp took the initiative a step further by highlighting their Ones to Watch in Black businesses, further aligning their purpose with the societal need of empowering small businesses that are essential to the health of the economy.[7]

Chime online banking provides financial opportunities through its Chime Spotlight: Chime in for Changemakers initiative.[8] Started in 2020 to help small communities impacted by the pandemic, the program identifies leaders and organizations that are using education and access to enhance the economic health of their communities. Chime then partners with them to overcome barriers to growth through the provision of mentorship, funding, and marketing guidance. With a focus on entrepreneurship and education, the company is forging a pathway to financial empowerment that is often allusive to historically-excluded communities. The company measures the program's success by evaluating the goals achieved by the individual recipients. Recognizing that each Changemaker has a specific challenge, Chime tailors its opportunities to the acceleration of their individual goals.

Another fintech company that's showing up for small businesses is Cash App. According to a Pew Research study, 59 percent of Black Americans report using Cash App, compared to 37 percent of Hispanic Americans and a much smaller percentage of white and Asian Americans.[9]

REAL TALK WITH RESPONSIBLE MARKETERS
Ryan Pearson

Founder at Design Staff Digital, and formerly Brand Marketing Lead at Cash App, Ryan is focused on the intersection of technology, culture, and entertainment.

How Cash App Found its Audience

It's important when we think about the audience and the community that Cash App serves to start with Cash App's mission. The mission at Cash App is to redefine the world's relationship with money. They want to do that by making money more relatable, more instantly available, and more universally accessible.

Traditional banking has always catered to individuals with high net worth. Oftentimes, those communities aren't Black and Brown folks. I think when Cash App was created, the thought was about this large community of folks who people in the traditional banking sector weren't paying any attention to. These people have specific needs that weren't being met by these other sorts of entities.

The impact that Cash App has been able to have on Black and Brown communities actually starts with the product. Sign-up is very easy to do. It's not a long and arduous process. You can do it basically within minutes, which is very different than if you were to try to sign up for a Bank of America account, for example. The ability to send money back and forth to anyone in your life in a matter of seconds was also amazing. Remember, Cash App came before Zelle and just a little bit after Venmo. Another very appealing aspect of the platform is direct deposit. Being able to get the money from your paycheck a few days ahead of your normal payday can make a big difference.

By really understanding the audience and designing the product around the needs of the audience, it naturally became something that people who were traditionally not being catered to gravitated towards. That happened to be the Black and Brown communities.

Reaching Your Audience Through Cultural Partnerships

When it comes to marketing Cash App, I think they do a really, really great job of meeting customers where they are. Where we began to see a lot of user interest, activity, and growth was from people in the American Southeast and the Midwest amongst mostly Black and Brown communities. A lot of times folks were younger, skewing Gen Z to younger Millennial, and generally making less than $50,000 a year.

So these pockets of the country where traditional banks maybe weren't so focused became the real focus of Cash App from a marketing perspective. A lot of our early initiatives were focused on social media activities. We began to partner with folks within culture, from musicians to influencers to artists and actors. We tried to dip into culture and connect money and culture in ways that no other brand or product or service had done before.

Doing Good the Way Only Your Brand Can

Partnerships are so important when you're trying to be a brand that's trying not only to be involved in culture, but also trying to do good for the world. If you take a look at Cash App's marketing work over the last few years, you'll see repeated characters and it's a testament to the great work that our partnerships team was able to do. Some of our favorite cultural figures that we work with are Serena Williams and Megan Thee Stallion.

We did some work with Megan Thee Stallion a few years ago centered around financial education. What we tried to do is figure out a way to make financial education fun and relatable and relevant for our audience. Usually, financial education would be taught by an expert, someone that an audience might not have a deep connection to, and it would be boring and a bit stale.

We always try to think about what we can do in a way that only Cash App could do. What's our take on financial education? Why don't we work with a celebrity and basically make that person the "expert" to teach their fan base about financial literacy? Based on that teaching, the fan base will also be able to reach the masses because the content that we create is so entertaining, so fun and so different.

So, with Meghan Thee Stallion, we created a series focused on teaching people about all aspects of money, from saving to investing to spending, etc. The focal point was teaching the audience all these things that maybe they didn't know but should. It was in such an innovative space, that it wasn't just about her giving definitions and talking to the audience. It was more so her educating the audience and speaking with them in a way that was very palatable.

We saw a bunch of really great results from that work, using the power of culture and celebrity to reach audiences in new ways.

Creating real opportunity can be a long game where actions may look like cheerleading at first blush, but if brands stay consistent with their goals, they can evolve into champions or even catalysts of change. For instance, some of America's top universities offer free AI certifications as part of their commitment to expanding access to education, while also addressing the growing demand for AI skills in the workforce. While these efforts may look superficial on the surface, the long game provides students with knowledge and skills in artificial intelligence, regardless of financial ability to attend college.

As AI technologies continually expand, so does the need for skilled professionals. The wider audiences, diverse backgrounds, and varied geographical locations that result from university online learning platforms, translate into more opportunities for historically-underserved communities. With these free AI certification offerings, universities promote lifelong learning, the development of valuable workplace skills, and a social impact with regenerative outcomes.

RESPONSIBLE TERMINOLOGY

Collectivism champions unity, mutual support, and shared responsibilities. It prioritizes the interests and values of the group—be it family, community, nation, or otherwise—over personal ambitions. This concept stands in contrast to individualism, which celebrates personal autonomy and individual rights. Collectivism advocates for aligning with group norms and working towards shared goals, underscoring the significance of social harmony and collective loyalty. It's about embracing "we" over "I," fostering a sense of solidarity and collective achievement.

Regenerative impact is all about doing good that keeps on giving. It's not just about avoiding harm or being less bad; it's about actively making things better. Think of it as the difference between simply recycling and transforming a vacant lot into a thriving community garden. It's about initiatives that heal the planet, empower communities, and spark positive changes that ripple outward. In essence, regenerative impact is about leaving things way better than you found them, creating cycles of goodness that regenerate and grow.

Economic equity refers to the distribution of opportunities and resources in a way that levels the playing field for everyone. This means adjusting the scales so that access to wealth, chances for advancement, and resource allocation are not just ideals but realities for all, aiming to correct imbalances and foster a just economic landscape.

Economic inclusion breaks down the walls that keep some on the outside looking in, ensuring every individual—regardless of background, race, or gender—gets a real shot at economic success. It's moving from exclusive to inclusive, where every player has the tools and the stage to win financially.

RESPONSIBLE MARKETING WIN
Netflix Fund for Creative Equity

In 2021, streaming entertainment platform Netflix announced a long-term commitment to increasing diversity in the entertainment industry by supporting the production of stories that reflect a range of experiences and perspectives.

Triple top-line score: 3/3

✓ **Social impact**

✓ **Reputation impact**

✓ **Commercial impact**

The Netflix Fund for Creative Equity was established with the goal of investing $100 million over five years into creating opportunities for talent from underrepresented communities on Netflix productions.[10]

According to the Netflix website, the fund met the objective of investing in emerging talent around the world by investing more than $29 million in more than 100 programs and partnering with over 80 organizations operating in 35 different countries. As of 2023, the Fund had also supported over 4,500 creatives by providing training and resources designed to help prepare them for work in their local industries.[11]

As we consistently see with most effective responsible marketing efforts, the Triple Top-Line Flywheel effect is regenerative here, exemplified by initiatives like Netflix's fund to support Indigenous creators in Canada that aims to increase representation in media and provide financial support and resources to filmmakers from Indigenous communities. It's an extensible, scalable, repeatable program that can be easily tailored for local relevance. This not only amplifies voices that have historically been marginalized but also fosters a more diverse and inclusive media landscape—one that Netflix understands will only lead to more of the novel, high-quality content their business model relies on.

Missed Opportunities to Create Opportunity

When brands fail to place social impact at the center of their marketing strategies, not only can they miss valuable opportunities to create opportunities, but they can also experience negative reputational impacts. Cultural appropriation and content colonizing are two examples of missed opportunities that can bring reputational harms to brands.

Cultural appropriation occurs when brands borrow cultural elements or practices from underrepresented groups and use them for their own financial gain, while ignoring—whether intentionally or ignorantly— the opportunities that exist to highlight individuals from the communities and move them towards some level of economic equity. It is ultimately an unjust taking of someone else's culture without acknowledgement or compensation.

When a brand misappropriates cultural elements, the resulting campaigns lack both cultural literacy and authenticity. They use customs, symbols, or physical aesthetics without any understanding of their cultural significance or context, creating outcomes that can be insulting, disrespectful, and even offensive to the members of the community, which only reinforces the cultural imbalances that drive inequity.

REAL TALK WITH RESPONSIBLE MARKETERS
Keni Thacker

Chief Diversity Creative at Keni Thacker LLC, Founder and Chief Creative Officer at 100 Roses from Concrete, Adweek's 2021 Creative Visionary Award Honoree/Change Creator of the Year, 2021 Advertising Club of New York's Innovator Award Recipient, Keni has over 12 years of experience as a diversity, equity, cultural, and inclusion change catalyst. Keni helps companies big and small show up with purpose where art and commerce meet, and humanity often falls short.

On the Inspiration For 100 Roses From Concrete

100 Roses is to be a platform for people of color in the advertising industry to connect, collaborate, and grow together. A place where they find strength, community, encouragement, and inspiration from veterans and their peers. Someone was like, but what about the men? And that's how 100 Roses came to mind. I hate using words like "safe space," but it's where you don't have to feel like you're one of one. Regardless, of whether you're Black, if you're Asian, if you're Latinx... you're just

home. It's the garden and we're there to provide that sunlight, that soil, and that water that we don't get through the agency side.

I created it so our people can be hydroponic and grow in the house. We're gonna grow our own. So, by being a member of 100 Roses from Concrete, you can get that key support that you need from like-minded individuals. We started letting women in, there was some snickering, but I had to think of what was best for the survival of the organization. As founder, I had to make that decision.

Recognizing the Diversity Gap

Before I left JWT in 2019, I had created a program called the Young Commodores Program because the agency had no pipeline to talent of color, period. Every summer, the interns were like 1 percent Black. I thought, "What if I brought in students from the advertising high-school and students from local colleges together and had them work on a project? What if I have them come into the office twice a week to be mentored by different people from different departments?" That's how the Young Commodores Program came about.

When I first got to JWT or even Ogilvy... there were no Black men that I could kind of chop it up with. It was very hard not having anyone I could relate to or even look up to as a mentor. When I got the opportunity to go do DNI as a contractor, I jumped on it. During my last week at JWT, I was finalizing what 100 Roses was going to be, sending out emails, and creating the website.

Impact of the GROWTH Initiative

The Growth (giving real opportunity with talent and heart) Initiative allows a select group of multicultural college students to gain advertising and marketing experience over a ten-week program. We started it in March of 2020, about two weeks before lockdown. When Covid-19 hit, I knew agencies were going to run away from summer internships. So, I pulled together our leadership team and told them that I wanted to put the Growth Initiative on steroids in the middle of a global pandemic. During the first summer, we took 54 young people into the program from all across the country.

In 2021, to get the Growth Initiative active again, we had a bunch of cultural celebrations for Women's History Month, Black History Month, and Pride. Since we were still kind of locked down, we did a lot of virtual events and informative panels. We took in 50 students during the second summer. They worked on nonprofit clients making PSAs, and all of them got televised. Now, we have a cohort of 20 students, in two groups of 10. We have also started the Growth Initiative Take Two, where we work with people over 40. No one in the country is doing that, helping people over 40 specifically.

Tangible Outcomes

What separates us from others is all the things that the Roses do. We have tangible numbers that show the results of the hard work that we're putting in. We put money on how great our talent is. Agencies that sponsor us have first rights to our talent lookbook, where they can see the beautiful faces of our members and their work. We've raised over half a million dollars in free media for all the nonprofits we make commercials for. Our spots get televised, providing real-world impact.

We're not getting rich over here. I don't take a salary. Our sponsors don't look like an alphabet soup. We can barely break 50 grand, but we make it work with tangible results. We're very transparent about the journey of the dollar. Your donation goes to program development, maintenance, scholarships, and membership programming.

Cultural Appropriation Masquerading as Fashion

The fashion industry is filled with brands that continually misappropriate rich cultural traditions and reduce them to fashion show statements with no regard for their origin or meaning. Spanish fashion brand Loewe faced accusations of cultural appropriation in 2018 due to textile patterns used in their spring/summer collection.[12] Traditionally, the utilized textile patterns were reportedly the work of indigenous craftspeople in Ecuador. Yet, they were given no credit or compensation for the creations that were utilized for commercial purposes.

Victoria's Secret has also been the source of cultural appropriation allegations over the years. In 2012, one of their most famous models walked the runway in a feather headdress, with suede fringe, turquoise jewelry, and leopard print.[13] The outfit was reportedly meant to represent a connection between indigenous people and Thanksgiving. A public outcry forced the company to issue a public apology and remove the look from the televised version of its annual fashion show.

In 2016, women who were not of Chinese descent modeled Asian-inspired clothing featuring feathered dragons, a qipao-like bolero, and Chinese knot tassels. And allegations about the appropriation of Native American culture arose again in 2017, when the brand introduced its Nomadic Adventures themed section, including a Native American inspired dress and feather war bonnet.[14] When incidents like this occur, it can create a hardship for the community of people whose heritage is borrowed by disregarding their talents, undermining their cultural agency, and perpetuating stereotypes.

Content colonizing is also disturbingly common in the age of social media content. It occurs when a brand takes content from a social media account without giving credit or compensation. Sometimes, this content has been scripted, recorded, and edited by the content creator. Other times, it reflects random posts about the everyday happenings of life. A 2024 dispute between a content creator and Cetaphil skincare line offers a useful example.

After seeing one of Cetaphil's Super Bowl ads, a TikTok user and her stepfather used their social media platform to share their concerns about Cetaphil's use of content that was very similar to theirs without any attribution or compensation.[15] In the Cetaphil commercial, a father is watching football and trying to get his daughter to look at a video on his phone. The daughter refuses to do so and continues putting on her makeup. When the father mentions a "famous fan" in attendance at a game, a perceived reference to musician Taylor Swift, the daughter finally turns her attention to the video.

According to the TikTok user, Cetaphil copied several elements of her videos, including the casting of a white father in the commercial to resemble her white stepfather that appeared with her on TikTok. "Y'all Cetaphil legit copied the TikToks I made with my stepdad back in September," she said in a social media video. "Like y'all could have at least given us some credit what's up?" In another video, her step father commented, "That's a beautiful story that you have, and your commercial is going to be on the Super Bowl, but it's our story." In response to the backlash, Cetaphil reportedly agreed to feature the TikTok creator and her stepfather in a future marketing campaign.[16]

Don't Cut Corners, Create Real Opportunities

As a LinkedIn nerd, I have a front-row seat to the brazen, shameless plagiarism that people you'd think would have higher standards say is "just how it works" or the even more baffling, "more about the Internet's virtuous mission to share information freely to benefit the greater good." (Oh yes, I've actually heard a version of this more than once before!)

Well, here's the reality. Social media did not change the rules of plagiarism. If anything, it led to some new more complicated ones. This issue is one of few I am only capable of seeing through the rose-colored glasses of a stringent purist. My stringent rule is if you share work that is not yours without including the most seamless possible access to the original work, you are a plagiarist. If you reshare a video from TikTok without a link to the original, you are a plagiarist. If you pull a quote card from Instagram and share it without a link to the original, you are a plagiarist. If you screenshot a tweet (or xeet, whatever they're called now) from X, the platform formerly known as Twitter, without a link to the original, you are a plagiarist. Let me spell out exactly why this argument is foolproof. The only reason not to share a link back to the original is to ensure attention doesn't get diverted from you. Does that make sense when you didn't do all the work to earn the attention? I don't think so. Deep down, neither do you. It is within our power to denormalize this vile practice. Think about this next time you engage with clearly plagiarized content. If your newsfeed is anything like mine, it's about every third post on LinkedIn.

It's like we all learned in elementary school: Just because everyone else is doing it doesn't make it right.

Content colonization never works as well as content amplification. If effective marketing is all about making a brand-relevant emotional connection, which storyteller has the best shot at maximizing that... the original, or the one faking it? Investing in creators vs. stealing their ideas is far more than the right thing to do for the creator. It's also the commercially responsible thing to do for the brand.

RESPONSIBLE MARKETING WIN
How Amex Small Business Saturdays Introduced A New Holiday
To Create Opportunity

While Small Business Saturday has become a standard part of the holiday shopping season, it did not begin until 2010, when American Express introduced the concept to encourage the support of small businesses during the holidays.[17]

Triple top-line score: 3/3

✓ **Social impact**

✓ **Reputation impact**

✓ **Commercial impact**

Between 2010 and 2022, consumers reportedly spent more than $160 billion at small businesses on the 12 annual Small Business Saturdays combined. The yearly campaign eventually evolved into Shop Small, a continuous initiative for Amex and a year-round opportunity for social impact across the globe. As stated on the Amex website, the company invested approximately $200 million in global small business initiatives in 2020.

In 2023, Amex gave cardholders multiple reasons to support small businesses. Statement credits were given to eligible members who made a single small business purchase of at least $50.[18] The company also instituted an augmented reality (AR) experience entitled Door to Shop Small. Pop-ups were set up in popular shopping centers in Chicago, Los Angeles, and New York. Shoppers scanned a QR code for instant access to products sold by small businesses. In addition to the physical locations, Amex also created an AR experience accessible through a website.

With these initiatives, Amex created valuable opportunities for small businesses to increase their visibility and potentially their sales. The initiative also reinforced Amex's reputation as a resource for entrepreneurs and a strong supporter of small businesses, an attribute that carries over to the commercial success of the card company among small business owners.

Don't Over-Rely on the Sausage Monopoly

A huge barrier to creator investment happening the way it should is over-reliance on agencies. It's all too easy for brand leaders to find themselves taking advice on how much to involve creators in "traditional" advertising from the very people who stand to lose (and frankly are currently losing) their monopolistic control of how the sausage gets made. While the savviest of creative agencies and brand leaders are at the forefront of creating a new model that proactively invites creators to the table and ensures their fair compensation, the rest become less and less trusted and more and more irrelevant, clinging to the old way of doing things instead of allowing themselves to evolve.

This pattern is nothing new. Old school Harvard Business School Professor Theodore Levitt wrote all about it in *Marketing Myopia*, which I consider one of the most important works of the marketing canon, even though it was written in 1960, long before the creator economy as we know it was a thing.[19] Levitt argues that businesses fail when they solely define themselves by what they sell instead of the customer needs they satisfy. It is a myopic view that prevents them from adapting to changing market conditions and evolving consumer preferences. A broader vision encourages continuous innovation and adaptability, which, for marketing agencies, looks like recognizing the shift towards creator investments. A greedy and shortsighted mission prevents brands from creating the real opportunities that move the Triple Top-Line Flywheel, so don't allow complacency and overreliance to frustrate the overall impact goal.

REAL TALK WITH RESPONSIBLE MARKETERS
Jessica Nordell

Jessica Nordell is the author of The End of Bias: A beginning *(2021) and a science writer with degrees in physics and poetry. She has been a finalist for the Royal Society Science Book Prize and received a Gracie Award from American Women in Radio and Television. Nordell has written for* The Atlantic, The New York Times, *and* Slate, *among others. She was a Visiting Scholar at MIT and a featured speaker at SXSW in 2022.*

Avoid Monolithic Representations

Avoiding monolithic representations is crucial. Marketers should recognize and portray the wide diversity within any group to help combat stereotyping and discrimination.

Varied Descriptions Reduce Discrimination

When people from a particular group are described in varied ways, it reduces discriminatory behavior. This highlights the need for marketers to showcase the diverse attributes within any demographic.

Rethink Segmentation

Rethinking segmentation is important. Traditional demographic segmentation often reinforces stereotypes. Marketing should focus on shared interests or needs, such as those who commute via public transit or those who have small children, rather than demographic categories.

Inclusive Campaigns Need Authentic Input

Creating inclusive campaigns requires more than just diverse representation in visuals. Campaigns should be developed with input from people of diverse backgrounds to ensure authenticity and relevance.

Carefully Consider Language

The language used in marketing materials should be carefully considered to avoid reinforcing stereotypes or biases. Descriptive language should reflect the diversity and individuality of people within a group.

Address Unconscious Biases

Unconscious biases can influence marketing strategies and decisions, leading to exclusionary practices. It's crucial for marketers to be aware of their own biases and actively work to counteract them.

Structured Decision-Making

Implementing structured decision-making processes can help reduce the influence of bias. Regularly reviewing and reflecting on marketing practices to identify and address potential biases is essential.

Market with Empathy

Marketing with empathy involves understanding and addressing the real needs and experiences of the audience. Building empathy can lead to more effective and responsible marketing strategies.

Long-Term Commitment

Responsible marketing requires a long-term commitment to diversity, equity, and inclusion. Continuous learning and adaptation are essential for sustaining responsible marketing practices.

Finding Inspiration

Staying inspired to create real opportunities with responsible marketing starts with looking at the world around you through a lens of radical empathy. My friend, Professor Terri Givens, who just happened to write the book that originated and introduced this concept, offers this advice: "Be open to learning and changing as you gain the knowledge that can be critical to becoming an inclusive leader." [20]

While you can't go wrong with gaining knowledge, the imperative to be open is just as important a takeaway, particularly when your social impact goal is to create real opportunity. For the opportunity to be real in terms of authenticity, it also has to be real in terms of urgency and impact to your intended beneficiary. To truly be open, you have to be not just comfortable, but enthusiastic about the fact that everyone your work may try to help knows more about the best way to help them than anyone else. To truly be open, you have to be willing to hear hard truths. Often, your own biggest opportunities are tangled up in all the stuff it's hard for us to hear. That is the magic layer. Don't be afraid of it.

RESPONSIBLE RECAP

- Creating real opportunity starts with a deep and genuine understanding of community needs.

- Identify and create opportunities that are both brand-relevant and positioned for regenerative impact.

- Consistent commitment to opportunity creation earns consumer trust, leading to repeat business and powerful word-of-mouth referrals.

- Avoid cultural appropriation and content colonization, advocating for genuine engagement and compensation for original creators.

- Address internal resistance by fostering an abundance mindset, emphasizing education and cross-departmental collaboration.

- Focus on everyday behaviors to signal and spread a commitment to creating opportunity with responsible marketing.

FIGURE 7.1 The importance of brands creating opportunities (% of respondents viewing activity as important)

Opportunity creation activities	
Partner with knowledgeable experts to spread awareness and educate others	77.8%
Provide support for non-profit organizations or advocacy groups to promote advocacy efforts	76.0%
Invest in advocacy programs and campaigns that help impacted communities or promote a cause	76.0%
Create programs to directly benefit underrepresented or impacted communities	75.7%
Participate in advocacy efforts alongside organizations	74.9%
Partner with brands or businesses owned by underserved, underrepresented, historically-excluded, or impacted individuals	74.1%
Create a platform for underrepresented or impacted communities or relevant organizations to share their work or message	73.1%
Distribute (retail) products to scale brands or businesses owned by underserved, underrepresented, historically-excluded, or impacted individuals	69.6%
Host special events or programs to combat relevant causes	69.1%

SOURCE Based on data from 2023 sparks & honey Responsible Marketing Index

Notes

1 McNees. McNees launches expanded legal equity program for Black-owned, Black-controlled businesses, McNees, February 7, 2023. www.mcneeslaw.com/mcnees-launches-leap/ (archived at https://perma.cc/59DY-QV7F)

2 A. Jordan. Tastemade and Blavity celebrate Black cuisine with new food vertical, BlackEnterprise, August 26, 2022. www.blackenterprise.com/tastemade-and-blavity-celebrate-black-cuisine-with-new-food-vertical/ (archived at https://perma.cc/QQX6-MT8J)

3 S. Guaglione. Tastemade teams up with Blavity to create video vertical centered on Black food culture, Digiday, August 26, 2022. digiday.com/media/tastemade-teams-up-with-blavity-to-create-video-vertical-centered-on-black-food-culture/ (archived at https://perma.cc/65ZK-WZEA)

4 T. Lewis. Yelp teams up with My Black Receipt to support Black-owned businesses, Yelp, June 18, 2020. blog.yelp.com/news/yelp-teams-up-with-my-black-receipt-to-support-black-owned-businesses/ (archived at https://perma.cc/LTR4-983W)

5 T. Lewis. Yelp teams up with My Black Receipt to support Black-owned businesses, Yelp, June 18, 2020. blog.yelp.com/news/yelp-teams-up-with-my-black-receipt-to-support-black-owned-businesses/ (archived at https://perma.cc/M2BH-A8A6)

6 Yelp. Yelp local economic impact report: A look at diverse businesses, Yelp, April 2021. data.yelp.com/diverse-business-report.html (archived at https://perma.cc/K3JH-T3FC)

7 B. Leary. Yelp names Black-owned businesses "ones to watch" in food, beauty and home for 2022, Yelp, February 3, 2022. blog.yelp.com/news/yelp-names-black-owned-businesses-to-watch-in-2022/ (archived at https://perma.cc/TRP9-LN5C)

8 Talent at Chime. Chime spotlight: Chime in for changemakers, Medium, October 19, 2023. medium.com/life-at-chime/chime-spotlight-chime-in-for-changemakers-fd22549cb77c (archived at https://perma.cc/W9LD-45RB)

9 M. Anderson. Payment apps like Venmo and Cash App bring convenience—and security concerns—to some users, Pew Research, September 8, 2022. www.pewresearch.org/short-reads/2022/09/08/payment-apps-like-venmo-and-cash-app-bring-convenience-and-security-concerns-to-some-users (archived at https://perma.cc/GYJ8-RX2R)

10 Netflix. Building a legacy of inclusion, Netflix, 2024. about.netflix.com/en/programs

11 B. Bajaria. Making progress: Our latest film and series diversity study and Netflix Fund For Creative Equity updates, Netflix, April 27, 2023. about.netflix.com/en/news/making-progress-our-latest-film-and-series-diversity-study-and-netflix-fund

12 J. Kong. 7 fashion brands that have been accused of cultural appropriation, and how they responded, Buro 247, February 7, 2019. www.buro247.my/fashion/style/fashion-brands-cultural-appropriation-response.html (archived at https://perma.cc/QY7P-EMF7)

13 J. Kong. 7 fashion brands that have been accused of cultural appropriation, and how they responded, Buro 247, February 7, 2019. www.buro247.my/fashion/style/fashion-brands-cultural-appropriation-response.html (archived at https://perma.cc/L45D-YWWZ)

14 J. Kong. 7 fashion brands that have been accused of cultural appropriation, and how they responded, Buro 247, February 7, 2019. www.buro247.my/fashion/style/fashion-brands-cultural-appropriation-response.html (archived at https://perma.cc/ZVR4-W8JJ)

15 Microsoft Start. TikTok user claims Cetaphil copied her videos for the Super Bowl ad, March 2024. thegrio.com/2024/02/12/cetaphils-super-bowl-ad-is-a-reminder-that-black-content-creators-are-the-blueprint/ (archived at https://perma.cc/FB67-QPR9)

16 A. Kaplan, F. Gariano, J. Neff, and J. Poggi. How the Cetaphil Super Bowl ad went from beloved to controversial, Today, February 12, 2024. www.today.com/popculture/cetaphil-super-bowl-ad-controversy-explained-rcna138404 (archived at https://perma.cc/3KKC-KP6C)

17 American Express. Show love. Shop small, American Express, 2024. www.americanexpress.com/en-us/benefits/shop-small/ (archived at https://perma.cc/F4FS-8WP9)

18 J. Suknanan. How American Express cardholders can get rewarded for shopping Small Business Saturday, CNBC Select, January 30, 2024. www.cnbc.com/select/small-business-saturday-amex-rewards/ (archived at https://perma.cc/FN6D-Y5NT)

19 T. Levitt (2008) *Marketing Myopia*, Harvard Business Review Press, Cambridge, MA

20 T. Givens (2022) *Radical Empathy: Finding a path to bridging racial divides*, Policy Press, Bristol

08

Influencing Real Policies

Why just make a difference when you can influence the system? Brands have a unique opportunity to utilize their platforms in bringing about systematic change far beyond their sphere of influence. Responsible marketing reaches for more than the necessity of commercial impact. It embraces the possibilities of what could happen if marketing centers purpose while also driving profit. Today, brands have the reach to shape public opinion, spark conversations, and encourage meaningful action on pressing social issues. By aligning their marketing messages and corporate actions with real world policies that resonate with their audiences, brands can make a tangible impact on society and maybe even change some laws in the process.

If making a meaningful, measurable social impact with responsible marketing is the fuel that powers the triple top-line, consider your opportunity to influence real policies as jet fuel that can supercharge responsible marketing success.

Driving Lasting Change

The social and environmental issues of today are increasingly urgent, and sometimes it is just not adequate for brands to practice surface level activism by writing a check or making a public statement. To drive lasting change, brands must courageously challenge the status quo, standing boldly against the entrenched systems of inequality, and advocating for structural change. Responsible marketers decide to tackle the root of a systemic problem instead of simply addressing the symptoms. Brands are uniquely qualified to create the type of widespread awareness needed to change policies and address systemic inequities at their core.

Taking the initiative on policy change is not an easy task, and a lot of brand leaders shy away from it by convincing themselves that it is not their burden to bear. But at the core of effective marketing is listening to the wants and expectations of consumers, and according to findings from Edelman's Trust Barometer, as well as the sparks & honey Responsible Marketing Index, consumers want the companies they patronize to take a stance on policy issues.

What's driving these expectations? Part of it is the harsh truth that consumers trust brands more than they trust the governments under which they live, and, as exemplified by the sparks & honey Responsible Marketing Index, they expect those brands to continue earning that trust through authentic civic engagement.[1] Consumers often perceive business as being more agile and responsive to their needs than government entities. They can quickly adapt, innovate, and meet consumer needs, which further drives that level of trust.

Conversely, government institutions lack the flexibility to adapt due to structural limitations like bureaucracy and voting cycles. Especially today, people perceive their political entities as inefficient and lacking the transparency that builds trust. So, it is not surprising that they trust brands more and expect brands to stand up for their wellbeing in exchange for their patronage.

RESPONSIBLE TERMINOLOGY

Brand activism occurs when a company takes a public stance or engages in activities to support or advocate for a particular social or political issue. It can involve actions such as donating to causes, participating in protests, or publicly advocating for policy changes. Brand activism is driven by a desire to align with the values of consumers and make a positive impact on society.

According to the sparks & honey Responsible Marketing Index, 73 percent of consumers rate public advocacy as an important attribute for brands. More than 70 percent also believe that brands should take public stances on issues, support social and political campaigns, and partner with agencies to push for policy change. These findings are a wakeup call for brands that remain content to sit on the sidelines even in the wake of needed policy changes. They may not see the value of getting in the game, but consumers are looking to them to address pressing issues such as climate change, social justice, and economic inequality.

RESPONSIBLE MARKETING WIN

How Nike's Colin Kaepernick Campaign Sought to Influence Racial Justice Policy Change

In 2018, Nike released a game-changing ad campaign featuring Colin Kaepernick as part of their "Just Do It" 30th anniversary.[2] Nike's marketing department saw the conversations around Colin as an opportunity to make a statement. An opportunity to stand for something bigger than just sneakers and influence systematic policy changes.

Triple top-line score: 3/3

- ✓ **Social impact**
- ✓ **Reputation impact**
- ✓ **Commercial impact**

To truly appreciate the risk that Nike took, first consider Kaepernick himself. He sparked a controversy by taking a knee during the national anthem at NFL games to protest racial injustice and police brutality. It was a move that ignited a firestorm of controversy and debate across the country. Nike took a stance, with full understanding that the inclusion of Kaepernick in their ads would alienate some customers. But the cause was bigger than the inconvenience. They went for it anyway because they believed in the cause, and it paid off in every area of the responsible marketing Flywheel. Commercially, Nike did what the shareholders wanted the company to do. They sold shoes. Sales soared and their stock hit record highs. Reputationally, they cemented themselves as a brand that stands for something more than just sportswear. A brand that does not back down to discrimination and threats.

And, most importantly, Nike also made a social impact by sparking important conversations around race, activism, and the role of athletes in societal discourse. The campaign served as a rallying point for activists and advocates of racial justice and civil rights, providing an incredible platform for Kaepernick's message and amplifying his efforts to raise awareness about systemic racism and police violence. Nike did not directly lobby for government policy, but they did contribute to the broader conversations about race, justice, and equality that have political implications. They boldly drew attention to issues that were being downplayed in mainstream political discourse, influencing policymakers to address them more directly.

This is what makes the campaign so groundbreaking. It exemplified that companies can—and should—use their platforms to champion important issues and influence policies that move the needle. Nike showed making a bold social impact, even when it's risky, can pay off in a big way, fueling the Triple Top-Line Flywheel.

Contrary to Belief, Brands Have Been Driving Policy For Decades

The use of marketing campaigns to influence and drive policy change is nothing new. We have seen plenty of campaigns that maximized their platforms to become catalysts for societal shifts. Clothing line Patagonia has long been involved in environmental advocacy. In the 1980s, the company established the 1 Percent For the Planet program, pledging 1 percent of its sales to the preservation and restoration of the natural environment.[3] In the early 1990s, outdoor clothing and gear company Patagonia pioneered organic cotton clothing, and its activism intensified over the years, leading to social and policy campaigns against dams, pesticides, and climate change.[4] The company has also been highly transparent and responsive when faced with allegations around labor practices in their supply chains, using the lessons learned to established rigorous standards for ethical sourcing and driving policy around labor conditions. Patagonia's decades-long commitment to influencing policy established the company as a global leader in responsible marketing.

The Ford Foundation's effort to support #MeToo offers another example of the history of policy impact by corporations. A movement that started on social media, #MeToo grew to have a profound real-world impact. By sharing personal experiences, it elevated conversations on sexual harassment and assault, resulting in policy reforms and increased accountability in workplaces. As #MeToo gained momentum in 2017, the Ford Foundation offered financial support to organizations and initiatives that addressed sexual harassment and publicly emphasized the importance of confronting the unsettling truth about gender-based violence.[5] The Foundation has remained consistent in these efforts and introduced the Ford Foundation's International Program on Gender, Racial, and Ethnic Justice Free Future

2023 Forum.[6] This inaugural event convened global experts on gender inequality and leaders of anti-violence movements to discuss the prevention of gender-based violence. It also featured dynamic leaders of the #MeToo movement, including its founder Tarana Burke.

Marriage equality campaigns were also supported by brands that recognized the importance of cementing marriage rights for the LGBTQ+ community. Retail giant Nordstrom took the bold step of offering life partner benefits to its employees back in 1998.[7] In 2013, Starbucks CEO Howard Schultz suggested that a shareholder sell all of their shares after the person voiced concerns about the company's support for gay marriage.[8] In 2022, more than 200 major corporations, including American Airlines, Harley Davidson, PepsiCo, and Verizon signed onto a letter urging the U.S. Senate to pass the Respect for Marriage Act.[9] Collectively, these companies represented over 8.5 million employees.

RESPONSIBLE INSIGHT

Sparks & honey Responsible Marketing Index – what we learned:

- Support a campaign: 71.4 percent rated it as important.
- Partner with government agencies or institutions to push for policy change: 70.5 percent rated it as important.
- Actively organize or participate in protests/demonstrations: 61.4 percent rated it as important.
- Boycott or dissolve partnerships that go against the interests of historically-excluded groups or relevant causes: 60.3 percent rated it as important.
- Endorse relevant political candidates: 58.4 percent rated it as important.

If a brand or business that one regularly purchases from actively pushes for a policy that one personally does not agree with, respondents varied in their reactions:

- 27.9 percent said their reaction depends on the policy.
- 22.8 percent said they would stop purchasing from them.
- 21.5 percent said they would purchase less often.

The Possibilities of Policy Change

Identifying Real Policy Opportunities

In today's business landscape, spotting opportunities for social impact is as much of a strategic necessity as it is a moral imperative. Brands need the ability to effectively identify opportunities and evolve them into a call to action. Before embarking on any new initiatives, a thorough assessment of the brand's current social impact efforts is needed. This includes the evaluation of existing programs, partnerships, and community engagements. Once that data is gathered, brand leaders should look to their stakeholders as a valuable source of diverse perspectives and experiences. An active engagement with customers, employees, and community leaders offers insights into the areas where policy issues are ripe for action. This type of collaborative approach helps to ensure that the identified initiatives are well-informed and genuinely important to people they seek to help.

Cheerleaders Can Make an Influential Impact

Ben & Jerry's has always been intentional about influencing policy. In 2019, the company introduced a limited batch of a flavor called Justice ReMix'd.[10] This ice cream featured a combination of cinnamon and chocolate ice creams, flavors curated in partnership with The Advancement Project National Office, a multi-racial civil rights organization. The brand's goal in releasing Justice ReMix'd was to drive more collaboration with grassroots racial justice organizations and raise public awareness about systematic racism within the legal system. The ice cream flavor and billboard didn't revolutionize police reform, but the impact was powerful nonetheless. This level of commitment to driving policy is nothing new for Ben & Jerry's. The company has built a strong reputation for taking stances on important social and political issues, no matter how loud or uncomfortable the pushback.

Keeping Brand-Relevant Policy Change Authentic

When an impactful call to action aligns with the brand's core values and purpose, it gives credibility to the messaging, earning the trust and support of brand customers. Whether it's addressing environmental sustainability, promoting diversity and inclusion, or supporting local communities, brands risk being seen as opportunistic or performative if they don't stay true to those guiding principles. Dick's Sporting Goods identified an urgent policy change initiative that aligned with its brand in 2018. In response to the Parkland school shooting, the company announced that it would no longer sell assault-style rifles or high-capacity magazines in its stores.[11] It also instituted a prohibition on the sale of any guns to customers under 21. This bold stance was part of a broader effort to advocate for stricter gun control laws, and Dick's has continued with its commitment, consistently donating to relevant organizations like the Sandy Hook Promise and Everytown.

Social impact endeavors are often more successful with collaboration and partnership. When brands actively build relationships with like-minded organizations, businesses, and community groups, they can better amplify the impact of the messaging and leverage available resources. When Hamdi Ulukaya, chairman and CEO of yogurt company Chobani, established the Tent Foundation in 2015, he enlisted the support of over 400 corporations. The nonprofit mobilizes the business community to implement systems that improve the lives of refugees across the globe.[12] The company have been very vocal about their advocacy, using their platform to share personal stories of refugees to influence and advocate for more supportive refugee policies.

RESPONSIBLE REFRAME

I experienced a new level of self-actualization (and even greater professional success) when I stopped wearing my long braided extensions and fell deeply in love with my now signature short natural haircut.

Think about how tragic it is that even the braided style I came to find (personally) oppressive is considered unprofessional to some.

RESPONSIBLE MARKETING WIN
How Dove Leveraged its Commitment to Showcasing Natural Beauty in Support of the CROWN Act

Dove demonstrated its commitment to policy influence by partnering with organizations and lawmakers to sponsor and support the CROWN Act campaign. An acronym for "creating a respectful and open world for natural hair," the CROWN Act prohibits race-based hair discrimination, defined as "the denial of employment or educational opportunities because of hair texture or protective hairstyles including braids, locs, twists or bantu knots."

Triple top-line score: 3/3

- ✓ **Social impact**
- ✓ **Reputation impact**
- ✓ **Commercial impact**

Created in 2019, the CROWN Coalition partnered with a California State Senator to "ensure protection against discrimination based on race-based hairstyles by extending statutory protection to hair texture and protective styles designed to maintain healthy hair, such as braids, locs, twists, and knots in the workplace and public schools."[13] The coalition was founded by Dove, the National Urban League, the Color of Change, and the Western Center on Law and Poverty.

In 2018, Dove extended its CROWN Act campaign by partnering with LinkedIn to conduct the New CROWN 2023 Workplace Research Study, which found that "Black women's hair is 2.5x more likely to be perceived as unprofessional."[14] Additional findings from the study highlighted the bias that Black women with natural hair and protective styles face during the hiring process and the overwhelming pressure that Black women feel to change their hair from curly to straight when interviewing for new positions.

Dove identified the social and economic impacts of systemic hair bias and discrimination as an opportunity not only to make a social impact, but also to extend themselves into the realm of influencing and advocating for real policy. The connection with hair perfectly aligns with their product offerings, and having already established their brand's body positive message, they took it a step further by centering an extremely important issue for Black women. The reputational impact reinforces the brand's commitment to uplifting women.

Though Dove receives a 3 out of 3 on the Responsible Marketing Flywheel, the campaign could have been improved by publicly recognizing Adjoa as the driving force behind The CROWN Act. This is an example of how the initial creator of a policy initiative can be progressively erased as the campaign's profile rises and corporate sponsors, like Dove, become involved. Ideally, Dove would have chosen to proactively put her at the forefront by making her the face of the campaign and ensuring that she and the Black women responsible for the push in momentum were duly recognized and rewarded for the impact of their efforts.

Find Your Call to Action

Crafting a successful social impact ad campaign is absolutely within reach, but it takes a strategic combination of finesse, creativity, teamwork, and complete authenticity. People can sniff out insincerity from a mile away, so it's crucial to lead with big transparency energy (BTE) every step of the way. When brands bring all these elements into play, they can create campaigns that drive transformative policies that can change people's lives.

In the middle of an extremely contentious political climate, the marketing team at Heineken recognized an opportunity to center their beer in the conversation around civil discourse and mutual respect. The Worlds Apart campaign offered thought-provoking and impactful ads aimed at promoting unity in a divided world.[15] It was part of the brand's Open Your World initiative, which encouraged dialogue between people from diverse backgrounds and perspectives.

Released in 2017, the World's Apart ads featured pairs of individuals with contrasting viewpoints on social and political issues like climate change, feminism, and transgender rights. Each pair was tasked with a series of challenges towards the goal of building a bar together. Successful completion of the challenge required collaboration and communication, and provided the perfect opportunity for participants to talk and get to know each other better.

What made the Worlds Apart campaign so compelling was its emphasis on genuine human connection and empathy. Without taking any specific side politically, Heineken was still able to actively influence political discourse by helping people demonstrate a willingness to find common ground despite their differences. The campaign highlighted the power of conversation in bridging divides and breaking down barriers between people. It resonated with audiences around the world, sparking widespread praise for Heineken.

We saw numerous brands use this type of strategy during the pandemic, where they connected their products and services to issues of public health. We've talked before about rideshare companies offering free or discounted rides to vaccination sites to help people with transportation barriers access vaccines, but they were not the only brand to take up the cause of incentivizing vaccines. The Krispy Kreme doughnut chain offered a free doughnut to customers who showed their vaccination card, with no purchase necessary.[16] Walgreens hosted vaccination events and offered incentives, such as discounts or rewards, for customers who got vaccinated.[17] Dating apps like Match.com and Hinge encouraged vaccines by creating new filter options for users to find potential matches by their vaccination status. They also offered bonuses for vaccinated site members, including free access to premium features.[18] Each of these companies influenced real polices by identifying a call to action brand, their offerings, and their values.

Dealing With Detractors

Finding Comfort in the Discomfort

Not everyone will appreciate brands that influence real policy, and that's OK. Engaging in policy advocacy carries risks. Many brands have come up against the backlash from consumers or stakeholders who perceive their advocacy as inappropriate, opportunistic, or insincere. It's unrealistic to expect that every person who sees or hears your campaign will fall in line with adoration. It can sometimes feel like walking a tightrope, where one misstep could mean alienating your audience. But to truly influence important policies and commit to a responsible marketing platform, brand leaders must become comfortable with the discomfort, which is much easier when you have done the work to ensure that those advocacy efforts are not just relevant but also genuine. Remember, if nobody hated it, chances are nobody cared, which is a far worse outcome.

When faced with this opposition, it is important for brands to respectfully engage without yielding to their complaints. The two words I always recommend my clients start with when addressing detractors are positivity and impact. The worst thing that a brand can do is to match negative energies with their detractors, even in the face of hostility. Responding with professionalism and courtesy reinforces the brand's commitment to respectful communication and can help de-escalate the situation. It costs nothing to show up from a place of positivity.

Impact involves reiterating the brand's rationale with established, publicly available messaging that explains how the action being critiqued aligns with the core identity and values of the brand. Model behavior that de-escalates tension by positioning yourself as a steward carrying out an established mission, not their adversary. Sometimes, people just want to be heard. We can listen and stay open to learning something new, but we can't afford to let detractors call the shots.

Managing Expectations is All About Influencing, Not Fixing

Unlike the quick-fix solutions often associated with short-term gains, the process of shaping policy through responsible marketing practices is a long game that extends far beyond immediate results. It's a journey that requires continuous advocacy, collaboration, and an unwavering dedication to creating lasting impact rather than mere appearances. Brand leaders must understand the complexities inherent in the policymaking process and stay committed to letting the brand's voice be heard. Attempting to rush through this process in pursuit of quick wins risks overlooking crucial factors and may lead to shortsighted decisions with negative consequences for the brand. Remember, responsible marketing goes far beyond surface-level actions or performative gestures. It involves a genuine commitment to ethical principles, sustainability, social responsibility, and consumer welfare.

Our marketing expert, Seth Matlins, Managing Director of the Forbes CMO Network, gave us an example of the influencing policy long game when he spoke about the Truth in Advertising Act. Also known as the Photoshop Bill, the Act was introduced in Congress in 2014 and reintroduced in 2016. It was crafted with the legislative intent of getting the Federal Trade Commission, to protect women and girls in particular, but also an increasing number of boys and men, from the false and deceptive ads that photoshopped the human body into something it wasn't. It never became law, but that did not stop some brands from implementing policies in advancement of the Act's goals. In speaking about the CVS Beauty Mark initiative, Seth said, "CVS announced that not only would they stop photoshopping—they didn't put out that much creative—but, more importantly, they insisted that all carried brands disclose any photoshopping. So, any of the biggest beauty brands in the world, as well as any emerging beauty brands, that sent them point-of-sale had to indicate whether the people in the ads had been materially altered by post-production digital means. Those that had not been photoshopped received the CVS Beauty Mark Watermark; those that had been photoshopped received an indication of digital alteration. You can go into any CVS right now, walk through their makeup aisle and see the watermark on probably 95 percent of creative. That was an effort that continues to literally change the face and shape of beauty on a global basis."

CVS is not the only brand taking a stand against photoshopping. Fenty Beauty often features unretouched images of its models to provide accurate depictions of a wide range of skin tones. UK-based fashion retailer

Missguided launched the #MakeYourMark campaign, featuring diverse mannequins and real women with various types of perceived imperfections, like scarring, freckles, albinism, and birthmarks.[19] In 2014, fashion retailer ModCloth signed a Heroes Pledge for Advertisers, committing to not alter the appearance of models in its advertising campaigns.[20] Achieving meaningful change requires a deep understanding of systemic issues, engagement with diverse perspectives, and a willingness to address root causes rather than merely addressing symptoms. These brands are not trying to boil the entire ocean. They have learned to be content with filling one or two pots at a time. Otherwise, brands can become overwhelmed and get frozen in place instead of maximizing their platform toward policy changes.

The weight of our environmental concerns easily feels like too much for one brand to tackle, but where would we be if every company took that stance? Look to other brands that have broken the issue down into bite-sized pieces and identify ways that your brand can do the same. Through its partnership with Parley for the Oceans, adidas creates shoes made from recycled ocean plastic to raise awareness about pollution.[21] Through the power of sports, adidas is helping to reduce the immense problem of plastic waste in the ocean, one shoe at a time.

Consumer goods corporation Unilever has consistently advocated for sustainable palm oil production with the goal of reducing deforestation and habitat destruction. In 2009, it was among the first companies to make a public commitment to a long-term goal of sourcing 100 percent of its palm oil sustainably.[22] By the end of 2022, the company was sustainably sourcing 94 percent of its core palm oil.[23] This showcases the importance of long-term commitment. Unilever set a goal in 2009 and has spent more than a decade chipping away at the goal with the aim of building a better tomorrow.

RESPONSIBLE RECAP

- Influencing real policy can solve systemic brand-relevant societal needs.
- This is nothing new! Brands have a long history of advocating for social change and driving policy reform.
- Laws don't have to change for this responsible marketing move to be considered a success. "Cheerleaders" can make an impact by showing support when everyone else is sitting on the fence.
- Advocating for brand-relevant policy change can be one of the most powerful responsible marketing moves... if it's done authentically.

- Keep it real. Mitigate the risk of being perceived as performative by leading with BTE (big transparency energy) every step of the way.
- Stay the course. Engaging in policy advocacy may attract detractors, but conviction is the key to drowning out the noise of the loud minority.

Notes

1 L. Rodrigues. The sparks & honey Responsible Marketing Index [proprietary research], 2023

2 S. Laferte. When big brands take social stances: An in-depth analysis of Nike's Colin Kaepernick ad, Greenbook, September 13, 2018. www.greenbook.org/insights/brand-strategy/when-big-brands-take-social-stances-an-in-depth-analysis-of-nikes-colin-kaepernick-ad (archived at https://perma.cc/7VG9-UBS5)

3 Patagonia. 1 percent for the planet, Pagagonia, 2024. www.patagonia.com/one-percent-for-the-planet.html (archived at https://perma.cc/AA6P-KWT3)

4 Y. Chouinard. How a reluctant businessman built the Patagonia brand, Marcom Central: A RICOH company, Marcom, January 18, 2024. marcom.com/yvon-chouinard-how-a-reluctant-businessman-built-the-patagonia-brand/ (archived at https://perma.cc/AWP4-NFK7)

5 B. Rothenberg. Grantmaking in the #MeToo era, Stanford Social Innovation Review, December 6, 2019. ssir.org/articles/entry/grantmaking_in_the_metoo_era (archived at https://perma.cc/C762-N3XK)

6 The Ford Foundation. The Ford Foundation to host inaugural Free Future 2023 Forum on preventing gender-based violence, September 13, 2023. www.fordfoundation.org/news-and-stories/news-and-press/news/the-ford-foundation-to-host-inaugural-free-future-2023-forum-on-preventing-gender-based-violence/ (archived at https://perma.cc/VJD3-35CL)

7 E. S. Webster. 10 companies that proudly stand with the LGBTQ community, Teen Vogue, June 15, 2016. www.teenvogue.com/gallery/10-companies-support-lgbt-community (archived at https://perma.cc/V5MS-G3AK)

8 E. S. Webster. 10 companies that proudly stand with the LGBTQ community, Teen Vogue, June 15, 2016. www.teenvogue.com/gallery/10-companies-support-lgbt-community (archived at https://perma.cc/V5MS-G3AK)

9 N. Goodkind. America's largest companies are fueling inequality, says new study, CNN, March 26, 2024. www.cnn.com/2024/03/26/investing/premarket-stocks-trading/index.html (archived at https://perma.cc/MV7G-5CK4)

10 Ben & Jerry's. New flavor alert: Justice remix'd, Ben & Jerry's, September 4, 2019. www.benjerry.com/whats-new/2019/09/justice-remixd-event (archived at https://perma.cc/UK4E-3RYU)

11 E. Hawkins. What happened when Dick's Sporting Goods took a stand on guns, Axios Communicators, June 19, 2022. www.axios.com/2022/06/19/guns-corporate-messaging-dicks-sporting-goods (archived at https://perma.cc/9QBM-SJWK)

12 Tent. We mobilize major businesses to connect refugees to work, Tent, 2024. www.tent.org (archived at https://perma.cc/3RSS-SET7)

13 The CROWN Act. About: Creating a respectful and open world for natural hair, 2024. www.thecrownact.com/about (archived at https://perma.cc/Q8TQ-CCJU)

14 Black Enterprise. Dove partners with LinkedIn in support of The CROWN Act to help end race-based hair discrimination in the workplace, February 17, 2023. www.blackenterprise.com/dove-partners-with-linkedin-in-support-of-the-crown-act-to-help-end-race-based-hair-discrimination-in-the-workplace/ (archived at https://perma.cc/HFA5-YKFX)

15 L. M. Segarra. Heineken ad pairs up strangers with opposing views on transgender rights, climate change and feminism, *Time*, April 27, 2017. time.com/4757540/heineken-ad-worlds-apart-commercial/ (archived at https://perma.cc/YQ32-HGQF)

16 J. Cheang. Krispy Kreme offers free glazed donut to those who show Covid vaccine card, NBC News, March 23, 2021. www.nbcnews.com/news/us-news/krispy-kreme-offers-free-glazed-donut-those-who-show-covid-n1261768 (archived at https://perma.cc/QWP3-78PP)

17 Deerfield, Ill. Individuals getting Covid-19 vaccines at Walgreens to receive $25 in Walgreens cash rewards, Walgreens Boots Alliance, June 22, 2021. www.walgreensbootsalliance.com/news-media/press-releases/2021/individuals-getting-covid-19-vaccines-at-walgreens-to-receive-25-in-walgreens-cash-rewards (archived at https://perma.cc/43P4-BZL8)

18 J. Breslow. Dating apps are making it easier to swipe right for a match who's vaccinated, NPR, May 21, 2021. www.npr.org/2021/05/21/999178100/single-dating-apps-are-making-it-easier-to-swipe-right-for-a-match-whos-vaccinat (archived at https://perma.cc/HH8V-LLKC)

19 C. Teather. Misguided launches body positive campaign and you need to see it... pronto, *Glamour Magazine*, May 10, 2018. www.glamourmagazine.co.uk/gallery/missguided-keeponbeingyou-body-positive-models-campaign (archived at https://perma.cc/9DLA-U8UC)

20 M. Gibson. One fashion brand takes the "no Photoshop pledge," who's next, *Time*, August 19, 2024. time.com/3144306/modcloth-pledges-no-photoshopping/ (archived at https://perma.cc/2J6J-4GYA)

21 Adidas. Adidas X Parley, Adidas, 2024. www.adidas.com/us/parley (archived at https://perma.cc/94L7-KBKJ)

22   Unilever. About: Sustainable and deforestation-free palm oil, Unilever, 2024. www.unilever.com/sustainability/nature/sustainable-palm-oil (archived at https://perma.cc/62HS-STZQ)

23   Unilever. About: Sustainable and deforestation-free palm oil, Unilever, 2024. www.unilever.com/sustainability/nature/sustainable-palm-oil (archived at https://perma.cc/5XFE-626A)

PART THREE

The Process

Make It Happen

09

Cultivating Cultural Literacy

Advertising is the number one influence in our lives that we have no control of.

ANDRE GRAY

I moved down to Austin, Texas to join Dell in the fall of 2011 as a newly minted NYU Stern Master of Business Administration (MBA). Unlike during my summer internship experience where I was one of only two Black recruits, I and the majority of MBAs onboarding that year got our offers at the National Black MBA Association's annual conference. We were the best and brightest with a bonus—adding much-needed diversity to Dell's marketing team. Our shared workspace was a cluster of tiny cubicles flanked on either side by two of the office's major thoroughfares. Suffice it to say, we were noticed. The air was thick with *Why Are All the Black Kids Sitting Together in The Cafeteria?*[1] vibes that were palpably present and impossible not to feel.

As our mostly white colleagues sped back and forth, very much noticing the novelty of "so many of us" in one place, people reacted in one of two ways. They either gave their best "I don't see color!" performance by looking away or down at their phones, or they indirectly and often awkwardly expressed their approval by saying something like "It's about time for this, right?" These reactions were more cringe than problematic until the day I fell into the trap door.

I was moving to a larger cube in a different area of the building after being promoted to a new role. Box in hand, I smiled at a passing colleague who happened to be a white woman and I heard her say brightly: "Congrats on making it out of Cabrini Green!" followed by the sort of knowing chuckle meant to attract one in return. I stood there stunned and speechless, smiling tightly as my brain tried to process what had just happened while she sauntered by without missing a beat. A hot flash of shock burned up through my body leaving my cheeks warm. Then an icy clarity froze me in place, sending a chill down my spine. What she said was unconscionable, but what I realized at that moment was far more upsetting. Even as a sophisticated marketing director at a Fortune 500 company, entrusted with millions of dollars in budget and the career trajectory of many, she was completely unaware that what she considered a casual quip was both deeply harmful and egregiously unethical. I was falling down the rabbit hole of what writer Aminatou Sow calls "the trap door of racism."[2] In a systemically racist and sexist society, invisible trap doors are everywhere just waiting to suck historically-excluded people into a disorienting abyss where any scraps of belonging we'd managed to internalize are replaced by the only protection we know, the exhausting hyper-vigilance that keeps us safe at the expense of feeling fully alive.

Here's why this *has* to matter to leaders like you. The American Marketing Association defines marketing as "the activity, set of institutions, and processes for creating, communicating, delivering, and exchanging offerings that have value for customers, clients, partners, and society at large."[3] When the intentional and continuous pursuit of improved cultural literacy isn't a consistent practice, we extract value from the world instead of creating it, a direct contradiction to the central mandate of our role. Responsible marketing requires high cultural literacy to avoid polluting the world with trap doors that inflict harm on the audiences and consumers we serve at scale.

REAL TALK WITH RESPONSIBLE MARKETERS
Myles Worthington

Myles is Founder and Chief Executive Officer of WORTHI, Ketchum's 2014 PR Week Campaign of the Year, and formerly Head of Global Audiences, Brand and Editorial Marketing at Netflix. Myles and his team across the country partner with major brands like Google, Apple, Disney, Paramount, Lionsgate, Bumble, Tubi, Max, Amazon, Hulu, Peacock, and many more to build and execute upon strategies that keep these brands relevant and resonant for Black, Latine, LGBTQ+, Asian and Pacific Islander, people with disabilities, and every intersectionality in between.

The Ethnographic Marketing Imperative

WORTHI is an ethnographic marketing, communications, and content company. Our mission is to unlock the business value and cultural impact of historically-underestimated communities. We steep ourselves in the behaviors and desires of specific communities and create the cultural relevance between their unique needs and a brand's unique story to create a lasting bond. Why? Not because of DEI, although that's a beautiful and necessary byproduct of our work, but because these audiences influence and define broader culture and offer inarguable and extensive bottom-line value to brands. Business longevity ultimately depends on their buy-in.

Why Words Matter

When it comes to the canvases we paint on, we don't limit ourselves by a certain function or marketing mix diagram. The people we are trying to reach on behalf of our client partners do not live in boxes, so we don't think in boxes. Using words like "minority" or "marginalized," for example, is ultimately harmful rhetoric because it diminishes and "other"izes groups of people, suggesting they're small and inferior. Marketers should see the opportunity to speak to these audiences as the ultimate business proposition, not something they have to do because of cultural pressure.

There are moments when we need to speak broadly about people who are not white, cis-gendered, straight, able-bodied men, and there are more impactful ways to do that. For every other instance, we should lean into the specificity of who is being referred to because if you speak generally, you'll get generic results.

When speaking broadly, we at WORTHI use the term "underestimated audiences" when referring to, well, folks who are not white, cis, straight, able-bodied men. We gravitate toward this phrase because the word "estimated" is closely tied to valuation and business impact.

Stop Underestimating Your Consumers

When you underestimate an entity, you miss out on maximizing results due to a miscalculation of effort. The act of speaking directly to Black, Latine, LGBTQ+, Asian American and Pacific Islanders (AAPI), people with disabilities (PWDs) and other audiences feels like it's inherently related to diversity, equity, and inclusion, or something done to be considered charitable. In actuality, the data shows these audiences are critical for business longevity due to their increasing size, outsized influence and buying power that rivals the GDP of many major countries.

While these audiences have historically been underestimated, marketers can now course-correct. Chart a stronger course for your brands not because of principles related to DEI, but because of principles related to profit. Weed out the apathetic language, lean into specificity, and be intentional about authentically and consistently connecting with these underestimated audiences. Your brand's success depends on it.

Why I Revel in My Own Irrelevance

Top-ranking diversity executives can sometimes be the only people of color operating at that level within any given company. When you are a junior to mid-level person of color, you see this person and think, "Oh great, I've got somebody who's thinking about me and my community."

My team at WORTHI is awesome. I could cry about how much I love these people and how brilliant they all are. One of my favorite things to do as a leader is to render myself irrelevant. Watching them rock without needing me is such an incredible feeling.

Cultural Literacy Defined

A Foundation of Understanding for the Integration of New Ideas

In 1987, American educator and literary critic E.D. Hirsch coined the term "cultural literacy" in his book *Cultural Literacy: What every American needs to know.*[4] In the book, he sternly argued that children in the U.S. educational system were being deprived of cultural literacy, a skill that he described as necessary for successfully functioning in contemporary society.[5] His use of the term centered on literary works, specifically the background information that writers and speakers omit from their works based on the flawed assumption that their entire audience shares the same background of knowledge. But the evolution of cultural literacy has taken it far beyond the literary space.

In the modern context, cultural literacy centers on the multiculturalism of our world and the ability of people to understand traditions, history, activities, and essential elements of cultures separate from your own. It is having a healthy appreciation for the uniqueness of individual cultures and taking those differences into consideration when engaging with diverse perspectives. In today's globalized society, where interactions with people from various cultural backgrounds are commonplace, effective communication and collaboration requires cultural literacy. It requires a recognition of the inherent value and richness of all cultural heritages and traditions, acknowledging that a universal standard for what constitutes "normal" or "correct" does not exist.

Moreover, cultural literacy involves actively seeking out opportunities to expand one's knowledge and understanding of different cultures. It cultivates a mindset of openness and curiosity about others' perspectives and experiences, buttressed with a commitment to empathy, respect, and inclusivity. When done correctly, cultural literacy goes beyond mere familiarity to intentionality. It recognizes and challenges the stereotypes, biases, and prejudices that hinder genuine intercultural communication.

RESPONSIBLE MARKETING WIN

Professor, St. John's University Tobin College of Business, author of Stop, Ask, Explore: Learn to navigate change in times of uncertainty, *Founder of WOMBLab, contributor to Harvard Business Review, Joan helps emerging and established leaders to build resilience, embrace hope, explore new possibilities and develop an experimental mindset.*

Imagine standing on the edge of a familiar meadow on the threshold of a dense forest with no map or compass. Leaving the meadow and reorienting to life in the woods might feel like an exciting adventure, a daunting chore, or a mix of both. Making sense of the transition from one involves zooming out and looking through multiple lenses at once. We need to know ourselves, who we're traveling with, the resources we have for the journey, and whether we're out for the day, a year, or for good. We also need to develop the capacity in ourselves and others to face the known (and unknown) barriers we'll inevitably encounter along the way—some of which we can plan for, and others that will require learning, improvisation, and adaptation in the moment.

The same could be said about the opportunities and challenges facing aspiring responsible marketers as we seek to bring new thinking, practices, and processes into environments that are conditioned to the industrial-era, profit-over-people environment of modern marketing. While it might be tempting to think that we can educate people into new ways of being and working, anyone involved in change initiatives knows that the space between knowing what should be done, what is possible to do, what we choose to do, and the intended and unintended impact of what we've done is often a chasm. That is one of the reasons that so many efforts to do what is right go so very, very wrong.

That's why, whether we're talking meadows and forests or organizations and societies, stepping into the ill-defined, liminal space between what is and what could be is so difficult for so many people—including people who are committed to the effort. Entering the unknown takes more than trite calls to "toughen up" or "get comfortable being uncomfortable" on one hand, or five-step prescriptions on the other. It takes a willingness to go off script, take risks and engage in active exploration and experimentation—with or without permission, support, or resources. It also requires the courage to take risks, the humility to be a learner, and the confidence to suspend certainty and be open to new possibilities.

And all of that takes practice.

When we face uncertain transitions—by choice or necessity—well-crafted plans with precise metrics, firm objectives, and clear timetables for measurable outcomes and ROI often fail us. Pivoting and "failing forward" are no more helpful—especially if the stakes are high and there is skepticism or lack of individual, team, or organizational support for the change. Instead, these moments invite us to shift from a focus on execution and create space for experimentation and liminal learning.

I can hear the skeptics as I type this. "We don't have time or money to invest in research and development or trial and error." I get it. This is not about trying something to see what sticks. Instead, I favor well-designed, time boxed experiments that: 1) are aligned with existing goals and objectives, 2) are geared toward contextual learning in practice, and 3) view resistance and barriers to progress as creative constraints rather than cause of frustration. These types of experiments challenge the binary between learn and do, and provide a way to build learning how best to bring responsible marketing into everything we do—keeping what works and learning from what doesn't.

I wish I could close with that motivational ideal, but I've observed something in my work with well-intentioned leaders and aspiring changemakers that is important to keep in mind.

Becoming learners in work we are passionate about can be easier said than done. Even the most committed among us have been marinated in centuries of narratives of what it means to do business well and decades of platitudes about doing good business. These shape our thinking, our actions and the means and methods we use to spark change. As a result, we inadvertently build upon the same foundations as the ones we hope to reimagine. To succeed. To get it right. To win. We fall into the trap of bringing the prescriptive ideas and activities from our favorite meadows into the forests of existing contexts and are frustrated when our best practices don't stick. We can be overly certain and immovable in our views of what "right" looks like, especially when the work involves more sacrifice and is more exhausting than we thought it might be.

Putting down scripts is the easy part. Working together to write them is the real challenge.

Culture Impacts Consumer Behavior

As brands operate in an increasingly globalized world, cultural literacy has become an essential aspect of the continuous learning and education it takes to craft effective marketing strategies. Today's consumers are far from monolithic, hailing from diverse cultural backgrounds and holding varying beliefs, values, and preferences. For marketers to resonate with their audiences and establish the meaningful connections that evolve into a loyal customer base, they must understand and respect the nuances of different cultures.

In his book *For the Culture: The power behind what we buy, what we do, and who we want to be*, Marcus Collins brilliantly examines the connection between culture and its impact on consumer behavior.[6] As the driving force behind some of the decade's most iconic ads, he sees culture as a powerful driver of influence that brands can use to effect action. This is because consumption, in and of itself, is a cultural act. "What we buy, wear, drive, how we style our hair, where we go to school, who we marry, if we marry, where we vacation, and how we bury the dead are all byproducts of cultural subscriptions," says Collins. "Culture moves forward based on one simple question: do people like me do something like this? If the answer is yes, we do it. If the answer is no, we don't. Therefore, if you have a vested interest in getting people to take action, then culture is your biggest cheat code."

According to Collins, while today's brands leverage culture in a way that speaks to people's sense of identity, tomorrow's brands will center on community. "We are tribal, given to gathering and communing in familiar groups. We want to belong. As we use brands to say something about ourselves, we find people who are like us, thus forming communities." In fact, according to the sparks & honey Responsible Marketing Index, 71.6 percent of respondents are likely to buy inclusive alternatives to products even if the need for an alternative does not apply to them (Figure 9.1).

Mastering the Art of Decentering

A lack of cultural literacy often results from one's inability to identify opportunity areas, let alone address them effectively. Instead of considering how diverse groups perceive interactions, they interpret all communications through the lens of their own cultural background and experiences. In a corporate environment, cultural differences are often disregarded in the pursuit of efficiency or for fear of being perceived as politically incorrect.

FIGURE 9.1 Likelihood of consumers buying inclusive alternatives to products, even if they do not apply to them personally (% of respondents)

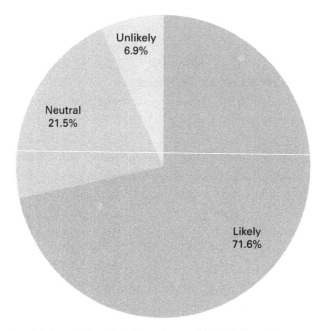

Unlikely
6.9%

Neutral
21.5%

Likely
71.6%

SOURCE Based on data from 2023 sparks & honey Responsible Marketing Index

The people who wield the most power across the marketing industry at large have continually demonstrated a pervasive unwillingness to acknowledge lived experience as exclusive expertise. They go through the motions of attempting to appear more culturally literate while demonstrating a stubborn fragility to criticisms, pushing back with denial and excuses, which only spotlights the depth of their cultural unawareness. For brands, consumer feedback should be a motivator for growth. It can be a difficult mirror, reflecting not only the strengths, but also the weaknesses of an advertising campaign. But it is also a priceless learning opportunity. Perspectives provided by different cultures are extremely valuable, especially when they are given the space and safety to offer them with unfiltered transparency. But feedback fragility closes the door to learning opportunities.

Once the problematic behaviors are identified, they must be unlearned and replaced with cultural literacy skills through programs like workshops, seminars, or experiences specifically designed to craft an understanding about the importance of the language and images used by marketers, along with the impact they have on consumers and society. When these behavioral adjustments are practiced consistently, they evolve into habits over time, arming marketers with the confidence and conviction it takes to navigate the consumer space in a more culturally literate way.

In 2007, a sports drink company introduced a television commercial featuring a Black NBA player as a 1930s-type milkman, complete with a white uniform and cap.[7] In the ad, he provides the new beverage to other athletes as they leave home to go play their respective sports. Each of those featured athletes are white. Meanwhile the only other Black athlete in the commercial is depicted as watering the lawn. The online debates were contentious, with consumers questioning the appropriateness of the commercial's portrayal of the white athletes as playing their sports, while the Black athletes were delivering milk and watering the lawn. One blog post about the commercial summarized a woman's negative response to the ad, saying that, while he initially did not find her opinion worth highlighting, he changed his mind when one of his coworkers also expressed an opinion that the commercial was racist.[8]

Some commenters opined that the brand only cast the Black NBA player due to his tall and lanky body type and explained the other negatively perceived aspects away as coincidences or overly analyzed.

Though their voices were represented in far fewer numbers, others weighed in with an education about the problematic cultural references of the commercial, specifically referring to the historically oppressive and anti-Blackness of its imagery. The vastly different perspectives represented in these comments offer a compelling example of feedback fragility as a response to cultural literacy.

RESPONSIBLE INSIGHT

We all deserve and yearn to feel seen. That is a core human need. Responsible marketing is a key part of having a holistic, end-to-end process that builds products that work for the world.

The research shows that consumers and users want to see the beautiful diversity of the world reflected back at them in marketing and storytelling. In fact, consumers are more likely to take the action businesses want them to take when there is representative marketing collateral. The myth that focusing on historically-marginalized groups takes away focus from the bottom line is simply not true. Demographics are shifting and shifting rapidly, and for businesses to be successful, they need to make sure that they build for everyone.

> The truth is, this work doesn't slow down the process—it's about being intentional from the onset. When planning your strategies for the year, what agencies are you partnering with? How can you get perspectives from groups that have been historically marginalized? How do you allow real consumers to tell their stories authentically? Planning up front leads to successful campaigns at launch.
>
> SOURCE Annie Jean-Baptiste, Head of Product Inclusion and Equity, Google

Underestimating the Relevance of Cultural Literacy

The Common Marketing Mistakes Cultural Literacy Solves

Today's dynamic marketplace requires a consistent infusion of culturally relevant insights into marketing campaigns. It's a challenge that marketers must meet, not as the latest marketing wave, but as a strategic imperative for commercial longevity and as simply the right thing to do. Culture shapes perception, life experiences, and buying choices, so underestimating its impact on consumer purchasing decisions is a costly mistake. Not to belittle the importance of decisions driven by data, but reliance on hard numbers alone can mask the "why" behind the data, resulting in potentially detrimental marketing mistakes.

When marketers craft messages and campaigns with no consideration for diversity and cultural complexity, without consideration for the impact on diverse groups, and a limited understanding of related cultural and experiential complexities, they can end up with messaging that is offensive to certain audience segments.

In 2012, a fast-food company announced a major rebranding and image change in response to declining sales. Desperate to turn things around, it recrafted its menu with numerous items, including its fried chicken wraps. The restaurant chose to bring in a Black R&B artist to sing about the wrap in the commercials and the backlash started before the ad was even released. A leaked version resulted in a resounding social media uproar against the restaurant for perpetuating stereotypes about Black culture. The chain quickly pulled the ad, citing problems with music licensing agreements. They also issued a public apology to the R&B singer, who also felt compelled to issue a public apology. This lack of cultural literacy demonstrated by the brand tarnished the company's reputation, particularly among Black consumers.

To mitigate the risk of stereotyping in their marketing campaigns, brands need to conduct thorough audience research, embrace internal diversity, and commit to inclusive messaging. Without these guardrails in place, marketers may overlook important cultural nuances when developing marketing campaigns aimed at more diverse audiences. They may consciously or unconsciously seek data that confirms their existing assumptions, while ignoring evidence that contradicts these culturally limited beliefs. These types of flawed approaches result in a flawed marketing campaign, absent of the authenticity and inclusivity that resonates with a broader range of consumers.

REAL TALK WITH RESPONSIBLE MARKETERS
John "JP" Petty, III

Global Executive Creative Director at Wieden+Kennedy Bodega, 2021 Ad Age Creative of the Year, 2020 Business Insider 40 Rising Stars of Madison Avenue, and Board Member at The One Club for Creativity, JP believes that being an Executive Creative Director of one of the most creative organizations on the planet means getting out of the way and helping the most talented creative minds do their best work.

Responsible Humans Make Responsible Marketers

I think at the core of responsible marketing is the people, the people that surround a creative process or the business of creativity as it relates to any particular thing, brand, project, brief, whatever it is. It's about making sure that those people are responsible themselves: first responsible human beings and then responsible marketers. Are these empathetic people? Are they inspiring? Are they doing the job of making space for other people, other voices and other perspectives?

It's really hard to be in the communications industry and lack empathy. You always have to keep other perspectives top of mind. Then I think about the workplace; are we creating the kind of environment fit for the best work of our lives? Finally comes the actual work. So it starts with the people, then the workplace, and then the output.

The Most Influential Marketing Moment For JP

I got into this business because I experienced some work that I saw myself in. I'm from Philadelphia, and back in the early 2000s, I remember watching the

Philadelphia 76ers going for their title run. Allen Iverson was like a god in the city at that point in time, and the first ad that I was exposed to, that I was conscious of, was a Reebok signature shoe for Allen Iverson. This thing was beautifully shot. It was shot by Hype Williams, a music director who I was familiar with, so I was paying attention to that. Jadakiss was rapping on this commercial, and it was shot black and white by Trackmasters who were a legendary production team. All this cultural glory was put on a pedestal there.

That commercial played like a music video. It jumped out of the screen and grabbed me by my collar. It made me pay attention. I remember thinking, holy shit! It was the first time I had seen myself in work like that, because these were some of my cultural heroes. I loved what they were doing, outside of whatever this commercial was. So I was locked in and paying attention and that made me attracted to not just the brand and the product but also the business. I thought, I want to do that when I grow up. I don't know who made it, but I want to be responsible for work like this.

I was probably about 10 or 11 years old. I didn't know what to call it because I didn't have the language. My brain wasn't saying, I want to be in marketing or advertising. It was just saying that's cool as shit. I want to do cool shit like that. Imagine seeing that spot between other ads at those times, which were really vanilla ads. They put that thing in between, and it was super disruptive and empathetic for me and people who looked like me. That was the moment for me.

The Cultural and Business Success of Nike's Yardrunners Program

Fast forward to last year. We got invited to work on this platform for Yardrunners, which is Nike's program dedicated to historically-Black colleges and universities (HBCU) culture. I am the product of the nation's first historically-Black university, Lincoln University, so I have a lot of love for higher education as it relates specifically to Black people and people that look like me or come from where I come from.

Yardrunners is a program that was started by two HBCU alumni in the Nike system. It is dedicated to carving out some space in the ecosystem to tell stories about the culture of historically-Black colleges and universities in areas related to sports.

I'm always a fan of doing work that people can see themselves in. To be able to contribute to a program like Yardrunners for a brand like Nike, when I grew up on Nike, was amazing. Nike has influenced and shaped my worldview. But outside of extraordinary athletic performance, it's not really created much space for me if I'm not LeBron James or Kobe Bryant. Very rarely did I see myself—it was always like looking up at Mount Rushmore at these athletic greats. To be able to humanize or present Nike in this new light, especially for HBCU students, is something that is really important for me. Then to see that, because of our program, business has thrived, is extra rewarding.

Black people helped build Nike. For us at Wieden to be able to contribute to a program like Yardrunners is a full circle moment. Obviously it has business implications, but the cultural and social implications that it has I absolutely love. I want to do that for the next 30 years. I hope that program never goes away.

How Yardrunners Authentically Represents the Community

Initially, it was about collecting a group of ambassadors who were representing their universities to help establish a more healthy communication line between Nike and Black students. Then it was about learning how Nike could support the community beyond selling them shoes. This past year, they selected former members of those collectors from the previous two years to design apparel.

Now, they have tapped these four Black women from North Carolina A&T University, Clark Atlanta University, Tennessee State University, and Florida A&M to design their own Nike Dunk shoes. So now they've got products. We have this system of customs and beliefs that we're feeding into Yardrunners, and now out of the third year we have actual artifacts that they've directly influenced or designed. The thing I love is that they're actually creating all of the elements of culture within this program. They're co-authoring that with their community. It's not just something that Nike is force-feeding HBCU students. They're building product, they're building sports apparel, they are building programs that come out of Yardrunners specifically for those respective universities. That's really cool.

Those contributors definitely get paid well. I love that. And by the way, they're not going anywhere. They're part of the family now. So they'll be around, and they'll be influencing product and stories beyond whatever this past line was.

Learning is Liberty

There's a reason why "learning is liberty" is one of my six core values. It truly is the thing that sets us free, allowing us to set others free. It's why one of the big things driving cultural illiteracy in the marketing and advertising industry is the lack of cultural literacy education at the core of our academic and training curriculums. I'm not talking about making sure people know what to say. I'm talking about making sure they know how to think. How many creatives, entrusted to create responsible, compelling work by the world's most resourced brands, were taught to do so by someone with low cultural literacy themselves, and what can we do about it? I explored these questions in a 2023 Adweek article I wrote advocating for the inclusion of cultural literacy within the standards of marketing education.[9] It centered around an advertising school dean who happily shared an ad created by one of the school's students on social media which depicted a white polar bear up against a blue sky with the words "White Lives Matter," sharing that, in his opinion, this was a great example of an attention-grabbing spec ad for the WWF.

After being bombarded with criticisms about the lack of cultural sensitivity displayed in the ad, the dean ultimately removed it from their social media account and apologized. Speaking with me about the incident, he said that he perceived the ad as an "in your face" moment at people who used White Lives Matter to belittle the Black Lives Matter movement. But the loud and public response that he received made it painfully clear that the ad's lack of cultural literacy made it not only inappropriate, but offensive.

The significance of training cannot be overstated for teams tasked with creating and disseminating messages within marketing departments. These marketers need exposure to the intricacies of cultural norms, customs, and communication styles if they are to gain insights into cultural differences, including the avoidance of stereotypes that may inadvertently creep into marketing messages and an appreciation for the traditions that shape consumer behavior within different cultural groups. This heightened sense of awareness drives messaging that rings with authenticity instead of relying on one-size-fits-all approaches. Equally as important, cultural literacy training equips team members with the skills to adequately address missteps that may occur when engaging with diverse audiences.

The marketing strategy of the Axe male grooming brand was one such misstep, earning the company a reputation for using stereotypical gender roles to target young male consumers.[10] For years, Axe consistently used female objectification and male hypermasculinity in its Axe Effect ads, with little thought to the cultural illiteracy of their toxic messaging. The brand's reputation took a hit as public criticism increased, and the social media sentiment grew louder. Between 2012 and 2017, its U.S. product sales declined by an estimated $150 million.[11] In response, Axe shifted its marketing strategy by launching the Find Your Magic campaign, with the goal of redefining masculinity and challenging the toxic male stereotypes in a way that demonstrated a greater level of cultural literacy.[12] Instead of messaging that men needed Axe to be sexually attractive, the campaign centered on other male attributes, the important things like personality, individuality, and the courage of self-expression.

Speaking about the brand's marketing shift, Rik Strubel, Global Vice President of Axe, said the brand wanted to encourage guys to be themselves and live more freely. By doing so, they hoped to break the stereotypes of men and toxic masculinity to create a healthier image that encompasses a broader cultural view.

In a 2017 Super Bowl ad, Axe's Find Your Magic campaign debuted its change in messaging by including images of men dancing in heels, caressing kittens, and engaging in other activities that differed from the traditional view of masculinity.[13] In addition to the ad campaign, the company also partnered with several nonprofit organizations to drive wider awareness among both men and women. More specifically, the company commissioned a study on the pressure inflicted on young guys as the result of masculine stereotypes. They also collaborated with anti-bullying campaign Ditch the Label to create a unique online community designed to help young men who were struggling with toxic masculinity. This is what cultivating cultural literacy looks like. Axe learned from its misstep and took it as an opportunity to infuse its marketing strategy with a heightened sense of cultural awareness.

There Are No Culture Wars

Let me be abundantly clear. There are no culture wars. There are people who deserve to exist as they are, and people who refuse to accept their existence. Using the term "culture wars" implies that hate and acceptance are two equally valid "cultural" perspectives, an implication more dangerous than we give it credit for. We need to reframe the "good people on both sides" narrative. I often hear the argument that most people agree with the values but not the implementation, but if we're really honest with ourselves, the evidence suggests the exact opposite. Think back to the genesis of the Civil War. Both sides would say they wanted the best for enslaved workers (shared values!), but only one side believed what was best for enslaved workers was to keep them enslaved (implementation).

This trend of framing cultural differences as a static battleground over-simplifies the dynamic nature of cultural interactions. Diverse cultures are not locked in perpetual conflict. The actual conflict stems from the willingness to indulge culturally illiterate messaging and excuse the actions of those who choose to perpetuate the systemic bias that continually impacts historically-excluded communities. Marketers that bow down to the boogeyman of culture wars intentionally choose to ignore the social ills perpetuated against their diverse stakeholders.

REAL TALK WITH RESPONSIBLE MARKETERS
Pam Yang

Executive Coach, Board of Directors Member at Welcome to Chinatown, Cofounder at Agency DEI, and named one of Business Insider's Most Innovative Career Coaches, Pam's mission is to help people build meaningful lives and careers so they have more to give to the world.

The Importance of Intersectionality

Some executives are shortsighted about what their target demographic looks like. They don't even realize it, because so many people in these roles don't have a broad scope of lived experiences. They don't naturally think about all the other groups that are potentially excluded. The teams doing the work are often ignorant, maybe not intentionally, about how else their target demographic could look.

For example, if they are targeting women with a campaign, what about transgender people who identify as women? Are they included as well? The concept of a target demographic is often more nuanced than they think.

The next issue is that marketers often don't think about anybody outside of that group that they are targeting. They don't consider other realms of impact. They should be asking questions: What are the potential ways that other groups can be impacted? Are we being mindful about how we're executing this? How is what we're doing either contributing to or having an impact on our physical environment? That consciousness is certainly lacking across the board in marketing.

Then we have the bottom-line impact. Marketing can be very wasteful. It can be wasteful from a budgetary standpoint within the company, being irresponsible about how dollars are being spent, but it can also have a larger negative impact. Marketers need to simply be more thoughtful and strategic about what they do and how they execute.

People often don't want to give strategy the time that it needs. When I say strategy, I also think about it in terms of effectiveness and efficiency. They can find themselves moving really quickly, just checking boxes. Then the physical impact on the environment and the impact on people are left unconsidered.

A Global Realm of Responsibility

We have a "global economy," but some people don't view capitalism as a collective effort. Before globalization, our economies were very localized, then regionalized, then nationalized. What matters is where you see your realm of responsibility sitting. If you're only thinking locally, then you are incredibly shortsighted. We would love every corporation to see themselves as a participant in the global economy with global impact on the physical world, as well as the human and animal populations.

Sometimes marketers may narrow their scope because it's just too much to think about. They can only think about selling this period product to these white women, because they're the largest demographic in this scope. With public companies in particular, who control the largest marketing budgets, there is inherent tension in building a company of long-term value versus building a company that returns short-term profits.

Why Marketing Needs to Be Redefined

We are trying to redefine how most people see marketing, to give them a way to do it better. First, we need to reset the context of where marketing sits and the impact that it has. It's so obvious to us that this is just what marketing should be. Now we have to redefine marketing for this current day and age where all of these things are interconnected. And they always have been, we just haven't been talking about it in that way.

To a degree, people might see this title, *Responsible Marketing*, and think, "Oh great, another thing I have to be mindful about..." Instead, you're saying that in order to do your job better, in a world that now currently looks like this, here's how you need to think about marketing.

Why Marketers Should Care About Doing Our Jobs More Responsibly

We spend the majority of our lives working. No matter what we do with the time, in one way or another, we are all contributing something to the collective. One of the biggest challenges that many of my clients face is a sinking feeling they aren't contributing anything of value. If it benefits both us and the collective, why wouldn't we contribute something more than checking the box, getting a paycheck, and making sure we don't get fired? When we commit to doing our jobs more responsibly, we give ourselves a chance to feel better about how we spend our time, the most precious and finite resource there is.

The Future of Cultural Literacy

Trust building, particularly with diverse audiences, must involve a respect for the cultural nuances that motivate their buying decisions. While it may not be obvious at first glance, big data will play a major role in providing the foundation for that respect as we move into the future of cultural literacy in brand marketing. Advanced analytics tools will provide the analytics needed to create strategies driven by data gathered through surveys, social media listening, and data mining. The valuable patterns and trends identified through these strategies will help marketers better understand cultural nuances for a more tailored approach to broader audiences.

The power of influencers within the brand marketing space will also expand into the future. Individuals with significant social media platforms have changed the game for consumer engagement, broadly expanding the consumer influence from traditional advertising channels. This new sphere of influencers come from vastly diverse backgrounds, and they command the attention of vastly diverse audiences. By partnering with influencers whose values align with their brand, companies will have the ability to engage with all types of diverse audiences. But doing so in authentic and relatable ways means moving into the future with an authentic commitment to cultural awareness and literacy.

To remain relevant in the ever-evolving landscape, brands must embrace cultural awareness and evolve their marketing platforms to continually meet consumer expectations. One thing that will not change is the importance of keeping commercial targets top of mind. Anastasia Karklina Gabriel is the author of *Cultural Intelligence for Marketers: Building an inclusive marketing strategy*. Using the 4Cs—culture, communication, critical consciousness, and community—she aptly explains the connection between inclusive marketing and cultural literacy. "Brands not only reflect culture but actively shape societal norms and values," states Gabriel. "Move beyond performative inclusive marketing and drive the cultural conversation."[14] She explains that inclusive marketing strategies integrate critical societal perspectives, recognizing the significant influence brands have in shaping cultural norms and values. In relation to the Triple Top-Line Flywheel, it's a leap beyond superficial inclusivity, where marketers seek to drive meaningful social impact while also achieving economic impact.

Cultural literacy isn't just a buzzword; it's the compass guiding marketing toward a future where authenticity, relevance, and purpose intersect. Marketers that nail it will develop a sense of cultural dexterity where their decentering is so robust, that their strategies in developing and evaluating creative, messaging, images, campaigns have internalized or more readily embody or incorporate cultural literacy regardless of audience. This is where the personification of responsible marketing lies.

RESPONSIBLE RECAP

- Culture-centric approaches emphasize genuine connections. Brands that actively participate in cultural conversations foster stronger bonds.

- Cultural understanding enables brands to define meaningful purposes while driving commercial impact.

- By analyzing cultural data, marketers can refine their messaging and campaigns.

- Embracing cultural literacy positions marketers to thrive in an era where imagination knows no bounds

---

Notes

1   D. B. Tatum (2017) *Why Are All the Black Kids Sitting Together in the Cafeteria? And other conversations about race*, Basic Books, New York

2   A. Sow, and A. Friedman (2020) *Big Friendship: How we keep each other close*, Simon & Schuster, New York

3   AMA (2024) Definition of marketing: What is marketing? AMA, 2024. www.ama.org/the-definition-of-marketing-what-is-marketing/ (archived at https://perma.cc/4JRT-M96R)

4   Britannica. E. D. Hirsch, Jr. Biography, books, and facts, Britannica, April 19, 2024. www.britannica.com/biography/E-D-Hirsch-Jr#ref661225 (archived at https://perma.cc/84T5-XLTJ)

5   E. D. Hirsch Jr. (1988) *Cultural Literacy: What every American needs to know*, Random House Inc, New York

6 M. Collins (2023) *For the Culture: The power behind what we buy, what we do, and who we want to be*, PublicAffairs, New York

7 Gatorade. Kevin Garnett Gatorade spot (2007), Garnettribute account on YouTube, 2007. www.youtube.com/watch?v=3VEJIFpqrOY (archived at https://perma.cc/GA4P-P7C6)

8 D. Rovell. Is the new Gatorade A.M. ad racist? Darren Rovell's Gatorade blog, TypePad, April 10, 2007. firstinthirst.typepad.com/darren_rovells_blog_on_al/2007/04/is_the_new_gato.html (archived at https://perma.cc/YSU9-JKUU)

9 L. Bakare. Cultural literacy belongs in every advertising classroom, Adweek, January 20, 2023. www.adweek.com/creativity/cultural-literacy-belongs-in-every-advertising-classroom (archived at https://perma.cc/TU39-F8CM)

10 S. McManis. Amusing or offensive, Axe ads show that sexism sells, *The Seattle Times*, December 4, 2007. www.seattletimes.com/life/lifestyle/amusing-or-offensive-axe-ads-show-that-sexism-sells/ (archived at https://perma.cc/3A2H-SQ3P)

11 Eightify. The decline of Axe body spray: A marketing strategy shift, Eightify, 2023. eightify.app (archived at https://perma.cc/TP4W-2J79)

12 T. Nudd. Axe is bringing its great "Find Your Magic" commercial to the Super Bowl, Adweek, January 28, 2016. www.adweek.com/brand-marketing/axe-bringing-its-great-find-your-magic-commercial-super-bowl-169249/ (archived at https://perma.cc/6E47-P34E)

13 T. Nudd. Axe is bringing its great "Find Your Magic" commercial to the Super Bowl, Adweek, January 28, 2016. www.adweek.com/brand-marketing/axe-bringing-its-great-find-your-magic-commercial-super-bowl-169249/ (archived at https://perma.cc/Q3SJ-FA8A)

14 A. K. Gabriel (2024) *Cultural Intelligence for Marketers: Building an inclusive marketing strategy*, Kogan Page, London

10

Choosing Cheerleader, Champion, or Catalyst

People who think about marketing all day tend to have at least a few things in common. One of those is the universal love of a memorable framework. Some of us may not admit it out loud, but all of us know how useful it is to have a relevant, not yet overused, impromptu presentation-friendly way of getting your key point across. The right framework easily lessens the challenge of arming stakeholders with takeaways that are digestible enough to be memorable, and compelling enough to believe in. (If you really nail it, you're compelling enough to believe and repeat.)

The other thing we all have in common? We all grapple with the question of how to approach our brand's level of involvement with the social impact opportunities your responsible marketing strategy aims to address. Of the many marketing professionals and C-suite execs with whom I've discussed responsible marketing, the most frequent questions I get are less about exactly what to do, and more about how deeply it makes sense to get involved.

Is it better to stand up in solidarity but show support with statements alone? Or should you play the more involved role of brand activist, in the game and side by side on the front lines, fighting the good fight? Further still, is that thinking too small? Could you be or should you be going for something greater? What if we did more than standing up or fighting for change? What if we became one of the brands that actually rewrites systemic rules in a more permanent way, or at least puts the process of systemic change in motion?

Keeping It Net Positive

When Paul Polman and Andrew Winston set out to write their book *Net Positive*, they did so in the face of immense pressure for corporations to evolve the age-old mechanisms of getting business done.[1] In a 2022 interview with Forbes, Polman talked about his goal of elevating the ambition of business leaders past the infamous corporate traits of self-interest and shareholder prioritization.[2] In the book, the authors talk about evolving from a stance of doing "less bad" to a commitment of doing "more good." The theory of net positive moves beyond the policies, actions, and metrics necessary to prevent harmful results—which is also extremely important—into a realm of creating a more healthful and thriving environment for all brand stakeholders. Winston and Polman steadfastly believe that nothing is bad if it creates a net positive impact.

During his tenure as CEO of Unilever, Polman understood that the short-term goal of maximizing today's profits could not be the endgame.[3] In 2010, the company launched the Unilever Sustainable Living Plan, its blueprint for shifting the brand towards a philosophy of serving society's interests across its entire business operations through three main pillars: improving health and wellbeing, reducing environmental impact, and enhancing livelihoods. Under the first pillar, recognizing the company's position as a player in the consumer goods industry that could offer healthier product versions, Polman led the company in initiatives around reducing salt, sugar, and saturated fats in its food products. Environmental impact is addressed through a commitment to minimizing Unilever's carbon footprint and reducing waste generation throughout its value chain, among other initiatives. And the company is making good on its dedication to enhancing livelihoods with programs to promote fair labor practices, empower women in the workforce, and support smallholder farmers through sustainable sourcing practices. The company has also committed to paying a living wage to all its employees and suppliers.

In an interview with the *Guardian*, Polman said that corporate wins do not have to come at the expense of others, and that those wins are inadequate without a purpose behind them.[4] He also warns against the pessimism that can creep in when the pace of change is slow, and the scale of societal problems is large. Polman summons CEOs to boldly lead the charge by empowering leaders at all levels of the company and laying the groundwork for moving all employees towards the mindset of long-terms goals.

Unilever's Sustainable Living Plan achieved significant milestones, including but not limited to reaching more than a billion people through its health and hygiene initiatives, the reduction of sugar in their sweetened beverages, meeting high nutrition standards across a majority of its food portfolio, moving in the direction of a gender balanced workplace at all levels of the company.[5] These accomplishments helped Unilever garner recognition as a leading example of what can happen when brands prioritize both profitability and sustainability.

A New Take on the 3Cs

In *Net Positive*, the authors acknowledge that the idea of regenerating the entire world may sound a bit too optimistic, but that does not create a pass for minimal effort.[6] Advancement takes time, and not all social impacts are appropriate for the same degree of action. Some require an aggressive approach, while others may be more suitable for support from the sidelines. However, done correctly and with good intent, every level of responsible marketing can be successful at effecting progress.

Brands can show up in a responsible marketing context in one of three ways: the cheerleader, the champion, and the catalyst. Each of these archetypes can play a substantive role and each comes with implications, both desired and less so. As shown in Figure 10.1, think of it as a "level of involvement" continuum spanning from encouraging action, where the degree of social impact is lower, to making systemic change, where social impact opportunities are much higher. The risk of negative business impact if you get it wrong increases as you move from cheerleader to catalyst. Conversely, the risk of not truly committing increases as efforts skew more toward cheerleader vs. catalyst. The risk of not truly committing increases with the extent to which your efforts skew more toward cheerleader vs. catalyst on the brand "level of involvement" continuum.

Cheerleaders Spark Meaningful Change

Cheerleaders tend to get a bad rap, especially in an environment filled with the performative obligations of thoughts and prayers, Black solidarity squares, and logos dressed in the colors of a cause. Then there's the one-time $100,000 donation from a multi-million-dollar corporation, a tactic that

FIGURE 10.1 Cheerleader, champion, catalyst continuum

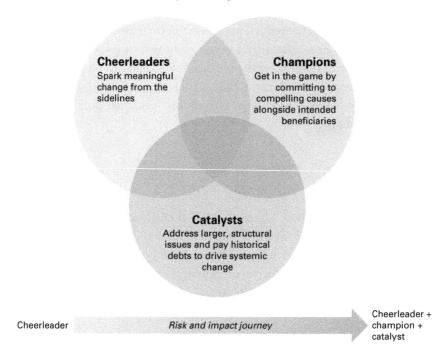

leaves ample room for a quick retreat and lack of commitment. But done correctly, cheerleading can move beyond performative actions into a space that encourages and inspires movement.

In 2019, Gillette publicized its support for the #MeToo movement by releasing a short film campaign featuring images of violence between boys and the objectification of women in movies and at work, as a voice asked, "Is this the best a man can get?"[7] Yes, it was a cheer from the sidelines, but it was also a compelling use of the brand to call attention to a serious societal issue. To cheerlead effectively, brands must be transparent and willing to openly acknowledge that they don't have all the answers. It is not about saving face. It's about doing what is in their ability to empower and enable the cause in an authentic way.

The *Disney World vs. The State of Florida* controversy offers an excellent example of how cheerleading can call attention to important social matters, even when done begrudgingly. In March of 2022, the Florida state legislature passed the Parental Rights in Education bill, also known as the "Don't say gay bill," which prohibited public school teachers from talking about sexual orientation and gender identity with students in kindergarten through third grade. As critics spoke out against the bill, Disney's CEO Bob Chapek announced that he would sign onto a statement by the Human Rights Campaign in opposition to laws targeting the LGBTQ+ community.[8] He also pledged a $5 million corporate donation to organizations fighting against such legislation.

In an unexpected turn of events, the Human Rights Campaign made it very clear that Disney's decision to cheer from the sidelines was unimpressive. The organization refused to accept its donation, instead calling on Disney to actively work against the passage of this and similar bills.[9] Many Disney employees also let their dissatisfaction with the company's response be known by calling for boycotts and staging walkouts at both the Florida and California Disney amusement parks. In response to this employee backlash, the CEO announced a variety of initiatives in support of the LGBTQ+ community and pledged to work towards getting the "Don't say gay" law repealed. Disney has long operated under an image of including everyone. While its cheerleader stance on this issue may not have initially provided the type of impact critics of the legislation hoped for, it did open the door for change opportunities.

Champions Take Risks

Are you a champion? Are you on the field taking part in advancing a collectively prioritized outcome to actually make things better? Being a true champion requires the willingness to take a risk. As anyone who plays a team sport knows, deciding to play means being OK with the fact that the outcome could be a loss. But the decision to play is about much more than one game, or even one season. It's about a commitment to something you feel compelled to take part in. Whether driven by economic gain, physical fitness, or the simple joy that comes from doing something you enjoy, the bigger picture drives you to take the risk and get in the game.

Most business leaders recognize that a certain level of risk comes with the territory of being successful, so they are willing to take them. They take the risk of introducing a new product line, or reaching out to a new consumer market, or even acquiring another company. Yet, when it comes to responsible marketing, far too many of these same risk-taking leaders are suddenly struck with fear. They would rather sit in the stands and watch the societal ills than risk making even one stakeholder slightly uncomfortable, even if that single stakeholder stands for hatred, bigotry, and oppression.

Champions take the risk. These brand leaders recognize that a certain level of risk is as necessary for a successful responsible marketing outcome as it is for any other successful business decision. As Polman pointed out in a 2022 interview with the Purpose 360 podcast, the danger of not taking these risks will impact the future of humanity.[10] He called out companies that choose to set small achievable environmental, social, and governance (ESG) goals, challenging them to close the gaps with more audacious actions than run-of-the-mill "round-up at the register" companies.

Partnering with frontline activists and agencies that align with brand values is a perfect way for champions to close that gap. These individuals and organizations often embed themselves within the communities they serve, giving them an intimate understanding of the issues at hand and the needs of those affected. Through partnerships with them, opportunities to champion their causes will surface as leaders learn more about the mission and work. For example, TenTree is an eco-conscious apparel brand that plants ten trees for every item of clothing purchased.[11] Through partnerships with nonprofit organizations such as Eden Reforestation Projects and One Tree Planted, the company is working to prevent deforestation, restore ecosystems, and mitigate climate change. The brand's message extends to its clothing line using its Earth-First approach, where all products are made in fair, safe working conditions, solely using sustainably sourced and recycled materials.

Frontline organizers know what resonates with their communities and what messages will spark meaningful conversations. They also have insight on the best strategies for building support for their causes. By partnering with them, brands can co-create campaigns that speak directly to the heart of the matter, resonating with audiences on a deeper level and driving real engagement and action. Eyewear brand Warby Parker partners with nonprofits like VisionSpring, a social enterprise working to deliver optic products and services to underserved markets globally. For every pair of glasses that Warby Parker sells, the company works with the nonprofit to donate a pair of glasses to someone in need.[12] Through this Buy a Pair, Give a Pair program, over 15 million pairs of glasses have been distributed. Champions take responsible marketing farther than raising awareness— they drive real-world outcomes.

RESPONSIBLE MARKETING WIN
How the Tory Burch Foundation Masters the Role of Responsible
Brand Champion

The Tory Burch brand embodies the ethos of a champion with its Tory Burch Foundation. Established in 2009 by fashion designer Tory Burch, the foundation works to empower women entrepreneurs by providing access to capital, education, and digital resources.

Triple top-line score: 3/3

- ✓ **Social impact**
- ✓ **Reputation impact**
- ✓ **Commercial impact**

The efforts of the Tory Burch Foundation have earned the Tory Burch brand a positive reputation for empowering women entrepreneurs and breaking down harmful stereotypes. Charity Navigator, a platform that evaluates nonprofit organizations based on financial health, transparency, and governance practices, awarded the Foundation the highest rating of four out of four stars.[13]

Since its inception, 600,000 small businesses received business building and finding identification support through the foundation's free online resources and $2 million in grants has been allocated to women of color founders.[14] Additionally, notable results include 12,000 business plans created through the foundation website and 50 fellows annually selected to receive ongoing education and networking support. In 2019, Bank of America contributed $100 million to support the #EmbraceAmbition global initiative, which highlights the Foundation's credibility and reputation.

From a commercial impact standpoint, results are no less impressive. The Tory Burch brand has consistently maintained impressive sales figures, reportedly bringing in $1.2 billion in sales annually. In 2022, the brand's estimated sales value increased to over $1.75 billion. Created by a woman known for savvy and style, it's no surprise the Tory Burch Foundation makes the frontlines of brand activism look good.

Catalysts Create Regenerative Impact

The catalyst is the ultimate goal for maximum impact, actually changing the way something works long term in a sphere of influence even bigger than their own. And if it doesn't cause systemic change, it at least sparks systemic change in a way that could have broad and lasting impact. If Champions follow the communities they care about into battle, Catalysts win the war. They move past the finite victory of a Champion to address an underlying structural problem. It's like a cellular change in the body that has a broader reach. For the brand, a catalyst change is broader than just the company, extending to a category or industry effect, and it is likely to influence at the broader level. For example, Mastercard partners with so many different banks that when they introduced True Name, a program that allows card holders to use their preferred name on their credit cards, they were able to influence industry-wide change. They provided the roadmap to a solution that impacted countless transgender and nonbinary consumers.

Catalysts have a long-term regenerative goal. When brand campaigns establish the social impact and reputation impact of the Responsible Marketing Flywheel, but miss the target on commercial impact, it generally means that their efforts are moving into something that is either long-term, or even better, regenerative. Regenerative efforts are more likely to be done on a larger scale, and that resonates with consumers. 67.80 percent of respondents to the 2023 sparks & honey Responsible Marketing Index agreed that businesses should help push for policies through activism.[15]

To be clear, none of the 3Cs are bad, and there are both situations and moments in time when brands are better off staying in the cheerleader lane. It depends on the level of urgency associated with the social impact opportunities, cultural causes, or sustainability initiatives you're pursuing as a brand. If there's a high urgency, the Ukraine War or children in Gaza for instance, a statement may be extremely powerful, but there are limitations to making cheerleading the focus of your brand.

RESPONSIBLE MARKETING WIN
How Rihanna's Fenty Brand Universe Became One of the Most Iconic Catalysts of All Time

Rihanna's Fenty brand universe, including Savage X Fenty, Fenty Skin, and Fenty Beauty has earned its spot as a catalyst by intentionally centering authentic diversity and inclusion in all of its products and marketing efforts.[16]

Triple top-line score: 3/3

✓ **Social impact**

✓ **Reputation impact**

✓ **Commercial impact**

Savage X Fenty has consistently offered inclusive lingerie sizes from its initial launch in 2018. The collection's bra and underwear options range from XS to 4X. The radical approach to inclusivity extends to the brand's fashion shows, which routinely feature models of different ages, sizes, and abilities. Savage X Fenty has also utilized pregnant models in fashion shows and marketing campaigns. This contrasts greatly to the traditional lingerie marketing that consumers are used to seeing, where the "plus size" models are still smaller than the average American woman, and campaigns unapologetically exclude specific audiences.

Though Fenty Beauty was not the first makeup brand to launch with 40 shades of foundation, it was able to capture the market when other more-established beauty brands had failed. Responsible marketing made all the difference. By making inclusive marketing a central part of their business model and using models from a wide range of ethnicities, Fenty sent a clear societal message about its mission to serve everyone. Speaking about the Fenty line of foundation, Rihanna declared that the line offered something for every hue of skin color, from the deepest dark to the lightest of light.

Savage X Fenty is also inclusive of all genders and gender identities, including men of various sizes, as well as nonbinary and transgender models in their shows.

Fenty Beauty was named *Time* magazine's Best Invention of 2017. Speaking about the brand, Time magazine said: "Fenty's unabashed celebration of inclusivity in their makeup campaigns put an unprecedented spotlight on the need for diverse beauty products."[17] The company was also named as the 2018 Women's Wear Daily Beauty Inc Digital Innovator of the Year for championing diversity across all its social media platforms.[18] From a commercial standpoint, Savage X Fenty generated an estimated $150 million in revenue in 2020 and is now valued at an estimated $3 billion. Within Fenty Beauty's first 15 months in business it made $570 million in revenue.[19]

The Fenty brand expertly identified and met its impact opportunities. First, they identified the societal harms that have been caused and worsened by the traditional beauty and clothing industries. These companies have been largely responsible for holding up unreasonable standards of beauty that exclude the vast majority of the global population. To meet this gap, Fenty elevated the emotional promises and functional benefits of its brand to market itself as more inclusive and made for every person. This is exemplified within their campaigns, their online presence, clothing sizes, and fashion shows. In addition, as the face of Fenty, Rhianna never misses an opportunity to champion the brand's commitment to diversity and inclusion. By addressing that impact insight, Fenty immediately captured a considerable percentage of the market for unprecedented commercial success, while also establishing its reputation as a responsible brand.

To Be a Catalyst, Think Like a Category Manager

In my experience working on the Gatorade brand, I learned about one of the unsung heroes of consumer-packaged goods success—the category management function. Category managers synthesize performance trends across a product's competitive landscape to advise retailers on the best shelf configuration for the entire category related to the brand. Their role is to paint a picture of what it would look like to maximize the impact of a "rising tide lifting all boats" theory to the benefit of all parties, including competitors. For example, our category managers at Gatorade would present a mutually beneficial vision for improving the productivity of the entire sports drink shelf. It's less "How can I beat them?" and more "How can we all win together?"

Choosing to show up as a catalyst in a responsible marketing context requires a similar mindset, and similar available opportunities to address. It's expanding the view to identify industry-wide systemic inequities and historical debts that can be addressed through the right innovation or campaign. When Citi launched the Action for Racial Equity Program following the murder of George Floyd, the brand endeavored to do just that. Through a number of wide-ranging and long-term programs, Citi leveraged its industry capabilities to help narrow the racial wealth gap and increase economic opportunities. The company's approach includes enhanced access to banking and credit for people of color, increased investment in Black-owned businesses, greater homeownership opportunities and the advancement of anti-racism policies across the financial services industry.

RESPONSIBLE MARKETING WIN
How Citi's Action for Racial Equity Shows Up as a Catalyst
by Facing its Real History

Citi acts as a catalyst with its Action for Racial Equity initiative by addressing the systemic inequities that have historically been at the core of the banking industry.

Triple top-line score: 3/3

✓ **Social impact**

✓ **Reputation impact**

✓ **Commercial impact**

Citi recognizes the lack of access to traditional banking services for communities of color and how that systematic deficit impacts the foundation of financial stability and thriving communities. These economic insecurities are made worse by insufficient access to credit, which impedes access to affordable mortgages and small business loan options. To meet these needs, Citi pledged to:

- Provide Minority Depository Institutions (MDIs) with up to $50 million in growth capital to strengthen their ability to serve racially diverse households and entrepreneurs.

- Generate revenue for MDIs by inviting them into up to $50 million in loan participation opportunities between the Citi Community Capital division in the Institutional Clients Group and its clients to finance affordable multi-family rental housing.

- Alleviate one of the biggest barriers to banking by expanding the Citi ATM Community Network program that removes out-of-network fees at Citibank ATMs for customers of participating minority-owned banks and community development credit unions.

- Put 1 million youth on the path to higher education by expanding the Citi Start Saving® platform—which initially was developed to power the City and County of San Francisco's children's savings program.

- Allocate an additional $50 million to the Citi Impact Fund exclusively to support businesses owned by Black entrepreneurs.

- Increase Citi business procurement spend with certified diverse suppliers from $700 million to $1 billion annually, including $250 million with Black-owned firms.

- Launch a new program called Citi Start CreditSM, which will work with Community Development Financial Institutions (CDFIs) to help underserved entrepreneurs increase their credit scores and access more affordable credit.

- Provide $200 million of equity and preferential financing through Citi Community Capital to affordable and workforce housing projects by minority developers who either are the sole equity owners or are in a joint venture with meaningful equity participation.

One year into the Action for Racial Equity commitment, Citi had invested $1 billion in initiatives for greater access to banking and credit in communities of color. These efforts helped them cultivate a reputation for increasing investment in Black-owned businesses, expanding affordable housing and homeownership among Black Americans, and committing itself to anti-racist practices in the company and in the financial services industry. Citi's efforts were on track to exceed the original goal of $1.1 billion years ahead of schedule.

Citi is consistently solving real systemic problems by working to close the economic inequities that exist for Black consumers and Black-owned businesses. They are creating real opportunities that have the potential to close the generational wealth gap that continues to impact the Black population in the United States. The brand is also influencing real policy by setting a higher standard within the banking industry as a whole. They publicly acknowledged the role that banks have played in creating the systemic inequities that have disproportionately affected Black communities, which is an admission that most financial institutions have been unwilling to make. They then examined the effects of those industry actions and identified their impact opportunities, implementing them in a way that advances prosperity while dismantling the legacy of colonialism, while also creating long-term, regenerative impact.

Heritage Months: What Cheerleaders, Champions, and Catalysts Teach Us

Celebrated both globally and regionally, heritage months honor a particular historically-excluded demographic or community in various ways including but not limited to commemorating their history, recognizing their achievements and societal contributions, and arguably most importantly, raising awareness of and/or endeavoring to address the ongoing implications of past and current injustices and systemic inequities. While heritage months present meaningful opportunities for brands to participate appropriately and authentically, especially in an increasingly multicultural and inclusive world, each year results in far too many examples of brands phoning it in or downright missing the mark. Beyond that, it's all too likely for a brand to assume the role of cheerleader alone without considering the brand and business-aligned ways they could show up more impactfully as a champion or catalyst.

REAL TALK WITH RESPONSIBLE MARKETERS
Taryn Talley

Head of Marketing at Position², Executive Member at Pavillion, Executive Member at Dreamers and Doers, Member at Only Influencers, and featured in NASDAQ and Bold Journey, Taryn is a data-driven marketer with 20+ years of experience who can think strategically while delivering tactically.

Taryn's Take on Responsible Marketing

Responsible marketing is marketing that does no harm. For me, marketing is communication, and responsible marketing is thoughtful, inclusive and empathetic.

Authentic Pride

I'm always hesitant as a marketer to jump on the bandwagon during celebratory months (like Pride Month) or holidays/days of recognition, because I feel they can be seen as insincere noise that distracts from messages from content creators. But that doesn't mean that they can't also be a success story.

As the Head of Marketing at a growth marketing agency, I was in charge of social marketing. In 2022, I oversaw a series of Pride posts that wove the main themes of Pride with digital marketing to create a relevant message that related to both what we did as a company and what Pride means to so many of us. Our Pride posts were our top performing posts for engagement in 2022, helping increase awareness of our brand as well as increase our follower count.

I'm not only the Head of Marketing, I'm also a Brown transgender woman. As a member of the LGBTQ2SIA community, I wanted to focus on authenticity, with an uplifting message that contained the voices of those in the community. I did that again in 2023 with similar success. If I wanted to replicate that for any other occasion, I would include folks from those communities that were the focus of a particular campaign.

Inclusion Means More Than Representation

In the world we operate in, the focus is on the shareholder and profits. Most brands are risk-averse, which leads to complete inaction. The few huge brands that have "tried," like Anheuser Busch and Target, retreated once a vocal minority rose up because that minority opposed any representation they saw as a threat.

As marketers and creatives, we can fight for stronger inclusion in everything we do. It can show up in our communications and designs. It's not enough to have simple "representation," it needs to showcase various communities as they are— living, working, and loving the people close to us. I'm reminded of an ad campaign for Biktarvy. There was a transgender woman in the commercial and over the course of the campaign she dated and eventually married her partner. That campaign was inspiring to me because it wasn't just representation. It showed a woman through stages of her life.

I think every marketer should commit to telling the stories of all people, like they did in the Biktarvy commercial. It is important to tell stories that we can all relate to.

As Taryn points out, authenticity is nonnegotiable when it comes to brand participation in heritage months, but how does that look in relation to each of the 3Cs?

Responsible brand cheerleaders complement a low barrier to participation with steadfast conviction and impeccable consistency. They show up on the sidelines to support the historically-excluded community being advocated for and honored not when it suits them, but when the community wants and needs it. At the cheerleader end of the continuum, brands use visual and artistic content to commemorate the observed heritage. They may create honorary clothing or change the visuals of their brand, and even though these actions may use an emotional connection to engage a more diverse audience, they typically do little to address the underlying inequities the historically-excluded community being advocated for faces. If their special edition Pride tee shirt is not benefiting the LGBTQ+ community in a meaningful way, then this marketing strategy is little more than a performative ploy with no impact.

The History Channel's Arab American Heritage Month series exemplifies a brand cheerleading effectively during a heritage month.[20] In 2022, it launched an Arab American Heritage Month page on its website. The page features educational articles about Arab immigration to the United States, Census data, and the background of the month's official national designation.[21]

Responsible brand champions invest in high-impact partnerships and sponsorships that fuel ongoing programs for and by the historically-excluded community being honored with otherwise unobtainable resources or access. We often hear companies say that they are going to allocate however many millions of dollars over a stated period of time, soliciting guidance from people within that community to make as much of an impact as possible. This champion approach is a bigger commitment than just one single investment. Take Pride Week, for example. Brands that consider themselves champions of the LGBTQ+ must truthfully consider some difficult questions:

- How much are you centering your subject?
- How much are you centering yourself?
- Have you thought about the vendors that you're using?
- Are they aligned with the cause itself?

If brand leaders have not given serious thought to these questions, then they likely are not filling the Champion shoes that they claim to fill.

The Champion level heritage month participation is why PepsiCo's Chief Marketing Officer Todd Kaplan praised his team's Dig In initiative on LinkedIn during Black History Month.[22] The ongoing initiative helps Black restaurateurs become successful. With Dig In, PepsiCo doesn't just show support, they offer it in the trenches where it is most urgently needed. It also doesn't hurt that this support is being offered to future customers. Like responsible marketing always does at its best, it serves its intended social impact beneficiary right alongside the long-term business objectives every brand steward is ultimately responsible for.

Responsible brand catalysts participate in heritage months by advancing the work they're already doing in furtherance of positive systemic change that the community being recognized is known to consider one of its most urgent priorities. Take Puma's 2023 approach to Black History Month in the UK. Instead of just celebrating, they took the opportunity to set a long-term initiative up for success by introducing one that would deliver catalyst-level impact year-round by empowering the next generation of up-and-coming Black designers. Selected designers were invited to present looks inspired by Puma footwear in a competition to win mentorship from fellow designer and Creative Director at Puma, June Ambrose. Participants beyond just the winner also received resources to inform and/or fund the launch or expansion of their own businesses and brands.[23] They are impacting the entire industry by opening doors to diverse brands that may not have had a way in otherwise.

REAL TALK WITH RESPONSIBLE MARKETERS
Shelley Zalis

Founder and CEO at The Female Quotient, Board of Directors Member at Makers Women, Board of Directors Member at Advertising Research Foundation, 2018 New York Women in Communications Matrix Award Honoree, and winner of the Advertising Research Foundation's Great Minds in Innovation Award, Shelley is a pioneer for online research and a champion of gender equality.

With the conviction characteristic of the most impactful champions, Shelley Zalis isn't shy about explaining why The Female Quotient's signature activation features a full schedule of completely free and open-to-the-public programming at the Cannes Festival For Creativity, the World Economic Forum, South By Southwest, Consumer Electronics Show, and more.

Why The Female Quotient's Equality Lounge is Free And Open to All Attendees, Even At the World's Priciest, Most Exclusive Conferences

Every woman is going to have access to my space, period. One of the main reasons women have been underrepresented at these major industry conferences is the cost of entry. Our equality lounges feature the same level of speakers and insights as the badged parts of the conferences we partner with, but at no expense to our attendees. It encourages more women of all levels to attend conferences that can be defining moments of their careers. More women feel welcome in spaces where the kind of networking that elevates professionals to new heights takes place. There are no badges or nametags required. Everyone is on an equal footing. We want early-career women to interact with C-suite executives. Those critical interactions have been confined to traditional "boys' clubs" for so long. It's time to leave all that in the past and bring forth a more inclusive, more prosperous future where women have opportunities to reimagine the scale of their potential impact. Nobody leaves an Equality Lounge thinking small.

How The Female Quotient's Volunteer-Only Speaker Policy is Actually Surprisingly Champion-Worthy

Keeping Equality Lounges free of charge to attendees while shouldering the cost of securing space at elite events and conferences isn't without its tradeoffs. Paying speakers is one of them, but it actually results in more diverse programming and pivotal learning experiences that unsilence the voices of women leaders who deserve to be heard.

Our celebrity speakers are there because they want to engage with our community. Some organizations draw a crowd by paying celebrities huge amounts and making their presence the story. I don't pay celebrities; our policy is the same no matter who you are. Everyone has something to say that is worthy of being heard and everyone's voice needs a chance to develop. It's not unlikely to see a Fortune 10 CEO sitting next to a Senior Manager or Director on any of our panels and we pride ourselves on always modeling a more inclusive, and in turn more effective, way of doing things that have always been done a certain way.

The Practice Shelley Zalis Has Turned Into a Habit That Could Make Brand Champions Out of All of Us

Simple changes to the way we use social media can create meaningful social impact while serving our business objectives too.

My favorite content to share on LinkedIn is my shoutout series. I post shoutouts celebrating big professional wins women in our community are experiencing. Promotions, big new jobs, board appointments—all the moves up the ladder that signify the much-needed gender representation gains we're fighting for, or should I say championing, one breakthrough at a time. It's a simple, highly impactful way to honor our community members, attract more women to engage, consistently showcase our values in action, and spread inspiration to keep shifting the status quo. It's just so rewarding. Anyone can do it and you won't see me slowing down anytime soon!

It's OK to Get Credit, But is it OK to Want It?

In the evolving landscape of responsible marketing, brands face a unique challenge: how to receive recognition for their socially impactful initiatives without overshadowing the genuine intention behind their efforts. Whether brands show up as cheerleaders, champions, or catalysts, the delicate balance between earning credit and maintaining authenticity should always be top of mind. While marketing responsibly must inherently be more motivated by driving meaningful change than seeking applause, it's natural for brands to desire acknowledgment for their contributions. That desire just can't become the defining characteristic of their work.

> ### RESPONSIBLE INSIGHT
>
> Social impact comes in a multitude of ways. How we're depicting consumers on camera in the advertising world. Are we leading with authentic relatable insights versus surface-level insights? Are we hiring a Black agency to do the spot? What is the percentage of diverse media in the media plan to ensure we're reaching the audiences appropriately? So there are levels to the social impact when you talk about how to drive that and I don't know that people often think about that full funnel.
>
> SOURCE Lizette Williams, Global Head of Vertical Solutions Marketing, Meta

As we've discussed, there's more than one way to make a real social impact that leads to real business impact when responsible marketing is done right. Cheerleaders support and amplify existing causes, leveraging their platforms to increase awareness. Champions take a more involved approach, leading initiatives and serving as frontline activists. Catalysts, on the other hand, are the innovators and disruptors, creating new pathways for change and shifting the status quo toward a more inclusive, equitable future. Each role is vital, offering unique contributions to societal progress in ways that align with a brand's authentic identity. As such, the approach to getting credit varies across each of these roles as well, starting with a nuanced understanding of visibility and impact.

The goal for brands should be to achieve invisible credit—recognition that is earned naturally through the authenticity and effectiveness of the initiatives vs. cringeworthy self-congratulation. When the pursuit of credit becomes visible within the work itself, it risks taking over and becoming the story, casting a shadow of performative allyship that inadvertently undermines the very cause it seeks to support. Invisible credit is earned through impact, not intent. When a brand acts as a cheerleader, its genuine enthusiasm and support for a cause can foster community engagement, encouraging others to join the effort. As a champion, a brand's leadership and commitment can set new standards, inspiring peers to follow suit. As a catalyst, the introduction of innovative solutions to social problems can earn a brand a place in history as a pioneer of change. In each role, the credit comes from the tangible difference made, recognized by those who benefit while observed and appreciated by everyone else.

The art of receiving credit also requires subtlety. It's about doing the right thing for the right reasons and allowing the work to speak for itself. Engagement metrics, impact reports, and community testimonials can serve as indicators of success, offering a mirror to the brand's efforts in a way that shows vs. tells. In today's digitally connected world, consumers are keen observers and willing heralds of authentic brand actions. When a brand's commitment to the role it plays is clear, consistent, and meaningfully impactful, recognition follows and in the best-case scenario is also amplified by the very communities and cultural causes a brand seeks to support.

Ultimately, the most revered responsible marketing works because it comes from a place of service. For cheerleaders, champions, and catalysts alike, the true measure of success is the positive change effected in the world—a legacy far more lasting than any award or acknowledgment. Brands that navigate this path with integrity and purpose will find that the most meaningful credit is often that which is never explicitly sought but comes naturally when a brand commits to the role those chosen as its stewards have chosen for it to play.

RESPONSIBLE RECAP

- Use the 3Cs framework for responsible marketing as a tool to guide your brand's approach to determining the ideal level of involvement in a particular responsible marketing scenario.

- Responsible brand cheerleaders let the communities being shown support determine how and when that support is needed.

- Responsible brand champions are the activists who are willing to join the communities they are advocating for side by side while taking action at the frontlines.

- Responsible brand catalysts actually make changes to the systems they operate within that benefit the communities they're focused on for good—or at least attempt to.

- Timing, cultural context, brand relevance, brand reputation, commercial implications, relative levels of risk tolerance and corresponding rationale are key factors that determine the ideal archetype for a brand to embody.

- Remember, there's no one right way to show up. There are defensible decisions about how to show up, and those can evolve and shift over time.

Notes

1   P. Polman, and A. Winston (2021) *Net Positive: How courageous companies thrive by giving more than they take*, Harvard Business Review Press, Cambridge, MA

2   A. Aziz. "Net positive" is the new rallying cry for CEOs: An interview with Paul Polman and Andrew Winston, Forbes, February 1, 2022. www.forbes.com/sites/afdhelaziz/2022/02/01/net-positive-is-the-new-rallying-cry-for-ceos-an-interview-with-paul-polman--andrew-winston/?sh=142ad15e1946 (archived at https://perma.cc/V3B2-AY2V)

3   P. Polman, and A. Winston (2021) *Net Positive: How courageous companies thrive by giving more than they take*, Harvard Business Review Press, Cambridge, MA

4   B. Reed. Paul Polman: "The power is in the hands of the consumers", *Guardian*, November 21, 2011. www.theguardian.com/sustainable-business/unilever-ceo-paul-polman-interview (archived at https://perma.cc/4EHH-DENK)

5   Unilever. Unilever celebrates 10 years of the Sustainable Living Plan, May 6, 2020. www.unilever.com/news/press-and-media/press-releases/2020/unilever-celebrates-10-years-of-the-sustainable-living-plan/ (archived at https://perma.cc/F9PB-MP33)

6   P. Polman, and A. Winston (2021) *Net Positive: How courageous companies thrive by giving more than they take*, Harvard Business Review Press, Cambridge, MA

7   A. Topping, K. Lyons, and M. Weaver. Gillette #MeToo razors ad on 'toxic masculinity' gets praise—and abuse, *Guardian*, January 15, 2019. www.theguardian.com/world/2019/jan/15/gillette-metoo-ad-on-toxic-masculinity-cuts-deep-with-mens-rights-activists (archived at https://perma.cc/2YC8-YSGA)

8   G. Petras, and J. Borresen. Graphics timeline illustrates the length, bitterness of Disney–DeSantis dispute, USA Today, May 16, 2023. www.usatoday.com/in-depth/graphics/2023/05/16/graphics-timeline-illustrates-bitter-details-of-disney-desantis-dispute/11750086002/ (archived at https://perma.cc/KC44-8RAJ)

9   E. Bibi. Human rights campaign refuses money from Disney until meaningful action is taken to combat Florida's "Don't Say Gay or Trans" bill, Human Rights Campaign, March 9, 2022. www.hrc.org/press-releases/human-rights-campaign-refuses-money-from-disney-until-meaningful-action-is-taken-to-combat-floridas-dont-say-gay-or-trans-bill (archived at https://perma.cc/8R8Z-YPCM)

10 C. Cone. "Bringing humanity back to business": 10 insights from Paul Polman, Sustainable Brands, October 5, 2021. sustainablebrands.com/read/leadership/we-need-to-bring-humanity-back-to-business-10-insights-from-paul-polman (archived at https://perma.cc/PK8Q-F8XT)

11 Tentree. About. www.tentree.com/pages/about (archived at https://perma.cc/9PUJ-FWVL)

12 Warby Parker. Buy a pair, give a pair. www.warbyparker.com/buy-a-pair-give-a-pair

13 Charity Navigator. Tory Burch Foundation Inc, Charity Navigator, 2009. www.charitynavigator.org/ein/263660127 (archived at https://perma.cc/B8KL-U773)

14 Tory Burch Foundation (2024) Our Mission: Empowering Women Entrepreneurs, www.toryburchfoundation.org/about/ (archived at https://perma.cc/E6AD-QYGB)

15 L. Rodrigues. The sparks & honey Responsible Marketing Index [proprietary research], 2023

16 T. McKinnon. How Rihanna's Fenty brand is leading in diversity and inclusion, Indigo 9 Digital, October 31, 2023. www.indigo9digital.com/blog/fentydiversityinclusion (archived at https://perma.cc/E6SY-ATEK)

17 C. Lang. Broadening makeup's palette, *Time*, October 3, 2018. time.com/collection-post/5412503/fenty-beauty/ (archived at https://perma.cc/8Z2L-JY3U)

18 A. Tietjen. WWD Beauty Inc awards: Fenty Beauty wins Digital Innovator of the Year, WWD, December 13, 2018. wwd.com/beauty-industry-news/beauty-features/wwd-beauty-inc-awards-fenty-beauty-digital-innovator-of-the-year-1202926816/#! (archived at https://perma.cc/KC7H-M7M7)

19 A. Tietjen. WWD Beauty Inc awards: Fenty Beauty wins Digital Innovator of the Year, WWD, December 13, 2018. wwd.com/beauty-industry-news/beauty-features/wwd-beauty-inc-awards-fenty-beauty-digital-innovator-of-the-year-1202926816/#! (archived at https://perma.cc/5CTU-8RFQ)

20 Arab America. History (Channel) Television Network launches Arab American Heritage Month on History.Com website, March 23, 2022. www.arabamerica.com/history-channel-television-network-launches-arab-american-heritage-month-on-history-com-website/ (archived at https://perma.cc/2RGU-VCGJ)

21 A. Onion, M. Sullivan, M. Mullen, and C. Zapata. Arab immigration to the United States, History, March 26, 2024. www.history.com/topics/21st-century/arab-american-heritage-month (archived at https://perma.cc/K7XW-WW7U)

22 T. Kaplan. Todd Kaplan's post, LinkedIn, 2022. www.linkedin.com/posts/toddkaplan_diginday-pepsicoproud-pepsidigin-activity-6851576751827644416-oaT7/ (archived at https://perma.cc/ZHQ2-RSXC)

23 Tirade World. Black History Month: Puma x June Ambrose champions up and coming designer, August 23, 2023. www.tirade.world/newspaper/puma-x-june-ambrose-champions-up-and-coming-designers (archived at https://perma.cc/Q7R2-7DTX)

11

Earning Stakeholder Buy-In

If you ask any of my CMO and marketing exec clients what I consider the most overlooked, yet most critical aspect of marketing success, chances are they'll repeat back something I often say: selling the work *is* the work. This succinct yet profound statement encapsulates the fundamental truth at the heart of each and every piece of effective marketing there ever was, ever is, and ever will be—it can't get results if it doesn't get launched.

Within a responsible marketing context or otherwise, our work can only be as good as what actually goes to market. Of course, we all fundamentally know this to be true. What we're less conscious of is the extent to which our approach—our daily professional practices and the way we show up—determines whether our work sees the light of day as much as, if not even more than, the inherent merit of the work that we do.

So, what happens?

We control what we think we have the power to control. We obsess about establishing clear objectives. We craft thoughtful, defensible, consumer-centric strategies perfectly poised to achieve the goals those objectives set forth. We create roadmaps packed with tactics to which our strategies align. We tell ourselves that as long as we get these parts right, our stakeholders are sure to give the green light.

The unspoken truth is more complex. The green light depends on one other thing... our ability to earn collective stakeholder buy-in. And whether or not perceptions match reality, this ability becomes more and more elusive with increasing levels of perceived risk. To succeed at fueling the Triple Top-Line Flywheel to drive outsized commercial impact, responsible marketers like you are faced with the often-daunting task of managing outsized (and often irrational) levels of perceived risk. With an empathetic understanding of why this is the case and an actionable toolkit to help you breakthrough to buy-in, what we'll discuss in this chapter will take you beyond knowing what responsible marketing is to being fully ready to get responsible marketing done, while also becoming a more capable leader at large.

This is even more true in a responsible marketing context, since responsible marketing encompasses a commitment to ethical principles, transparency, and accountability in all aspects of marketing activities. In this context, selling the work isn't just about persuading stakeholders to invest in marketing initiatives; it's also about ensuring that those initiatives align with ethical standards, respect consumer rights, and contribute positively to society.

What Makes Earning Buy-In For Responsible Marketing So Hard?

I sincerely hope that I don't need to say this at this stage in the book, but in case someone still needs to hear it, I'll make it very plain. Your team's lack of diversity is negatively impacting stakeholder buy-in, and here is why. A lack of diversity significantly narrows the range of perspectives and experiences being represented in marketing strategies and campaigns. Without diverse voices at the table, those initiatives may fail to resonate with various target audiences. Stakeholders are questioning why your marketing efforts do not consider the diverse needs, preferences, and experiences of their intended audience. Campaigns developed by non-diverse teams may unintentionally include messaging, imagery, or cultural references that are insensitive or offensive to certain demographic groups. This can result in damage to the brand's reputation and loss of trust among consumers. Stakeholders are hesitant to support marketing initiatives that are perceived as tone-deaf or culturally insensitive.

Marketing campaigns developed without diverse representation often struggle to effectively target and communicate with diverse consumer segments. Without insights into the unique needs, preferences, and behaviors of various demographic groups, strategies may miss the mark and fail to drive engagement or conversion. Stakeholders want a positive ROI and they are not going to buy in if they have concerns about ineffective targeting and messaging.

You Worry About Ending Up on the "Cancel" List

If you fear cancel culture so will your stakeholders, and who wants to jump aboard a ship with an unconfident captain? It's irrefutable that there is a certain amount of risk involved with responsible marketing, especially in a culture where the most diversity-adverse people seem to have the loudest voices. I get it. You fear the potential backlash that being "cancelled" can have on your brand's reputation, financial stability, and overall success. Getting it wrong could mean a blow to your reputation as a responsible brand, driving a wedge of distrust between your brand and its loyal customers. And that's a scary thing. Even Dove has gotten it wrong before when they released a 2017 Facebook advertisement that showed a Black woman removing her shirt to reveal a white woman underneath. The brand was widely criticized for being racially insensitive and perpetuating racist stereotypes about cleanliness and beauty. Dove quickly apologized and pulled the ad, stating that it had missed the mark in representing diversity and inclusivity.

But here is the other side of the coin. You can also get cancelled for doing it right. In 2013, a popular breakfast cereal brand dealt with controversy over a television advertisement that featured an interracial family. While the commercial was generally well-received by the public, it also sparked a substantial backlash from critics who objected to the portrayal of an interracial family. Social media platforms were filled with complaints, racist sentiments, and calls for a boycott. In response, the company released a statement standing by the commercial and reaffirming its commitment to diversity and inclusion, stating that it reflects the reality of modern families in America. It also disabled the comments section on the advertisement's YouTube video due to the overwhelming number of offensive and inappropriate comments. However, the advertisement continued to air on television. Brand leaders had a choice to make. They could either cave into the objections or move ahead, fully committed to the social impact goals behind their decision.

RESPONSIBLE REFRAME

Conversation isn't cancellation. During a recent presentation at the annual Sustainable Brands "Brand-Led Culture Change" conference, I asked the audience to raise their hands if they could think of a single company that had ever actually been "canceled" to the point of no longer existing.

None were raised—because being canceled is a made-up notion concocted to protect the status quo and those in power from uncomfortable yet necessary/normal things like critique and accountability.

Think about it! The fear of being canceled doesn't serve the advancement of society, consumers, or brands... it only aids in enabling silence that sets us all back.

What if brands considered it an honor to be called for conversation instead of fearing cancellation? After all, we spend our budgets on focus groups to hear negative feedback so it can be considered and addressed. When consumers come to us with their thoughts, why consider their time and effort anything else but a gift to be met with gratitude?

As Harvard Business School Professors David M. Bersoff, Sandra J. Sucher, and Peter Tufano advise, how companies respond to being called for conversation can be the difference maker between a costly controversy and a shift toward a historically-excluded community gaining much-needed validation and acceptance. Consider their analysis of two similar calls for conversation and their opposite commercial impacts.[1]

On April 1, 2023, transgender influencer Dylan Mulvaney promoted Bud Light on Instagram when he uploaded a sponsored post to Instagram. The immediate backlash boiled over with condemnation and vitriol, followed by calls for boycotts from social conservatives across the United States. Anheuser-Busch, the brand's parent, did not make any public statements until two weeks after the event, and even then, the company failed to directly mention the issue or defend Mulvaney. The controversy reportedly cost Bud Light about $395 million in U.S. sales.

Conversely, when Brazilian cosmetics giant Natura hired transgender actor Thammy Miranda to promote its Father's Day campaign in 2020, conservatives took to social media with words of hatred, demanding a company boycott. Without missing a single beat, Natura publicly stood by the decision, stating that there are many ways to be a man, free from stereotypes. It took only two days for the company's shares to increase, along with its social media followers.

Management Fears Distractions From Bottom-Line Priorities

Resistance to responsible marketing initiatives often stems from a short-term mindset that often permeates management teams. In today's fast-paced business environment, where quarterly results dictate decision-making, the immediate financial gains take precedence over the long-term benefits of investing in DEI. Some managers may view diversity efforts as costly and time-consuming endeavors without clear and immediate returns on investment, leading them to prioritize the brand initiatives they perceive as more directly tied to the bottom line. But this approach exemplifies a state of intentional ignorance to the business case for enhanced diversity. Despite the growing body of evidence demonstrating the positive impact of diversity on innovation, employee engagement, and overall business performance, some managers choose to remain unconvinced by these substantiated benefits. Without a regard for how responsible marketing initiatives drive organizational success, they default to prioritizing initiatives that appear more directly linked to financial outcomes.

I have also witnessed this resistance in response to unwanted change within an organization. Real diversity efforts require unapologetic challenges to existing power dynamics, norms, and practices. These are changes that the beneficiaries of these inequities do not want to see. They fear any disruption to the established hierarchies or resistance from shortsighted shareholders. So, they choose to uphold the status quo, perpetuate inequities, and hinder organizational progress, instead of advancing responsible marketing interests. Effective leadership requires the courage to drive meaningful change toward a more inclusive and equitable society for all.

REAL TALK WITH RESPONSIBLE MARKETERS
Lauren Kelly

Chief Commercial Officer at ThoughtExchange, Lauren is a transformational business executive with proven success launching innovative products and repositioning established businesses for sustainable growth.

Even For a Card-Carrying Pragmatist, the Triple top-Line Flywheel Has its Merits

In a world where we as marketers, or just plain business folks, are trying to manage and balance a lot of different things, making it easier for leaders to take affirmative steps, even if they are small, is something that I've thought a lot about. And while, of course, we want to keep our standards high and continue to aspire to something that maximizes all three of those goals, I also have observed that, in some cases, the higher we raise the bar, the more people opt out. And that's kind of where, from a ThoughtExchange perspective, we've spent a lot of time refining our purpose.

We've landed someplace that required a lot of internal conversation and debate because we have a really diverse workforce, many of whom came to ThoughtExchange because it has such a deep purpose. The work is purpose-driven, but in some cases we must be sure not to apply our own lens as to what is good purpose versus less good purpose. And so, we landed on an articulation to accelerate change for good through inclusive problem solving.

Equitable Decision-Making isn't Top-Down, it's All Around

The point of ThoughtExchange is not as a marketing output, but rather as the compass for the whole company around how we are achieving what we want to achieve in the world. And there are a couple of different components. One is, there are lots of different ways to solve the world's problems, and the world's problems can be massive, or they can be relatively small within your own organization.

We believe in, and we've seen evidence of, the successful outcomes that come when you leverage the wisdom of crowds, or, more technically, the collective intelligence. That differentiation allows you to bring in more perspectives and understand what's actually most important, not just those who are the loudest and most passionate about their perspectives. You can utilize these types of conversations, at scale, to first define the problem. Defining the problem to solve is super critical. And often you have to peel back and ask "Why?" a few times to discover, "OK, no, *this* is the actual problem we're trying to solve." And then you do so in an inclusive way that looks at the problem from all different angles and takes perspectives from all different angles.

When Everyone Gets to Weigh In, the End Result Will be a Win For Everyone

We have people with very different worldviews in our organization, so we spent a little bit of time identifying certain things that we would not support. But what I like about the purpose, and then clearly about our platform, is that chances are if you bring together a big enough, diverse enough set of people, they won't lead you in the wrong direction. For instance, we are not there to judge whether this might be the right way for an organization to pursue their sustainability goals, but we *do* know that if you ask enough stakeholders who are impacted by the outcome, and that could be your internal employees, your constituents, your community, you will likely not miss some major kind of unintended externalities or implications of your decisions. And chances are, if you involve all those folks, they won't collectively come up with a solution that massively disadvantages certain people over others.

Solving Society's Problems With Society's Input

The concept is that if you put it out there for society to solve, and you really let society work to solve the problem, then it will produce a positive kind of momentum and change for good. And that's where it's trying to recognize that any small change can be meaningful. If a lot of organizations make small changes to how they're operating, to how they're treating their people or to how they're caring for their communities, then that will be much more impactful than that very small number who are trying to create just within themselves some type of seismic shift.

That's part of what we've aligned on, at least internally. It's good for us, though, because definitions of problems really are also something that we spend a lot of our time thinking about. More often than not, we find that our organizations are not solving the right problem before they come to us. So they're not going to get to something that creates really positive change.

What Makes Earning Buy-In For Responsible Marketing Easier?

Responsible marketing encompasses a commitment to ethical principles, transparency, and accountability in all aspects of marketing activities. In this context, selling the work isn't just about persuading stakeholders to invest in marketing initiatives; it's also about ensuring that those initiatives align with ethical standards, respect consumer rights, and contribute positively to society. Responsible marketers understand that gaining buy-in from stakeholders requires more than just demonstrating financial ROI; it also involves demonstrating a commitment to ethical behavior, social responsibility, and environmental stewardship. It emphasizes the importance of building long-term relationships with customers based on trust, respect, and mutual benefit. When stakeholders resist responsible marketing goals, identifying the point of discomfort and finding a way around it is imperative. Brands must arrive at a place where stakeholders feel compelled to buy in.

Discover Your Inner Diplomat

While it may seem counterintuitive, nation-building across functions is the best foundation for successfully earning stakeholder buy-in. There's a reason why diplomats have immunity—it's because they play a role that is perceived as being steeped in goodwill, not personal interest. In essence, they embody the principles of collaboration, diplomacy, and mutual respect—qualities that are indispensable in building bridges and fostering understanding across diverse stakeholders. Just as nations comprise diverse populations with varying cultures, backgrounds, and interests, stakeholders consist of multifaceted demographics and interests. By fostering unity amidst this diversity, brands can harness the collective wisdom, perspectives, and strengths of their stakeholders to seize opportunities collaboratively.

Like those international diplomatic missions that seek to advance common goals, organizational building promotes alignment of interests among colleagues. By fostering a culture of shared vision and mutual respect, your inner diplomat can harmonize individual pursuits with collective objectives for greater cohesion and effectiveness in stakeholder engagement. Goodwill among peers cultivates a positive work environment characterized by openness, transparency, and mutual support, an atmosphere of goodwill that also extends to external stakeholders. That exchange of ideas and information enhances the decision-making processes and fosters consensus-building, two keys for securing stakeholder buy-in.

The Power of FOMO

The fear of missing out (FOMO) is a psychological phenomenon that has become increasingly prevalent in today's world of interconnection. I've witnessed firsthand the powerful impact that FOMO can have on internal and external stakeholder behavior, driving them to take action, make purchasing decisions, and engage in meaningful ways. A little envy can go a long way. Highlight the wins of companies that have made a significant social impact while also reaping the rewards of economic impact. Share data and case studies that demonstrate business growth, innovation, and profitability to encourage a sense of urgency among stakeholders who don't want to miss out on similar opportunities. Showcase the preference for responsible marketing among today's consumers and illustrate how those brands that put in the work are outperforming their competitors. Emphasize responsible marketing as not only a moral imperative but also a strategic business imperative. Outline the reputational damage that can accompany inaction and emphasize that internal stakeholders who fail to get on board may be left behind as the stakeholders who recognize the value of responsible marketing increasingly demand action.

FOMO among external stakeholders can be crafted through social validation, the theory that people are more likely to adopt behaviors or beliefs if they see others doing the same. Call attention to testimonials, positive results, and endorsements of responsible marketing initiatives to demonstrate its value. This social proof triggers FOMO. As stakeholders experience the fear of missing out on the benefits enjoyed by their peers, they become increasingly motivated to buy in to avoid being left behind. Our world is in a state of urgency, which escalates the sense of urgency around responsible marketing. Make it clear to stakeholders that time is of the essence, so immediate action is needed before it's too late.

Social media rules the world of FOMO and brands can take advantage by recruiting happy stakeholders and asking them to share their experiences on their social platforms to be seen by others. By creating valuable content or experiences that champion responsible marketing, brands can tap into that insatiable human desire for social validation and recognition. Stakeholders see others sharing their experiences with the brand, experience FOMO, and join in. There's an additional bonus to this strategy as well. It also creates a sense of community among stakeholders, an even more powerful driver of FOMO. Stakeholders want to feel a part of something larger than themselves and interactive communities meet that need.

Define Success on Their Terms

Inside a single organization, different leaders can define success according to different metrics. And when you are trying to secure a stakeholder buy in, the ability to tailor messages to fit the right definition is critical for success. For instance, a board member or chief finance operator is most concerned with financial performance. They want financial metrics and numbers, like revenue, profit, and return on investment. For stakeholders in this category, a success generates healthy profits, maintains positive cash flow, and delivers strong returns to shareholders.

Marketing professionals may gauge success based on a company's market share within its industry or market segment. A campaign that gains market share is viewed as potentially successful and worthy of a buy in. These organizational members may also consider the impact on brand reputation and perceived trustworthiness.

Human resources professionals may focus their concerns on employee satisfaction and engagement when making decisions. A successful business creates a positive work environment where employees feel valued, supported, and motivated to perform at their best. They may want to know how the proposed plan will help to maintain or improve organizational culture.

The bottom line is that success looks different for everyone. So, getting the buy in may require figuring out how that stakeholder views success and defining the idea in terms that are relevant to their interests.

Share the Spotlight

Sharing the spotlight is not only the right thing to do but also a strategic imperative for brands seeking to build trust, foster engagement, and create sustainable relationships with their stakeholders. First, it demonstrates humility and respect for the contributions and perspectives of all stakeholders. Power dynamics are shifting with diverse voices increasingly being heard, so brands cannot afford to operate in isolation. By acknowledging the expertise, experiences, and insights of others, it shows a value for collaboration and inclusive decision-making processes. Trust and credibility are foundational pillars of any successful brand. As such, stakeholders expect brands to be forthcoming and honest in all interactions. Sharing the spotlight demonstrates a commitment to honesty that leads to stronger relationships and increased buy-in.

Another valuable outcome of sharing the spotlight with stakeholders is the promotion of diversity and inclusion, critical variables for meeting the needs of today's diverse customer base. Involving stakeholders from different backgrounds, perspectives, and experiences ensures that a wide range of voices are represented and heard. This not only enriches the decision-making process but also helps brands to identify blind spots, anticipate challenges, and develop more innovative and inclusive solutions. By actively seeking out input from diverse stakeholders, brands can tap into the collective knowledge, skills, and experiences of their communities. This not only benefits the brand but also empowers stakeholders to play an active role in shaping the brand's future direction.

Sharing the spotlight also enhances engagement and ownership among stakeholders. When stakeholders feel valued and respected, they are more likely to actively engage with the brand, advocate on its behalf, and contribute to its long-term growth and sustainability. Empower stakeholders to take ownership of the brand's success and become champions of its mission and values.

Dispel the Myth of "the Cancel Culture"

I know social media makes brand stakeholders believe otherwise, but it's important to make them understand that "getting canceled" isn't a real thing. Now, bear with me while I explain. When a brand faces challenges, the response is crucial to the long-term outcome. Humility, empathy, and a commitment must be present for the brand to survive what may initially look like "being cancelled." The first step is acknowledgment and taking ownership of the misstep. It cannot be about making excuses or deflecting blame but rather about demonstrating accountability and a genuine desire to make amends.

Next, take concrete steps to rectify the situation and prevent similar incidents in the future. This may require the implementation of new policies and procedures, or diversity programs to ensure greater accountability and sensitivity to social and cultural issues. Stakeholders must believe that your brand is actively working to address the root causes of the problem, and the only way to communicate that is through engagement. Don't shy away from stakeholders when problems arise. Be open to feedback and dialogue. By listening to their concerns, demonstrating empathy, and seeking their input on how to move forward, your brand can rebuild trust and credibility while dispelling the myth of cancellation.

Lastly, always remember that actions speak louder than words, so brands must demonstrate their commitment to change through tangible initiatives. Implement necessary steps like diversity and inclusion efforts, community outreach programs, or partnerships with organizations working on related issues. Active pursuit of positive change shows stakeholders that your brand takes potential problems seriously.

Rebuilding a damaged reputation takes time and effort, so brands must focus on consistently delivering on their promises and providing exceptional products or services. By consistently upholding their values and delivering value to customers, brands can avoid being cancelled by rebuilding trust and credibility. Remember that every setback presents an opportunity for learning and growth, so use the experience of being cancelled as a chance to reflect and improve. Learn from mistakes and making meaningful changes,

In 2018, Starbucks faced a public relations crisis following an incident at one of its stores in Philadelphia where two African American men were wrongfully arrested for trespassing while simply waiting for a friend at the store.[2] The event sparked accusations of racial profiling and discrimination after going viral on social media, resulting in widespread calls for boycotts of Starbucks.

In response, Starbucks CEO Kevin Johnson issued a public apology and announced a series of measures to address racial bias and discrimination within the company, including mandatory unconscious bias training for all employees, changes to store procedures, and a commitment to fostering diversity and inclusion. The company also reached a monetary settlement with the two men involved in the incident. Starbucks' immediate and meaningful response to the situation helped the company to rebuild trust with customers while demonstrating a commitment to social responsibility and accountability.

Build From Your Brand's Enduring Identity

Establishing a strong and enduring brand identity is essential for gaining buy-in from stakeholders, including customers, employees, investors, and partners. However, the true value of a brand identity lies not only in its creation but also in its consistent reinforcement and alignment across all aspects of the organization. At the core of stakeholder buy-in is authenticity—the genuine alignment between a brand's actions, messaging, and values. Building from your brand's enduring identity ensures that every interaction with stakeholders reflects the true essence of your brand. When stakeholders perceive authenticity, they are more likely to trust and engage with your brand on a deeper level.

Maintaining stakeholder trust requires consistency. Your brand's enduring identity serves as a guiding compass, ensuring that all touchpoints—from marketing communications to product design to customer service—are aligned seamlessly. Consistency reinforces your brand's promise and values, making it easier for stakeholders to recognize and connect across different channels and experiences. Without the differentiation that comes with a standout identity, your brand will not stand out in the crowded marketplace. It is what defines your unique value proposition, making your brand distinct and relevant to stakeholders. Whether it's a commitment to sustainability, a focus on social justice, or your dedication to policy influence, an enduring identity gives you a competitive advantage that resonates with stakeholders.

Beyond rational decision-making, even the most stoic stakeholders are influenced by emotions. Building from your brand's enduring identity allows you to tap into the emotional drivers that foster deeper connections with stakeholders. When stakeholders feel aligned with your brand's values and purpose, they develop a sense of belonging and loyalty that goes beyond transactional relationships. That is where the door to long-term engagement opens. On the other side, you will find advocacy and repeat business from customers, as well as commitment and support from employees, investors, and partners. Your brand's enduring identity provides a solid foundation for nurturing these relationships over time. By consistently delivering on your promise and maintaining alignment with your core values, you demonstrate reliability and integrity, earning the loyalty and support of stakeholders through thick and thin.

Remember, it's inevitable that your brand will face unforeseen challenges at some time, such as crises, disruptions, or changes in the market landscape. But a strong and enduring brand identity acts as a source of resilience during these times of uncertainty. When stakeholders have a clear understanding of your brand's values and purpose, they are more likely to stand by you, offering support, understanding, and even forgiveness when needed. An enduring brand identity symbolizes stability and reassurance, guiding stakeholders through turbulent waters and helping your brand emerge stronger on the other side.

RESPONSIBLE RECAP

- Creating real opportunity starts with a deep and genuine understanding of community needs.

- Identify and create opportunities that are both brand-relevant and positioned for regenerative impact.

- Consistent commitment to opportunity creation earns consumer trust, leading to repeat business and powerful word-of-mouth referrals.

- Avoid cultural appropriation and content colonization, advocating for genuine engagement and compensation for original creators.

- Address internal resistance by fostering an abundance mindset, emphasizing education and cross-departmental collaboration.

- Focus on everyday behaviors to signal and spread a commitment to creating opportunity with responsible marketing.

Notes

1 D. M. Bersoff, S. J. Sucher, and P. Tufano. How companies should weigh in on a controversy, Harvard Business Review, March–April 2024. hbr.org/2024/03/how-companies-should-weigh-in-on-a-controversy (archived at https://perma.cc/EJ42-MA7A)

2 T. Relihan. What Starbucks got wrong—and right—after Philadelphia arrests, MIT Management Sloan School, May 18, 2018. mitsloan.mit.edu/ideas-made-to-matter/what-starbucks-got-wrong-and-right-after-philadelphia-arrests (archived at https://perma.cc/WMX7-QRXM)

12

Getting It Wrong the Right Way

It's always amusing how surprised people are to learn that I love getting feedback. Perhaps it's that first-gen growth mindset we've talked about. After all, Nigerian mothers everywhere are known for their quickness to give a note and mine is no exception. Beyond being taught to welcome feedback, I think it also has to do with the thing that's always brought me the most joy, adventure, inspiration and discovery. I might be known as someone who is ferociously opinionated, but what's even more of a defining characteristic is my endless desire to learn. At the boarding school where I spent my high school years, this was described as a "zest for knowledge." If you've got a zest for knowledge and a passion for learning, what could be better than the opportunity to learn about the person who matters to you most? If you think about it, the moments you spend receiving feedback are some of the most intimate learning opportunities you'll ever experience— even more so when it comes from someone you respect, and more than that when it comes from someone you admire. Receiving feedback from someone you truly love? There's no more intimate learning experience than that.

Consumer Intimacy

So, what happens when we extend this thought process to the loves of a brand's life, the people who a brand exists to deeply understand and distinctively serve? You'd think there wouldn't be a brand leader who wouldn't see it as the greatest honor to be gifted an intimate learning experience from the consumers that matter most to the brand in their charge. You'd think such an intimate learning experience would be welcomed with open arms, celebrated even. It would make perfect sense, right? So why then is it so seldom the case? Even worse, why are such precious moments of consumer intimacy so often met with arms crossed? Why is it that not only is consumer intimacy not welcomed with open arms, but it is met with arms crossed, brows furrowed, a mouth full of choice words, and a petulant, forlorn frowny face?

When the Tarte Cosmetics brand was reportedly confronted with some unexpected feedback from one of their Black content creators, what happened next could have easily made things right, but ended up taking a turn that could be considered surprisingly wrong.[1]

According to the influencer who shared this feedback, one of the brand's lavish luxury excursions left her in tears upon learning that she received a smaller room and a shorter stay than her fellow content creators.

While curling her hair and applying makeup, the brand's CEO spoke up about the reported unfair treatment during a TikTok "Get Ready With Me" post. Centering the experience from her own vantage point, she effusively and emotionally denied any wrongdoing, insisting that the company had not and would never treat content creators differently based on ethnicity or background. There was no apology or mention of the influencer by name. There was, however, what some considered a defensive reaction that attempted to change the narrative about who had actually been victimized and why.

Given the imbalance in power dynamics between Tarte's CEO and the company's hired influencer, this response was unsurprisingly and immediately met with backlash. Past claims of racial injustice surfaced. A lack of inclusive product offerings, including its range of foundation shades, was pointed to as further justification the influencer's treatment was intentionally wrong. Then, the right thing happened. A formal apology and statement addressing DEI shortcomings with humility and transparency were shared, and the process of reconciliation had belatedly begun. This left me with a burning question. When a different response could have easily led to a more positive outcome, why didn't the company respond more effectively in the first place? A better path seemed obvious to me, yet the story was one in a long line of many that risked a brand's reputation by succumbing to corporate fragility. There is indeed a better way, and it doesn't have to be hard. By practicing responsible marketing instead, meeting these moments more effectively can easily happen in the first place. By embracing the growth mindset that creates all outsized marketing success, every brand leader can harness the positive societal, reputational, and commercial impact that awaits when we shift from a posture of corporate fragility to corporate humility. While our base human nature guarantees we will at some point get it wrong, we can leverage the very same human nature to get it wrong in the right way—to the benefit of all of our stakeholders and, perhaps even more importantly, our internal sense of career satisfaction and long-term professional success.

Corporate Fragility

For many brands, corporate fragility is the Achilles' heel that prevents them from admitting wrongdoing or accepting criticism, even at the expense of their own credibility and integrity. Instead of embracing feedback as an opportunity for growth, fragile organizations recoil from criticism, opting to deflect blame or bury their heads in the sand. This defensive posture stems from the misguided belief that admitting fault is a sign of weakness rather than brand strength.

One of the most glaring manifestations of corporate fragility is the phenomenon of "brand ego." In an age where image is everything, brands often become overly protective of their reputations, viewing any hint of criticism as a direct threat. This defensive stance can lead to a culture of denial, where inconvenient truths are swept under the rug in the name of preserving brand image. But anything that is fragile is likely to break. Companies need the ability to bend and be malleable when facing criticism. If they can't, they will also lack the ability to be responsive.

Most importantly, corporate fragility can create a toxic culture of silence within organizations, where employees are discouraged from speaking up or raising concerns for fear of reprisal. This lack of transparency and accountability stifles innovation, hampers collaboration, and erodes trust between employees and leadership.

But here's the kicker—corporate fragility doesn't just harm internal dynamics; it also has profound implications for consumer trust and loyalty. In an age of unprecedented connectivity and transparency, consumers expect brands to be honest, authentic, and accountable for their actions. When brands fail to meet these expectations, they risk alienating consumers and damaging their reputation irreparably.

So, how can organizations break free from the shackles of corporate fragility and embrace a culture of accountability and transparency? It starts with leadership—leaders must lead by example, demonstrating humility, integrity, and a willingness to admit when they've made a mistake. Organizations must also foster a culture of psychological safety, where employees feel empowered to speak up, ask questions, and challenge the status quo without fear of reprisal.

Open and honest communication with consumers is a must. Transparency builds trust, and trust is the currency of the modern marketplace. Brands that cling to a defensive posture, refusing to acknowledge wrongdoing or accept criticism, do so at their own peril.

It's All About What Happens Next

The premise of this chapter is exceedingly simple, but that doesn't make it easy to master. In any endeavor, and especially in the practice of responsible marketing, it's more than OK to get things wrong. The ever-accelerating evolution of the way we live and what we value makes it impossible for anyone creating content for mass consumption to get it right every time. While we can't always control the extent to which the impact of our work matches its intention, what we can always control is how we react when we're made aware that something has gone awry. We can't always control what happens, but we can control what happens next.

Suspense, Defense, or Repentance?

This one applies to each of us as much as it applies to the brands we steward. In every successful example of getting it wrong the right way we'll discuss in this chapter, getting it wrong the right way always starts with avoiding suspense, skipping the defense, and seeking repentance.

In June 2021, a popular Broadway composer became the target of a controversy that emerged around the release of the film adaptation of his Broadway musical.[2] Critics and viewers raised concerns about the lack of dark-skinned Afro-Latinx actors in leading roles, highlighting an issue of colorism within the casting choices. The movie, set in the predominantly Dominican neighborhood of Washington Heights in New York City, was expected to reflect the community's diverse racial backgrounds.

In response, the composer quickly addressed the criticism on social media, acknowledging the concerns raised about colorism in the film's casting. He expressed regret for the pain the film's casting choices caused and recognized the missed opportunity to represent the Afro-Latinx community in a more inclusive manner. His statement did not attempt to deflect blame or minimize the concerns raised, which is a mistake that many brands make when faced with criticism.

The composer also made a commitment to learning from the criticism and doing better in the future. This promise to acknowledge and address issues of representation and inclusivity in his work signaled a proactive approach to change, rather than a reactive or defensive stance. He then continued engaging by having open and honest discussions on representation and his support for diverse storytelling in the arts suggested a long-term commitment to addressing these issues.

Not delaying a response demonstrated a willingness to listen and engage with the community's feedback. His apology was seen as sincere, which helped mitigate some of the backlash and demonstrated a model for how individuals and brands can constructively respond to criticism and calls for greater inclusivity. This composer initially got it wrong, but he addressed the problem in the absolute right way.

HOW TO AVOID A FAUXPOLOGY

1   Recognition: Do you know what you did wrong? It's important to say "I'm sorry," but an apology is meaningless if you don't know or recognize what it is you're apologizing for.

2   Remorse: Do you feel bad about what you did? If/when you know what you did, it's important to have an emotional sense of culpability for the apology to make a difference.

3   Repair: What are you going to do differently moving forward? It's not sufficient to have just recognition and remorse; it's also vital to express your intentions (and follow through) for how you plan to make changes in the future so the issue or crisis does not happen again.[3]

SOURCE Robert Livingston, Harvard social psychologist and author, *The Conversation*.[4]

Listening to Learn

Today's marketing game is all about listening, learning, and, most importantly, engaging. I know that may sound easier said than done, but most brands already have the listening systems in place. They just aren't actually listening. Let's make this easy. Start with social media. That buzzing hive of activity where consumers chatter, vent, praise, and sometimes even rant about your brand is not just a platform for broadcasting your latest promo. It is also a goldmine of insights waiting to be unearthed. By taking the time to scroll through those comments and reply to those messages, brands can show their consumers that they are not just there to talk—they are there to listen.

Social media gives brands a two-way street, a digital conversation where every comment, like, and share is an opportunity to forge a deeper connection with your audience. So, brands should not be afraid to wade into the fray and engage in meaningful dialogue with consumers. Whether it's addressing a complaint, thanking someone for their support, or simply sharing a laugh, every interaction is a chance to show your consumers that their voices matter.

Data analytics are also powerful listening tools for brands that pay attention. Those numbers reveal trends and the hidden gems buried within. Consumers leave breadcrumbs everywhere they go—from their browsing history to their purchase patterns. It's up to the brand to piece together the puzzle and tailor offerings accordingly. Because let's be real, nothing says "We're listening" quite like serving up exactly what consumers want, even before they know they want it.

Let's talk feedback, and not those generic surveys that gather dust in your inbox. I'm talking about real, meaningful conversations with consumers. Open up those lines of communication, invite them to share their thoughts, their ideas, their dreams. And here's the kicker—actually listen to what they have to say. It's not about nodding along and then carrying on with business as usual. It's about taking their feedback on board, incorporating it into the brand strategy, and showing them that their voices matter.

I dedicated an entire chapter to storytelling for a reason. Consumers aren't just numbers on a spreadsheet; they're real people with real stories to tell. So, give them a platform to share those stories. User-generated content, testimonials, case studies—the possibilities are endless. Let their voices be heard, let their experiences be shared, and watch as your brand comes alive in ways you never thought possible.

Take note. The key to success in today's consumer-driven world isn't about shouting the loudest or flashing the brightest. It's about listening, learning, and engaging.

Salesforce took listening to the next level with its Idea Exchange platform.[5] Customers can post new ideas for product features and those ideas are voted on by other Salesforce customers. Once an idea reaches 250 votes or 2,500 points, the Product Development Team reviews it for implementation.[6] This initiative screams active listening in so many ways. Not only is Salesforce collecting feedback and using it in decision-making, but it is also making customers feel valued and heard by involving them directly in the product development process and creating features that directly serve their needs.

We Were Wrong (Just Say It!)

Transparency is like a breath of fresh air in a world full of smoke and mirrors. When brands open up about their inner workings—their processes, values, and even their missteps—it's like they're saying, "Hey, we're not perfect, but we're real." And let me tell you, authenticity like that? It's like catnip for consumers. They can smell the real deal from a mile away, and when they find it, they are all in.

Consumers crave something with substance, something with heart—and when they find a brand that's willing to let down its guard and show the real deal, they are all in. That kind of respect goes a long way in building trust. Because in a world where skepticism runs rampant and trust is hard to come by, finding a brand that's willing to be vulnerable, to admit when they've made a mistake and learn from it, is like striking gold.

E-commerce platform Groupon found a way to turn their apology into an outreach of social responsibility after facing accusations of discrimination in their hiring practices.[7] After reaching an agreement with the United States Equal Employment Opportunity Commission, the corporation established a \$350,000 fund to support Black students in science, technology, engineering, and mathematics.

Own Not Having it all Figured Out

Brands that engage in virtue signaling essentially put on a show. They want to flaunt their moral superiority for all to see, making a big fuss about their supposed values and beliefs, but without any real substance behind it. It's all about looking good, rather than actually doing good, and it is a huge turnoff for consumers. In today's dynamic business landscape, authenticity reigns supreme. Consumers crave genuine connections with brands that embody sincerity and transparency. Humility serves as the cornerstone of authenticity, allowing brands to showcase vulnerability and integrity. It's about more than just admitting mistakes and shortcomings; it's demonstrating a willingness to be open and honest with stakeholders.

Being "self-aware" is not enough, especially when your brand is part of the problem. That is where the value of humility really lies. It allows brands to acknowledge their mistakes and move forward to influence policy change in an authentic way. Vulnerability can go a long way in humanizing a brand, making it more relatable and trustworthy to consumers. It encourages empathy and understanding. By humbly engaging with their audience, brands can gain valuable insights into their needs, preferences, and concerns. This empathetic approach enables brands to create marketing campaigns that resonate on a deeper level with their target audience, leading to stronger brand–consumer relationships.

Most importantly, humility demonstrates respect for the intelligence and dignity of a brand's audience. It acknowledges that consumers are discerning individuals with their own unique perspectives and experiences. By approaching marketing initiatives with humility, brands show a genuine appreciation for their audience's perspectives and feedback. Rather than diminishing the brand's value or expertise, this marketing approach fosters a culture of openness, authenticity, and mutual respect. Brands that embrace humility in their marketing efforts are better positioned to build long-term loyalty and advocacy among consumers.

Airbnb gave us a playbook on marketing with humility when addressing allegations of discrimination by Airbnb hosts. Instead of trying to "virtue signal" their way out of it, the company acknowledged the flaws in their booking services that allowed for biased behaviors. In 2018, they modified their policy on requiring renter profile photos. They also added a nondiscrimination clause to their Airbnb Community Commitment. In 2020, the company launched Project Lighthouse, an initiative focused on understanding and combating racial discrimination on their platform, and through its We Accept campaign Airbnb promotes inclusivity and acceptance by featuring stories of hosts welcoming guests from diverse backgrounds.[8] They have also been consistent in their transparency, providing periodic updates on the status of their initiatives. The success of Airbnb's campaign underlines the importance that humility plays for brands as they seek to maintain connections with the public.

How Transparency Breeds Trust

Transparency is a brand's best friend. Gone are the days of hiding behind closed doors and smokescreens. Today's consumers crave authenticity, they crave honesty, they crave transparency. So, open up those doors, pull back those curtains, and invite your consumers in. Show them the real faces behind the brand, the real stories behind the products. Because when they see the humans behind the logo, they'll feel a connection like never before.

But transparency isn't just about being honest; it's about being accountable too. When brands lay it all out there for the world to see, they're inviting scrutiny—and that's a good thing. It keeps them on their toes, making sure they're walking the walk, not just talking the talk. And when consumers see that a brand is willing to own up to its mistakes and learn from them, well, that's when the trust really starts to build.

Now, let's talk about empowerment. Transparency hands the keys to consumers and says, "You're in charge now." When brands are upfront about their practices and policies, it empowers consumers to make informed choices about what they buy and who they support. And let me tell you, there's nothing more empowering than knowing you're voting with your dollars for a brand that shares your values.

Which leads right into loyalty. When brands are transparent about what they stand for and how they operate, it creates a bond with consumers that goes beyond just transactions. It's like having a friend you can trust—you're going to stick with them through thick and thin because you know they've got your back. And when consumers feel that kind of loyalty, they become your biggest cheerleaders, spreading the word far and wide.

Last but not least, transparency drives innovation. When brands invite feedback and listen to their consumers, it's like opening up a treasure chest of ideas and insights. Consumers know what they want, and when brands are willing to listen and adapt, everybody wins. It's a recipe for constant improvement and growth, and consumers can't help but respect and trust a brand that's always striving to be better.

Transparency isn't just a buzzword; it's the secret sauce that turns consumers into brand advocates. So here's to keeping it real, staying accountable, empowering consumers, building loyalty, and driving innovation—all in the name of trust.

Humility Over Hubris

In 1982, Johnson & Johnson faced one of the most notorious public relations crises in corporate history after seven people died after consuming cyanide-laced Tylenol capsules.[9] This incident posed a significant threat to public health and tested the company's crisis management and corporate responsibility practices. The company's handling of the crisis set a benchmark for effective crisis management and corporate transparency.

The tampered capsules were part of several lots distributed in the Chicago area, sparking fear and panic among consumers nationwide. In the immediate aftermath, Johnson & Johnson faced a monumental challenge in addressing the crisis and restoring public trust in its most popular product.

Within hours of learning about the tampering incidents, the company took the extraordinary step of issuing a nationwide recall of all Tylenol products, encompassing more than 30 million bottles to a cost of an estimated $100 million. While financially costly, Johnson & Johnson was celebrated for demonstrating a commitment to prioritizing consumer safety over profits.[10]

James Burke, the company's CEO at the time, took an unprecedented approach to crisis communication by agreeing to media interviews and issuing public statements to provide updates on the investigation.

Johnson & Johnson also cooperated fully with law enforcement agencies and regulatory authorities, including the Federal Bureau of Investigation and the Food and Drug Administration, to investigate the tampering incidents and identify those responsible.

In the months following the crisis, Johnson & Johnson worked tirelessly to rebuild trust with consumers and restore the reputation of the Tylenol brand. They introduced new tamper-evident packaging that included tamper-resistant seals to reassure consumers about safety. The company also launched an extensive advertising and public relations campaign to showcase their quality control measures and commitment to integrity.

Johnson & Johnson's handling of the Tylenol crisis became a textbook example of effective crisis management and corporate responsibility. Their swift response, transparency, and commitment to consumer safety set a new standard for corporate behavior in times of crisis. By prioritizing consumer safety, transparency, and accountability, Johnson & Johnson navigated the crisis successfully and set a benchmark for corporate responsibility that continues to inspire companies worldwide.

Anticipating Objections

Anticipating objections to responsible marketing campaigns isn't just a smart move—it's a strategic imperative. Brands can't afford to ignore the concerns and reservations that our customers may have.

By proactively identifying potential objections, they can tailor their messaging to resonate more deeply with their audiences and show them that they are not just there to sell a product or service but to solve a problem and improve people's lives.

Brands can't afford to wait for problems to rear their heads before acting. Instead, they must be proactive, constantly scanning the horizon for potential threats and taking decisive action to address them before they escalate. Brand leaders need to be attuned to the pulse of customers, whether it's through direct feedback, social media chatter, or market research. By understanding their concerns and expectations, brands can better nip issues in the bud.

But defense isn't the only way to play. By anticipating objections early, brands can offensively seize opportunities to push boundaries and shape the conversation. It's about preparing for the worst while hoping for the best, knowing that no matter what challenges come, your brand has the foresight, the fortitude, and the flexibility to weather the storm and emerge stronger on the other side.

The Customer *isn't* Always Right

We've all heard it, "The customer is always right." But while prioritizing customer satisfaction is crucial, there are situations where the customer's expectations or demands may not align with the brand's best interests or those of society at large. Businesses operate within certain parameters, whether it's policies, procedures, or ethical standards, and sometimes a customer's stance simply falls outside these boundaries. Furthermore, brands have a responsibility to shape the world into what it could and should be, not pander to the status quo of the day.

And let's not forget about brand reputation. Accommodating every customer's whim—especially the voices of the loud minority who might be invested in upholding the systemic inequities that most of us know do harm to us all—ultimately damages a brand's credibility, integrity, and continued cultural relevance—the trifecta that we see lead to many an industry leader's eventual extinction.

In the quest to satisfy every customer, brands may inadvertently create an environment where certain customers receive preferential treatment over others. When one customer's demands, no matter how unreasonable, are consistently met, it can create perceptions of favoritism among other customers, leading to feelings of frustration and disillusionment among those who perceive themselves as being treated unfairly.

There are also financial implications to consider. Marketing campaigns don't come cheaply, and changing directions can be extremely costly, potentially affecting the brand's ability to invest in customer experiences that benefit all customers in the long run.

Brands must strike a balance between meeting customer needs and upholding the values and integrity of the brand. That requires careful evaluation of customer complaints and critiques. By maintaining transparency, consistency, and fairness in their interactions with customers, brands can preserve trust, loyalty, and goodwill among their customer base while safeguarding their own credibility and integrity in the marketplace.

Sainsbury's is the second largest chain of supermarkets in the United Kingdom. In 2020, it released a series of Christmas ads, one of which featured a Black family preparing for a holiday.[11] Though the ad was intended to celebrate the diversity of families in the UK, some viewers objected to the placement of a Black family in the campaign. They took to social media to voice their disapproval and called for a boycott. The backlash was widely condemned by customers who appreciated Sainsbury's inclusive portrayal of British families.

Sainsbury's issued a statement defending its campaign, stating that it aimed to be "the most inclusive retailer" and that the company was proud of the representation in its advertisements. The statement emphasized the company's commitment to celebrating diversity and insisted that the ads represented a modern, more diverse Britain.

The controversy highlighted broader issues of racism and representation in media and advertising in the UK. It also sparked widespread support for Sainsbury's from the public. Other organizations praised the company's inclusive messaging in the face of backlash. Sainsbury's customers that called for boycotts were wrong in their stance, but instead of bowing to their demands, the supermarket stood by its commitment to responsible marketing.

Consistent Brand Values, Evolving Interpretations

Consistent brand values provide a solid foundation for building trust and credibility with consumers. However, as interpretations of those values evolve, brands must remain vigilant and adaptable, finding ways to stay true to their core principles while also remaining relevant and responsive to shifting consumer preferences. By striking this balance, brands can ensure that they continue to resonate with consumers and thrive in an ever-changing marketplace. The connection between the *Rolling Stone* scandal and the Rock & Roll Hall of Fame standards offers a perfect example.

Rolling Stone, the iconic music magazine, found itself in hot water when allegations of serious misconduct came to light, including reports of sexual harassment, discrimination, and abuses of power within the magazine's inner circles. For years, the Rock and Roll Hall of Fame had leaned heavily on *Rolling Stone*'s recommendations when it came to nominations and inductions. But with *Rolling Stone*'s credibility called into question, the Hall of Fame had to rethink its entire approach.

As a result, they introduced a series of major changes aimed at making the nomination and induction process more transparent, accountable, and inclusive.[12] A big part of the change involved setting up an independent committee to review nominations, ensuring a fair shake for artists of all stripes. The Hall of Fame also brought fans and industry insiders into the decision-making process by opening up the nominations to public input through online surveys and forums. This savvy move democratized the process and broke down barriers that had locked many artists out.

Finally, the Hall of Fame placed a renewed focus on artistic merit, cultural impact, and historical significance. They cast a wider net, making sure to shine a spotlight on the unsung heroes and underrepresented voices that had been overlooked in the past.

Now, did the scandal tarnish *Rolling Stone*'s reputation? Absolutely. But it also sparked a much-needed conversation about diversity, integrity, and accountability in the music industry. A crisis became an opportunity for evolved interpretations.

Brands are challenged in establishing consistent values and adapting to evolving interpretations of those values. While a brand's core values may remain steadfast over time, the ways in which they are perceived and interpreted by consumers can shift in response to changing societal norms, cultural trends, and market dynamics. But at the heart of every successful brand is a set of core values that define its identity, mission, and purpose. Though the interpretation may change, these values must remain at the foundation.

REAL TALK WITH RESPONSIBLE MARKETERS
Joan Ball

Joan Ball is an author and marketing professor. In her book Stop, Ask, Explore, *Joan Ball outlines a framework for decision-making and problem-solving that elegantly lends itself to empowering brand leaders looking to get it wrong the right way.*[13]

If organizational leaders take a step back from the noise and chaos of the moment, they can gain a fresh perspective on the situation at hand before moving forward with a strategy, avoiding the perils of becoming so focused on proving themselves right that they fails to truly hear what customers have to say.

Next up is asking the questions that unlock deeper insights and expand our understanding. When brands ask questions, they demonstrate humility and a genuine desire to learn that customers appreciate. It demonstrates an appreciation for knowledge and the humility to admit that there is more to learn.

But asking isn't just about seeking answers—it's also about sparking dialogue by creating a safe and inclusive space for shared thoughts and ideas.

Now it's time to explore what has been learned, dive into the depths of possibility, and push beyond the boundaries of what we know. Brands that dare to venture into uncharted territory allow themselves to think outside the box and experiment with new ideas, which fuels innovation and growth and strengthens adaptability in the face of change. Consider Professor Ball's three key change myths as you stop, ask, and explore to embark on becoming a more responsible marketer:

Change Myth #1: Change and uncertainty are scary.

"From the moment you open your eyes in the morning until the moment you close them again at night, you are constantly changing and adapting in uncertain situations. The vast majority of these changes come so easily that you don't even register them in your conscious mind. The changes and transitions that register as scary are the ones we perceive as a threat to ourselves or others, which means it's the threat, not the change, that prompts fear and discomfort."

Change Myth #2: Some changes are good, and others are bad.

"We all react differently to change, depending upon who we are and the context in which we find ourselves. A change that one person might perceive to be threatening is someone else's adventure. While we may be more vulnerable to viewing certain kinds of changes as difficult or threatening, to characterize change as good or bad outside of its context can be unhelpful and limiting."

Change Myth #3: I can't deal with uncertainty, so I'm not good at change.

"If you have stepped into a car, onto a bus, or crossed a street, you have proved you can deal with uncertainty and change. Human beings are built for change and adaptation. We are born for it and spend our lives doing it. Learning to apply those fundamental skills to other situations—even threatening ones—is possible with attention, resources, and practice. These myths point to the critical role that context plays in our perception of change and whether or not we view it as a threat."

Humanity First

It's easy for brands to get caught up in the bottom line. But prioritizing humanity is not just a moral imperative—it's also a smart business strategy. At the heart of every successful brand is a genuine connection with its audience. People don't just buy products or services—they buy into your stories, values, and experiences on a human level. The world is increasingly diverse and interconnected, which makes empathy and understanding more important than ever. The brands that prioritize humanity demonstrate a genuine concern for the wellbeing and needs of their customers, employees, and communities. Consumers recognize the effort made to listen, learn, and respond with compassion, empathy, and respect. This strengthens relationships and builds a positive reputation and goodwill that can withstand challenges and setbacks.

As influential entities in society, brands have a unique opportunity—and obligation—to positively impact the world. By prioritizing humanity, brands can align their values and actions with larger social and environmental goals, such as sustainability, diversity, and inclusion. This benefits society as a whole, enhances brand reputation, attracts socially conscious consumers, and drives long-term business success.

It is important to remember that a brand's humanity is not only measured by its outreach. It is also demonstrated in the way it treats its people. Prioritizing humanity means understanding the importance of investing in the wellbeing and development of employees. These brands create inclusive and supportive work environments where individuals feel valued, empowered, and motivated to do their best work.

Brands that prioritize humanity are ultimately investing in their own long-term value and sustainability. By building meaningful connections, fostering trust, and positively impacting society, these brands create a strong foundation for enduring success. They recognize that true value lies not just in short-term profits but in lasting relationships and a legacy of positive impact that extends far beyond the balance sheet.

Prioritizing humanity is much more than just the right thing to do—it's also the right business thing to do. Brands that place a premium on authentic connections and social responsibility are better positioned to thrive.

RESPONSIBLE RECAP

- Corporate fragility never pays off. Recoiling from criticism and maintaining an unwavering stance undermines consumer trust and can damage a brand's reputation long-term.

- Make the most of mistakes with open acknowledgment. While missteps are inevitable on every brand's responsible marketing journey, candor can become a powerful competitive advantage when brand leaders avoid ego getting in the way. Humility signals strength, not weakness.

- Conversation isn't cancellation. Active listening is an art that demands a brand's full engagement and the freedom from unnecessarily prohibitive fear. In the face of critiques, a simple "thank you" conveys that a brand values all feedback, not just praise.

- De-escalate negativity by authentically fostering community. Brands brave enough to amplify dissenting voices reap the rewards of more real and substantial relationships with their consumers.

- Brand evolution doesn't require a revolution. A consistent brand identity can bend without breaking by being flexible enough to embrace new interpretations and adapt to changing times without abandoning its core essence.

Notes

1   S. McCord. Bria Jones, Tarte, and how negligent influencer marketing can end your brand, Sara McCord Communications, 2023. www.saramccord.com/blog/bria-jones-tarte-miami-trip (archived at https://perma.cc/ZDH4-5GEM)

2 M. Garcia, S. E. Garcia, I. Herrera, C. de León, M. Phillips, and A. O. Scott. "In the Heights" and colorism: What is lost when Afro-Latinos are erased, *The New York Times*, June 21, 2021. www.nytimes.com/2021/06/21/movies/in-the-heights-colorism.html (archived at https://perma.cc/MP8T-EQCE)

3 R. Livingston. Robert Livingstone's post, LinkedIn, May 18, 2024. www.linkedin.com/posts/robertwlivingston_socialpsychology-antiracism-leadership-activity-7196494581004206081-2YZy (archived at https://perma.cc/5PDF-R252)

4 R. Livingston (2021) *The Conversation: How seeking and speaking the truth about racism can radically transform individuals and organizations*, Currency, Sydney

5 Idea Exchange. Idea Exchange, 2023. ideas.salesforce.com/s/search (archived at https://perma.cc/3LV5-4JGU)

6 S. Dubey. How top 15 brands use customer feedback effectively, May 10, 2024. qualaroo.com/blog/the-best-ways-big-companies-use-customer-feedback/ (archived at https://perma.cc/AUB9-7H42)

7 S. Keenan. Groupon commits $350k to Black STEM students as it settles race discrimination investigation, People of Color in Tech, January 2, 2024. peopleofcolorintech.com/articles/groupon-commits-350k-to-black-stem-students-as-it-settles-race-discrimination-investigation/ (archived at https://perma.cc/5QHJ-Y7JJ)

8 Airbnb. A six-year update on Airbnb's work to fight discrimination, December 13, 2022. news.airbnb.com/sixyearadupdate/ (archived at https://perma.cc/UZG2-XW6C)

9 N. Belludi. Tylenol made a hero of Johnson & Johnson: A timeless crisis management case study, Right Attitudes Ideas, March 11, 2021. www.rightattitudes.com/2021/03/11/crisis-management-case-study-tylenol/ (archived at https://perma.cc/MAW5-J6NK)

10 J. Rehak. Tylenol made a hero of Johnson & Johnson: The recall that started them all, *The New York Times*, March 23, 2022. www.nytimes.com/2002/03/23/your-money/IHT-tylenol-made-a-hero-of-johnson-johnson-the-recall-that-started.html (archived at https://perma.cc/6ENB-CJ8T)

11 A. Bray. Sainsbury's Christmas advert: Advertising watchdog rules out investigation and shuts down complaints after racist backlash, *Metro*, November 19, 2020. metro.co.uk/2020/11/19/sainsburys-christmas-advert-wont-be-investigated-after-backlash-13622238 (archived at https://perma.cc/UA6W-QBU7)

12 B. Sisario. "We're making progress": How the Rock Hall of Fame is trying to evolve, *The New York Times*, November 1, 2023. www.nytimes.com/2023/11/01/arts/music/rock-and-roll-hall-of-fame-john-sykes.html (archived at https://perma.cc/D5AG-XTVR)

13 J. Ball (2022) *Stop, Ask, Explore: Learn to navigate change in times of uncertainty*, Kogan Page, London

RESPONSIBLE MARKETING INDEX 2023 SURVEY

Key Takeaways

Below includes details and highlights from the 2023 study conducted by sparks & honey in partnership with Lola Bakare in which 1,300 people from diverse backgrounds were surveyed on attitudes and behaviors related to responsible marketing. Research was led by sparks & honey Human Intelligence Analyst, Leslie Rodrigues, with survey thought leadership provided by Lola Bakare and Davianne Harris, sparks & honey Managing Partner, Chief Client Officer and Head of the Equitable Futures Practice.

Respondent Demographics

Gender

Male—42.70 percent

Female—57.20 percent

Other—0.10 percent

Age

16–17—1 percent

18–24—21.50 percent

25–34—27.30 percent

35–44—22 percent

45–54—13.80 percent

55 plus—14.40 percent

Income

Under $25,000—24 percent

$25,000–$49,999—23 percent

$50,000–$74,999—17.90 percent

$75,000–$99,999—13.40 percent

$100,000–$124,999—8.50 percent

$125,000–$149,999—3.70 percent

$150,000 plus—5.40 percent

Prefer not to say—4.10 percent

Education

High school—36.30 percent

Vocational/technical school—14.30 percent

University—36.30 percent

Post-graduate—13.10 percent

Ethnicity

White—30.50 percent

Black—25 percent

Hispanic—25 percent

Asian—15 percent

Multiracial—3 percent

Other—1 percent

(Those that identified as Native, if any, are included among Multiracial and Other.)

Survey Highlights

Concern for Social Issues

- When it comes to national social issues, 86.30 percent said they are concerned ("Very concerned" and "Somewhat concerned").
- *64.40 percent* of respondents said they discuss with their peers and family members about social issues.
  - *63.10 percent* educate themselves and do further research on social issues.
  - Few said they do nothing.

- *71.50 percent* of respondents said they typically first find out about social issues through social media.

Social Media

- The social media platforms most used were YouTube with 72.70 percent of respondents selecting it.
  - *Facebook* was next most used with 69.40 percent.
- There is a wide range of trust when it comes to media brands:
  - *39.40 percent* said they trust CNN the most when learning about social causes.
  - *Fox News* came in second with 36.90 percent.
  - *NYT* was third with 34.10 percent.
  - There are generational differences, with many Gen Zers saying TikTok, and Millennials and older saying either CNN or Facebook, but a considerable amount still selecting Fox News.

Brand Involvement

- *80.80 percent* agreed ("Completely agree" and "Somewhat agree"): It is important for brands and businesses today to play a role in addressing social issues impacting their consumers and audiences.
- Despite the majority agreeing that brands should play a role, some feel there is a limit:
  - *39.60 percent* of respondents said brands should solve a relevant problem related to their business, not just take a stance.
  - *35.10 percent* said they should take a neutral stance.
  - *34.70 percent* feel brands should always take a stance.
  - Few said brands can take a stance as long as it is relevant in the open-ends.
  - Others said they don't mind neutrality as long as it is not harmful and it depends on the social issue.
- To what extent do you feel it is important that brands and businesses do the following when addressing social issues—Top 2 Box (T2B) ("Very" and "Somewhat important")?
  - Brands and businesses should donate to organizations that help with efforts—77.50 percent.

- Brands and businesses should partner with relevant organizations to address social issues—76.90 percent.

- Brands and businesses should create products or solutions to solve root causes of social issues when they can—76.50 percent.

- Brands and businesses should provide resources and information to help educate the public on social issues—76.50 percent.

- Brands and businesses should use authentic and inclusive storytelling—72.90 percent.

- Brands and businesses should help push for policies through activism—67.80 percent.

- About 1/3 of respondents said they find a brand or business to be "somewhat authentic" if they just publicly share its stance and do nothing else.

  - *50.10 percent* said authentic (T2B).

  - *19.8 percent* were neutral.

  - *30.10 percent* said inauthentic (Bottom 2 Box (B2B)).

- For those that said they view the brand as inauthentic:

  - *49.17 percent* said they view it as performative.

  - *48.84 percent* said they are joining a movement just because it is currently "trending."

  - *48.17 percent* said they only care about commercial gain.

- If a brand one regularly purchased from took a public stance and showed no further action, respondents showed divergent reactions.

  - *22.70 percent* said they would purchase less often and look for a replacement brand.

  - *21.60 percent* said they would still purchase but *also* for a replacement brand.

  - *But* if the brand or business also took further action, there was more of a consensus with 49.60 percent saying they would still purchase and not look for a replacement brand.

Solve Real Problems

- To what extent do you feel it is important that brands and businesses do the following when addressing social issues—T2B ("1—Very" and "2—Somewhat important")?

- o Run a program to make resources and/or products accessible to an impacted community—76.40 percent rated it as important.
- o Create an innovative solution that is not a product but helps a community or a relevant cause—73.60 percent.
- o Donate part of sales from a product to benefit a community or relevant cause—73.30 percent.
- o Update a current product with features that improve the lives of a consumer impacted by a social issue—73.30 percent.
- o Create a unique product that benefits a consumer impacted by a social issue—71.60 percent.
- o Provide inclusive alternatives to current products—71.10 percent.
- o Design a special-edition packaging inspired by the social issue—57.00 percent.
- *71.60 percent* said they would be likely ("Very" and "Somewhat likely") to still purchase a product even if it didn't apply to them.
  - o "Somewhat likely" was the most common response individually with 37.10 percent.
  - o Many said it depended on the quality of the product and price.
  - o Others said they would buy it to support those impacted and support the cause.
  - o Some said they would not want to take a product away from someone that needs it.
- If a social issue does not apply to them and they see a brand putting in effort to address it, respondents overall react positively.
  - o *36.20 percent* of respondents said they would do further research on the brand or business.
  - o *31.20 percent* said they recommend the brand to others.
  - o *28.80 percent* said they purchase from them.
  - o *28.50 percent* said they follow the brand on social media.

Tell Real Stories

- To what extent do you feel it is important that brands and businesses do the following when addressing social issues—T2B ("1—Very" and "2—Somewhat important")?
  - o Educate and provide information to the public on a social issue—76.20 percent rated it as important.

- o Feature and amplify the real stories of historically-excluded people and communities being impacted by a relevant social issue—74.40 percent.

- o Dismantle or help audiences see beyond stereotypes—73.90 percent.

- o Provide exposure and advertise for an organization dedicated towards a social cause—72.40 percent.

- o Foster a sense of belonging and inclusivity through characters/actors/models that resemble underrepresented individuals—67 percent.

- o Create exclusive content (TV specials, commercials, documentaries, etc.) solely focused on a social issue—66.50 percent.

- o Come up with a fictitious but relatable story inspired by communities being impacted by a social issue for the public to rally around—51.30 percent.

- o Use a celebrity or influencer as the spokesperson—48.10 percent.

- *54.20 percent* believe brands and businesses should not fail to give appropriate credit to impacted individuals or communities.

  - o *50.30 percent* said brands should *not* choose a celeb or influencer with no connection.

  - o *43.20 percent* said brands should give a call to action or resources at the end on how others can get involved.

Create Opportunities

- To what extent do you feel it is important that brands and businesses do the following when addressing social issues—T2B ("1—Very" and "2—Somewhat important")?

  - o Partner with knowledgeable experts to spread awareness and educate others—77.80 percent rated it as important.

  - o Provide support for non-profit organizations or advocacy groups to promote advocacy efforts—76 percent.

  - o Invest in advocacy programs and campaigns that help impacted communities or promote a cause—76 percent.

  - o Create programs to directly benefit underrepresented or impacted communities—75.70 percent.

o Participate in advocacy efforts alongside organizations—74.90 percent.

o Partner with brands or businesses owned by underserved, underrepresented, historically-excluded, or impacted individuals—74.10 percent.

o Create a platform for underrepresented or impacted communities or relevant organizations to share their work or message—73.10 percent.

o Distribute (retail) products to scale brands or businesses owned by underserved, underrepresented, historically-excluded, or impacted individuals—69.60 percent.

o Host special events or programs to combat relevant causes—69.10 percent.

• *52.60 percent* feel it is more important for brands to come up with solutions themselves but also partner with other organizations and experts.

o Between the two, more said partnering with other organizations and experts (27.30 percent) than doing things themselves (20.10 percent).

Influence Real Policies

• To what extent do you feel it is important that brands and businesses do the following when addressing social issues—T2B ("1—Very" and "2—Somewhat important")?

o Publicly advocate—74.90 percent rated it as important.

o Take public stances and speak out—73 percent.

o Support a campaign—71.40 percent.

o Partner with government agencies or institutions to push for policy change—70.50 percent.

o Actively organize or participate in protests/demonstrations—61.40 percent.

o Boycott or dissolve partnerships that go against the interests of historically-excluded groups or relevant causes—60.30 percent.

o Endorse relevant political candidates—58.40 percent.

• If a brand or business one regularly purchases from actively pushes for a policy that one personally does not agree with, respondents varied in their reactions:

o *27.90 percent* said their reaction depends on the policy.

- o *22.80 percent* said they would stop purchasing from them.
- o *21.50 percent* said they would purchase less often.

Brands That Do a Poor Job

- A variety of companies were mentioned for doing a poor job on social initiatives for different reasons:
  - o *Nike*—Many still find their support of Colin Kaepernick offensive, while others feel Nike is not as diverse or inclusive as they make themselves out to be. Some mentioned their lack of diversity in models and how their products designed for underrepresented people are more expensive than regular products (ex. shoes for disabled people).
    - – Some feel Nike needs to do a better job at educating the public on BLM, especially after Colin Kaepernick's kneeling during the national anthem.
  - o *Pepsi*—Not only was their protest ad insensitive to some, but others did not like how they chose Kendall Jenner, a non-POC person who cannot relate to POCs.
  - o *Chic-fil-a*—Many do not appreciate Chic-fil-a for their anti-LGBTQ+ stance and pushes for such policies. Others noted how the brand sometimes tries to flip the coin but they always slip back to their anti-LGBTQ+ policies.
  - o *Balenciaga*—Many were angered by the brand's recent photos showing children's toys with bondage and their inability to apologize and address the issue, as well as not allowing their influencers or ambassadors to speak out on it.
  - o *Starbucks*—Many are against how the brand did not allow its employees to wear BLM apparel considering the brand's dark history with DEI among their employees and promise to "better train" them.
  - o *Disney*—While some are against Disney speaking out on political issues, others feel they do not speak out enough or defend themselves.
- Despite the brand, some have stated they have stopped purchasing or interacting with brands when they have done a poor job on social initiatives.

- If a brand or business one regularly purchases from actively remains neutral or does not get involved, 46.60 percent said their purchasing behavior would not change.

  o This was similar across all income groups.

- If a brand's social impact initiative or marketing campaign came off as inauthentic or performative, 35.40 percent said they would purchase less often from them.

  o *28.50 percent* said they would stop purchasing completely and 25.50 percent said their behavior would not change.

  o *65.10 percent* said they at least appreciate the effort.

  o This was similar across all income groups.

INDEX

Looking for another book?

Explore our award-winning
books from global business
experts in Business Strategy

Scan the code to browse

www.koganpage.com/business-
strategy

More from Kogan Page

ISBN: 9781789668247

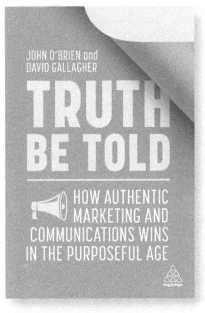

ISBN: 9781398600164

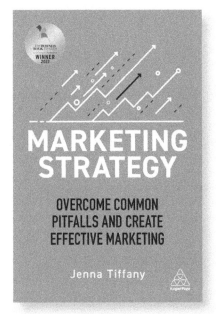

ISBN: 9781789667417

ISBN: 9781398607316

www.koganpage.com